THE
DAWN OF
CHRISTIANITY

By the same author

Roman Córdoba
Invisible Romans

THE
DAWN OF
CHRISTIANITY

PEOPLE AND GODS
IN A TIME OF
MAGIC AND
MIRACLES

ROBERT KNAPP

P

PROFILE BOOKS

First published in Great Britain in 2017 by
PROFILE BOOKS LTD
3 Holford Yard
Bevin Way
London WC1X 9HD
www.profilebooks.com

1 3 5 7 9 10 8 6 4 2

Typeset in Palatino by MacGuru Ltd
Printed and bound in Great Britain by
Clays, St Ives plc

The moral right of the author has been asserted.

A CIP catalogue record for this book is available from the British Library.

ISBN 978 1 78125 207 9
eISBN 978 1 78283 021 4

FSC
www.fsc.org
MIX
Paper from
responsible sources
FSC® C018072

CONTENTS

Maps   vii
Preface   xv

1   The Journey   1
2   Polytheists, Jews and the Supernatural   11
3   Ordinary Jewish People   26
4   The Justice of Yahweh   41
5   Polytheists in Their World   59
6   Paths to Change   88
7   Charismatics and Messiahs   114
8   Christianity in the Jewish and Polytheistic World   130
9   Hostility to Christianity   147
10 Christianity's Appeal: Magicians, Miracles and Martyrs   178
11 When Prophecy Fails   208

Valedictory   236
Who's Who and What's What   238
Sources   251
Further Reading   257
Acknowledgements   264
List of Figures   265
List of Plate Illustrations   267
Notes   270
Index   289

MAPS

1 The Land of the Hebrews
2 The Assyrian and Babylonian Empires
3 Galilee and Surrounding Areas
4 The Hellenistic Kingdoms, about 170 BC
5 The Roman Empire at the death of Augustus, AD 14
6 Palestine in New Testament times
7 The Eastern Mediterranean Lands in the First–Second Centuries AD

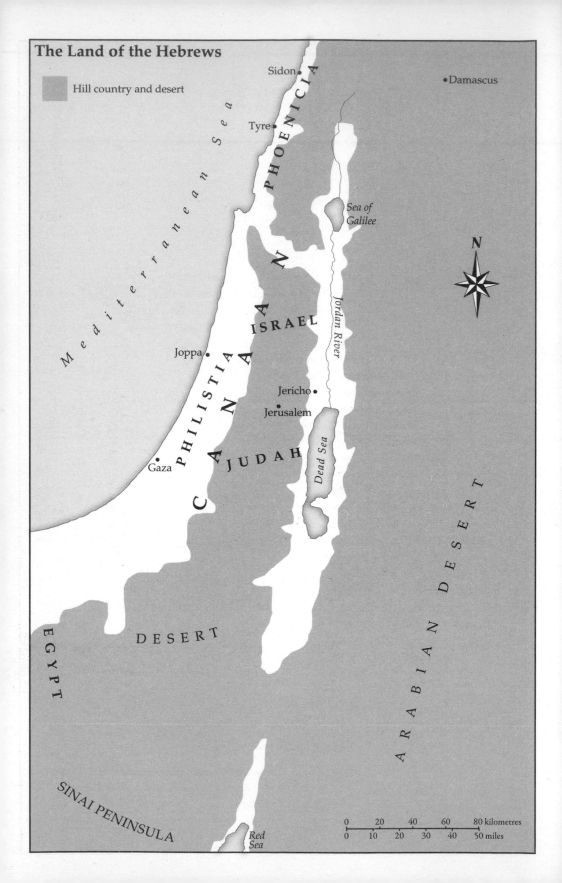

The Land of the Hebrews

Hill country and desert

Damascus

Sidon

PHOENICIA

Tyre

Mediterranean Sea

Sea of
Galilee

Jordan River

C A N A A N

ISRAEL

Joppa

PHILISTIA

Jericho

Jerusalem

JUDAH

Dead Sea

Gaza

DESERT

EGYPT

ARABIAN DESERT

SINAI PENINSULA

Red
Sea

N

| 0 | 20 | 40 | 60 | 80 kilometres |
| 0 | 10 | 20 | 30 | 40 | 50 miles |

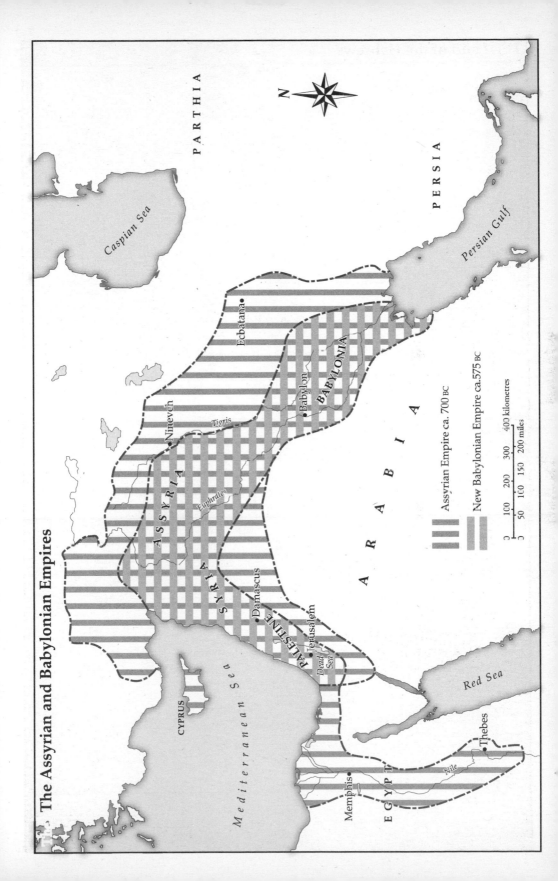

The Assyrian and Babylonian Empires

Assyrian Empire ca. 700 BC

New Babylonian Empire ca.575 BC

0   50 100 150 200 miles
0 100 200 300 400 kilometres

PARTHIA

Caspian Sea

PERSIA

Persian Gulf

Ecbatana

BABYLONIA

Nineveh

Tigris

Babylon

ASSYRIA

Euphrates

ARABIA

SYRIA

Damascus

PALESTINE

Jerusalem

Dead Sea

CYPRUS

Mediterranean Sea

Red Sea

Memphis

EGYPT

Nile

Thebes

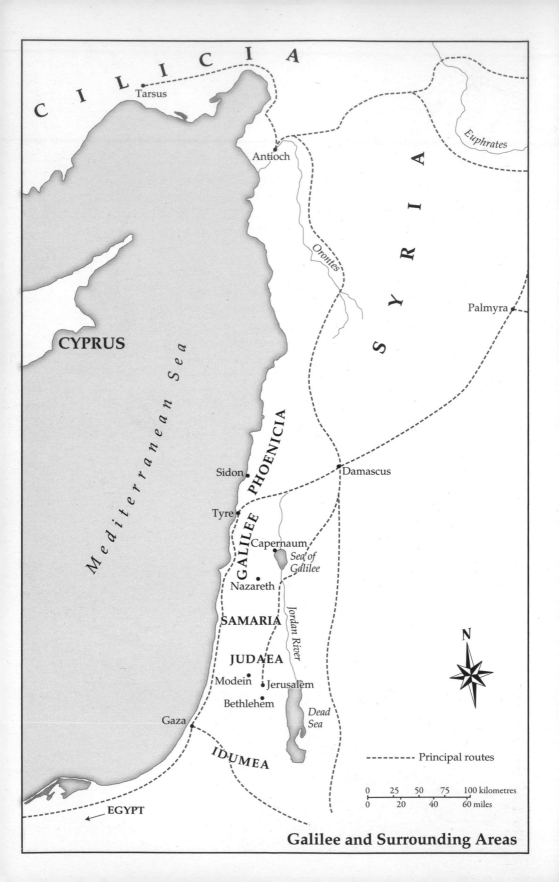

Galilee and Surrounding Areas

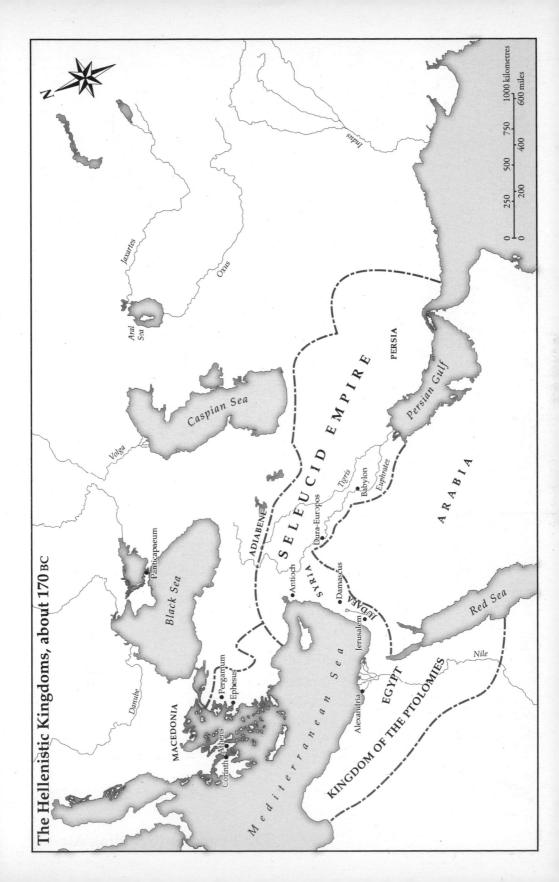

The Hellenistic Kingdoms, about 170 BC

MACEDONIA

Corinth
Athens

Pergamum
Ephesus

Panticapaeum

Black Sea

Mediterranean Sea

Antioch

SYRIA

Damascus

JUDAEA

Jerusalem

Alexandria

EGYPT

KINGDOM OF THE PTOLOMIES

Nile

Red Sea

ARABIA

ADIABENE

SELEUCID EMPIRE

PERSIA

Dura-Europos

Babylon

Tigris

Euphrates

Persian Gulf

Caspian Sea

Aral Sea

Volga

Oxus

Jaxartes

Indus

0   250   500   750   1000 kilometres
0   200   400   600 miles

N

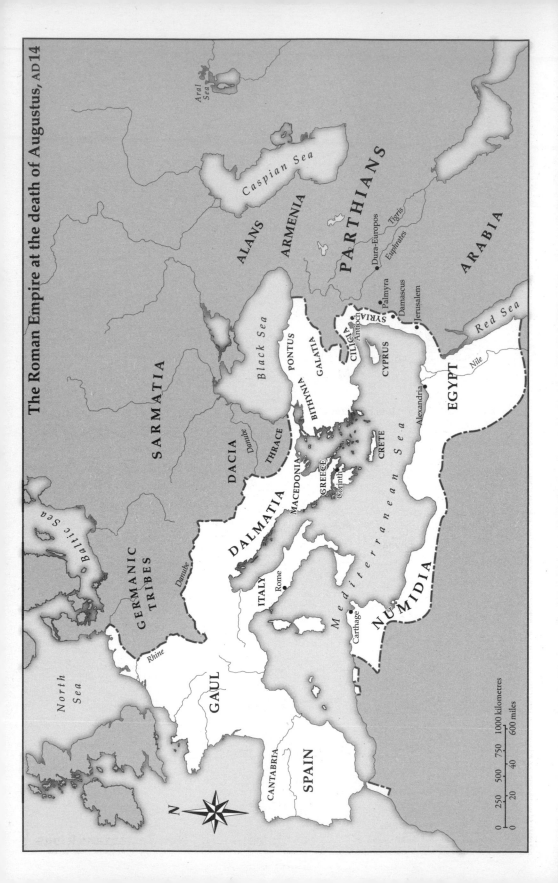

The Roman Empire at the death of Augustus, AD14

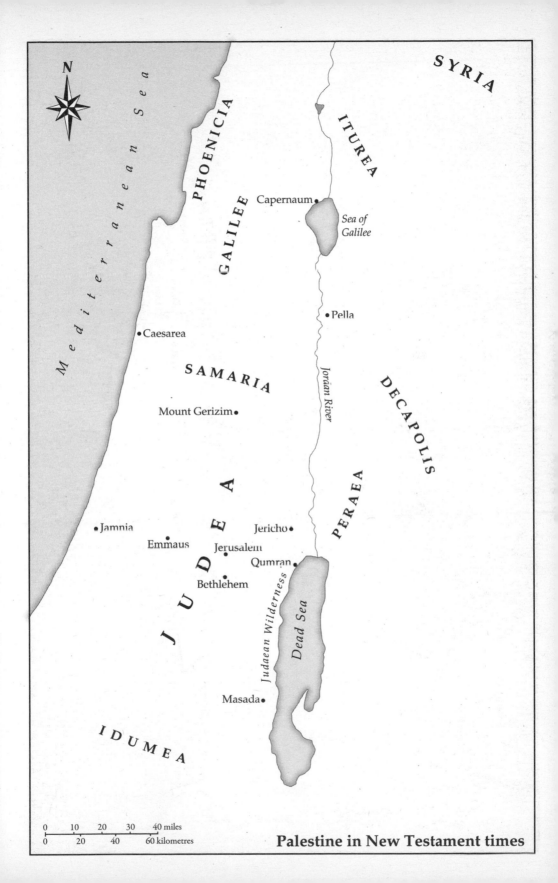

Palestine in New Testament times

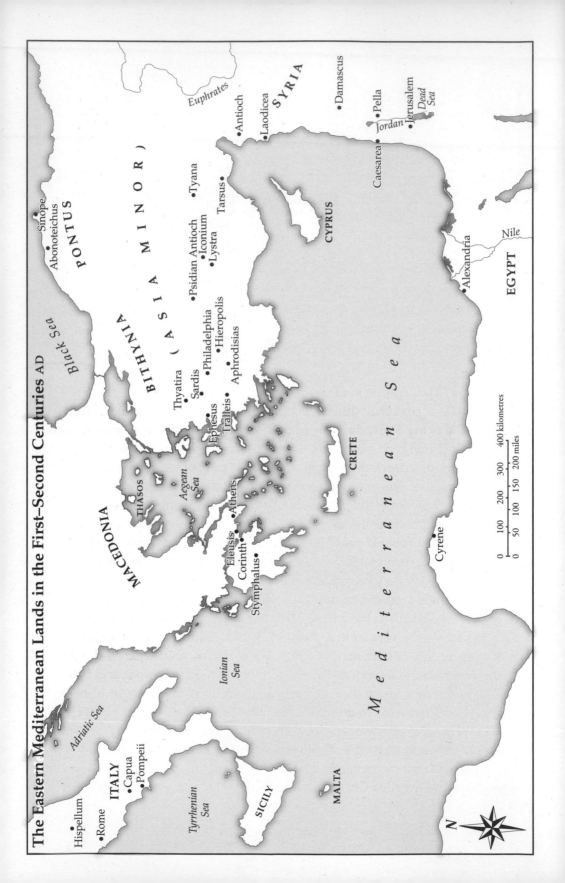

The Eastern Mediterranean Lands in the First–Second Centuries AD

PONTUS

Sinope
Abonoteichus

BITHYNIA

(ASIA MINOR)

Euphrates

Antioch
Laodicea

SYRIA

Damascus
Pella
Jerusalem
Jordan
Dead Sea

Tyana
Tarsus

Psidian Antioch
Iconium
Lystra

Caesarea

CYPRUS

Nile

Black Sea

Thyatira
Sardis

Philadelphia
Hieropolis
Aphrodisias

Alexandria

EGYPT

Ephesus
Tralleis

Thasos

Aegean
Sea

Athens
Eleusis
Corinth
Stymphalus

MACEDONIA

CRETE

Cyrene

Mediterranean Sea

Ionian
Sea

Adriatic Sea

ITALY

Hispellum
Rome
Capua
Pompeii

Tyrrhenian
Sea

SICILY

MALTA

0   100   200   300   400 kilometres
0   50   100   150   200 miles

N

PREFACE

HISTORIANS DEVOTE THEMSELVES TO discovering and revealing the past – a past that shimmers, fades in and out, its protean nature always seeking to evade our present. As I take on this huge project of the past, I make no claim to be able to divorce myself from my own ideologies of historical research or social justice, or contemplations on the meaning of life, or any other of a long list of thoughts and emotions colouring how I see the past world while bound by that present. With certainty impossible, the challenge is to approach the past as a series of more or less probable possibilities. Sorting out the 'probable' from the 'improbable' requires a self-awareness of our own limitations, as well as the inherent limitations of the evidence we have to work with.

Acknowledgement is necessary and honest, especially when the topic is as difficult as the religious life of ordinary people. The task set is to trace how the very ordinariness of their lives underlies and explains the emergence of Christianity. Those lives, inextricably entangled with the supernatural as well as the natural world, looked to gods and Fate, sought an orderliness they saw as justice and actively brought to bear magic and miracles in solving their problems. Their simple goals to survive and, if possible, to thrive forced them to be extremely careful and cautious in dealing with those supernatural powers. Yet, many in the end did embrace something new.

Jews and gentiles. Christians and pagans. The more traditional view holds that two traditions of the ancient Greco-Roman world stood at odds; that Christianity emerged as a better answer for humans' concerns than either Jews or pagans had. The experience of ordinary people blurs this artificially clear distinction made between those of the Jewish tradition, those who found religious experience with many gods – the polytheists – and, later, the Christians. The journey to understanding emphasises the commonalities of all three traditions. The experiences of supernatural power that ordinary people shared are the key to understanding the dawn of Christianity.

1

THE JOURNEY

When the day was already beginning to decline, Emperor Constantine saw with his own eyes the trophy of a cross of light in the heavens, above the sun, and bearing the inscription, CONQUER BY THIS. At this sight he himself was struck with amazement, and his whole army also, which followed him on this expedition, and witnessed the miracle.

Eusebius, *Life of Constantine*

ON 28 OCTOBER IN AD 312 a sign of the cross appeared to Constantine as he prepared for battle at the Milvian Bridge outside Rome with Maxentius, his rival for Roman imperial power. Some sixteen hundred years earlier, according to rabbinic tradition, Moses had stood atop Mount Sinai and received from the Jewish god Yahweh (Jehovah) the Ten Commandments that became the foundation of a covenant between the Israelites and their one god. The polytheist cultures elsewhere in the Mediterranean world conceived of a cosmos that contained many gods, all capable of being helpful or harmful. The Israelites' monotheism was different. Many centuries later Yahweh's covenant provided the seed bed for the teachings of a Jewish prophet called Jesus of Nazareth who, by the miracle of the resurrection reported by his disciples, set in motion the events that culminated in Constantine's cross nearly three centuries later.

1. Constantine sees a cross in the sky in this nineteenth century imaginative rendering of the event.

The Israelites' history goes back a long way from the birth of Jesus. By contrast, the history of polytheists, insofar as it is relevant to the rise of Christianity, goes back for only a few hundred years. If we take 1250 BC as the approximate date for the Israelites' exodus from Egypt and covenant with Yahweh shortly thereafter, then we can break their subsequent history into fairly clear periods. For about 250 years they lived in Canaan, now modern Palestine, the land they had invaded and more or less conquered. Their twelve tribes were each led by consensus leaders called judges. The tribes sometimes cooperated in military adventures but they were only loosely united until about 1020, when Saul, their first king, took control of all of them. David succeeded Saul in about 1000 and ruled for approximately forty years, during which he made the city of Jerusalem his capital. Here his son, Solomon, who reigned from about 961 to 922, built the first temple of Yahweh. After Solomon's death the kingdom split in two: the northern kingdom, Israel, and the southern kingdom, Judah. There followed a fractious period of intrigue, war and civil war, occasionally interspersed with

		1300 BC	
		1200	**Moses – Ten Commandments – Covenant**
		1100	
	Old Testament Period	1000	King David
		900	King Solomon builds first Temple
			Two kingdoms, Israel (north) and Judah (south)
		800	
		700	Assyria conquers Israel
		600	
			Babylon conquers Judah & Temple destroyed
		500	Return from exile – Persian hegemony – Second Temple built
		400	Persian hegemony
		300	Greek hegemony
		200	
	Second Temple Period	100	Maccabean Revolt – Dead Sea Scrolls Period
			Hasmonean Kingdom
			Romans intervene – Jerusalem captured
			King Herod the Great
		AD 1	**Birth of Jesus of Nazareth**
			Herod Antipas rules Galilee
			Crucifixion of Jesus
			Paul of Tarsus writes first New Testament works
New Testament written			Romans destroy Jerusalem & Temple
		100	Gospels written
			Last member of Jesus's family dies
			Last books of New Testament written
	Rabbinic Period		Pliny and Tacitus write about Christians
Apostolic Fathers Period			Apostolic Fathers live and write
		200	
		300	**Constantine sees cross in the sky**

Timeline of Major Periods and Events

peace. The great imperial power of the time, the Assyrians, conquered the northern kingdom in 722 and carried ten of the twelve tribes of the Israelites off into exile. They were never to return and are known still as the Lost Tribes of Israel. Those northerners who escaped exile and later mixed with other peoples called themselves Samaritans. In the south the two tribes of Benjamin and Judah continued in the independent Kingdom of Judah. Meanwhile, however, the aggressive empires of Egypt, Assyria and, later, Babylonia competed to control this important pathway between Egypt and the greater Near East. In 587–586 Judah succumbed to Babylonia: its elite were sent into exile in Babylon and the nation left devastated: 'By the waters of Babylon we sat down and wept when we remembered thee, O Sion,' the psalmist sang. This inaugurated a period of subservience to one imperial power or another that, with the exception of a few minor intervals, continued for the next two and a half thousand years.

This time, exile was not permanent, for Cyrus the Great of Persia (576–530 BC), having overthrown the Babylonian Empire, sent back those exiles who wished to return from Babylon to Judaea beginning in 537. A king was enthroned and his kingdom existed under the thumb of the Persians as their client state. By the end of the sixth century BC the returnees from exile had built a new temple, inaugurating what is known as the Second Temple Period. This lasted until the Romans destroyed that temple in AD 70.

It was during the period of Persian hegemony that the Greeks first appeared on the scene. From minor beginnings as raiders and merchants in the eastern Mediterranean, the people of the Greek mainland and islands coalesced into warring factions that, led by the Spartans and the Athenians, fought an exhausting series of internecine wars in the fifth and early fourth centuries BC. Finally, a new, semi-Greek, power emerged to conquer them all: Macedonia, led first by Philip II and then by his son Alexander the Great. Macedonians invaded the Persian realm in 334 BC. Like the Near Eastern conquerors before him, in 322 Alexander seized Palestine. At his death, Alexander's five main generals divided his conquests into warring empires. Seleucids, based in Syria to the north, and Ptolemies, based in Egypt to the south-west, fought over Palestine. By 303 the Seleucids had won out, installed puppet rulers to their liking and controlled Palestine completely. The Seleucid king

2. Pompey the Great captured Jerusalem in 63 BC, but he did
not sack the city or temple. Thereafter, Judaea was a subjected
client state except when ruled directly by a Roman official.

Antiochus IV Epiphanes compromised control of the area by alienating
a nativist faction that resented the Seleucids' hostility to their ethnic cult
of Yahweh. The Maccabean revolt began. This uprising for a very brief
time threw off the Seleucid yoke. Within decades, however, the independent Judaean kingdom had to bow to the pressures exerted upon
it by powerful enemies all around. There followed a hundred years of
manoeuvring by the leaders in Judaea, trying to play one faction against
another and one empire against another in order to maintain at least a
semblance of independence. At this point Rome entered the picture.

Rome, founded traditionally in 754 BC on the hills of central Italy,
at first only slowly spread its political power beyond nearby areas. But
after the defeat of the powerful rival empire of the Carthaginians in the
third century BC, the Romans rapidly pushed into the eastern Mediterranean. By the time of the Maccabees they were meddling in the affairs
of the Seleucid Empire. Jewish kings sought to use the power of the

Romans to counteract the power of the Seleucids. As a result, in 64 BC the Roman general Pompey the Great arrived with an army. He defeated the last of the Seleucid kings, turned Syria into a Roman province and entered Judaea to aid one faction in a civil war. He captured Jerusalem, but did not destroy it or its temple of Yahweh. He and his contemporary Roman leaders installed client kings to control Palestine. From then until the armies of the Islamic caliphate conquered the area in AD 637 Palestine was ruled either by men subservient to Rome or directly as a Roman province.

Christianity

Although some elements of this investigation stretch well back into distant times, the dawn of Christianity begins in earnest about 300 BC, when the Greeks after Alexander the Great controlled much of the Near East. Rome was as yet not a player. The Seleucid kings ruled what is now Palestine and the Israelite nation existed in the thrall of that empire. The narrative moves towards AD 33 when Christianity began with the crucifixion and resurrection of Jesus of Nazareth.

The ancient eastern Mediterranean world was early Christianity's environment. Stretching from the boot of Italy to the edge of Palestine, from the shores of France, Italy and Greece to the sands of Libya and Egypt, this vast area was home to a variety of peoples. Their social structures were widely similar. A small elite, perhaps 1–2 per cent of the population at most, controlled a large preponderance of political, economic and social resources. At the community level, this tiny elite managed all things political, either directly or through formal or informal delegation to sub-elites. A modest element of the general population, perhaps 10–20 per cent, lived fairly secure economic lives, although they had little power socially or economically. The rest of the population lived in various states of precariousness. Social structure was highly and rigorously stratified. All elements accepted this situation as a fact of life. The common people lived and breathed that strongly stratified, hierarchical world. The essence of political and social life for these people was existence within the established order. Outbursts, sometimes quite violent, from time to time did not shake or even actually challenge this order, but rather were almost always directed at specific ills and their correction by those in authority, not to a fundamental change in the established order (although, of course, there was exceptional unrest from time to time). The hierarchy in the community was evident at the family level as well. It was a patriarchal system, with the father at the top of the pyramid. Few would have contested these cultural arrangements.

The religious lives of virtually all people treated the world as full of gods. This was the polytheist ('many-gods') world – a world of powers and gods and demons and all sorts of supernatural emanations. Their polytheism shaped responses to good fortune and bad in people's lives, but had no political aspect other than functioning to confirm and defend the status quo dominated by elites. The people of the Jewish tradition, on the other hand, built religious views around their single god, Yahweh. Jews had within the previous two hundred years rebuilt their destroyed temple in Jerusalem and come to a general consensus both about what Yahweh's covenant on Mount Sinai meant and about what written material of history and prophets and songs were considered basic to religious life. While polytheists went about their daily lives without great concern for political processes well beyond their direct control, people of Judaea (including Galilee) thought not only about their daily lives, but also about their covenantal relationship to Yahweh. As their political life slipped ever more into the hands of hegemonic imperial powers, their faith in a unique relationship to a unique god fortified a belief in exceptionalism. With that, some became radically determined to maintain the covenant and, if possible, to regain political as well as religious freedom.

The religious story of polytheists and Jewish people run at first in parallel paths. Polytheism, the supernatural belief array (religion) that almost everyone in the ancient Greco-Roman world subscribed to, involved an elaborate but unorganised, incoherent, contradictory and idiosyncratic mixture of super-gods, minor gods, animistic powers and mixed-race gods and humans. No detailed dogma unified these beliefs, although everyone subscribed to the general basic principle: namely, that supernatural powers were active in the natural world. Interacting with this world populated by supernatural power involved acts, not dogma. Acts themselves were organised and coherent. A specific bundle of acts could define a particular worship or, on a larger scale, a particular religion – a particular approach to the supernatural – as a sub-set of all possible approaches. Quite naturally, the followers of one set of customs might think that another set was odd at best, dangerous at worst. But while a person might disparage a particular approach to the supernatural, no one (or, at least, none but a minuscule number) denied the supernatural web that infiltrated and even knitted together the natural world. A particular polytheist culture had its political ups and downs, but nothing much changed in the bedrock belief in a multitude of gods interacting with humans in a wide variety of ways.

Jewish people, the descendants of Abraham, Isaac and Jacob (Israel), were different. They had a set of behaviours and guidelines related to their god, Yahweh. This set of actions defined adherence to the group. So 'Israelites' distinguished themselves from 'not-Israelites' (polytheists) by practices such as circumcision, the Sabbath observance and avoidance of specific foods. As Josephus stated, maintaining the ancestral customs was the definition of a Jew. However, from the beginning there were internal disagreements about what those customs were and should be. In particular, the contradictions between covenantal expectations and the results of Yahweh's interventions led to religious questionings and active debate about how the covenant played out in everyday lives.

Jesus of Nazareth emerged from that ferment. He was a Jew among Jews and always remained so, but his later followers reached out to the polytheist culture and found acceptance even though a different cultural dynamic worked in each tradition. The Jewish covenantal relationship to their god determined the parameters of people's lives. Non-Jews lacked this unifying, foundational relationship and instead had a (to us) dizzyingly wide array of gods, beliefs and practices. Yet there was much common ground. On the one hand, Jewish ideas of the covenant between that people and Yahweh led to stresses and, eventually, solutions that early Christianity responded to well. On the other, non-Jews' attitudes and expectations of the supernatural left them open to what Christianity offered them. Early Christianity answered to basic issues, for Jews that Jesus was the Messiah and for polytheists that Jesus's monotheism had enough practical value to make them change their ways. A monotheist–polytheist hybrid promised a new relationship with the supernatural, one in which Jesus prophesied that he would return and would create a new world in which individuals could expect in death the ease and comfort that were usually denied them in life. Christianity was born.

Then two faith-altering events occurred. In AD 70 the Romans destroyed the temple in Jerusalem, the spiritual and political centre of Jewish life for hundreds of years. Jewish traditions were shaken to their foundations and only slowly regrouped as the rabbinical tradition gradually established its primacy over the next two centuries. About the same time as the temple disappeared, death took its toll on the generation of men and women who had known Jesus and had been his disciples, apostles, witnesses and followers. In no uncertain terms, Jesus himself had predicted a final apocalyptic event within the lifetime of his followers, an event that would destroy the world and replace it with a Kingdom of God. Yet, no such event happened. The message of Jesus had to be rewritten to accommodate this failed prophecy, or it would perish. In the face of these twin disasters, a Jewish–non-Jewish product emerged that amalgamated the Jewish roots of early Christianity with elite philosophical 'way of life' ideas of the non-Jewish classical world. Still an outcast religious community because of the firm belief in monotheism inherited from Jewish roots, persecuted because of its anti-cultural habits, the early Christians struggled to make a difference in the Roman Empire, and at times even to survive. The truth proclaimed by Jesus and his immediate successors had died in the failed prophesy. The successor faith might well have died too, but for Constantine's cross in the sky. A second miracle resurrected Jesus a second time. This time the faith he inspired, carried on the shoulders of empire, spread throughout the Mediterranean lands for good.

Engaging the ancient past is always a challenge. We depend on the scattering of sources left to us. These never offer as much information as we would like. They are seldom consistent among themselves. Each has its own point of view, something that determines the selection and arrangement of facts into a particular narrative. Patching together a coherent picture can be frustrating, even exasperating. The array of sources is like a giant smorgasbord. I pick an appetiser here, a main course there, a dessert at the end; wash down with a favourite beverage. My meal. My friend, however, makes completely different choices, producing another meal entirely. We each argue our selection is the one intended by the purveyor. So it is with the sources. A wide variety of 'meals' can be prepared. One might have logical integrity, but differ from all others. Arguments about which is best follow, but tend to be inconclusive.

This book features as wide a variety of sources as, I hope, it reasonably can. From the Jewish tradition there is the Old Testament (or Tanakh), often accompanied by the Apocrypha, additional books which, as a group, claim to be Jewish documents from the tenth to the second century BC. They include history, songs, prophecy, wisdom literature, religious instruction and more. Much continued to be written and preserved after this period. The Dead Sea Scrolls, first discovered in the late 1940s, added a large body of so-called inter-testamental literature – material written between the 'close' of the Old Testament documents and the writing of the New Testament. During this period Philo of Alexandria and Josephus of Jerusalem are two important Jewish sources. Both range widely, but Philo mostly writes extensively about the Jewish traditions, while Josephus gives us evidence and interpretations of the history of the Jewish people. After the destruction of the temple in AD 70 rabbinic authority gradually asserted itself in the Jewish tradition and during the period 200–400 rabbinic teaching was recorded in the Mishnah and Talmud. Occasionally, these documents throw light on earlier times, although mostly they reference a different, later Jewish world.

The New Testament material began to be laid down about AD 50 in letters (especially Paul's), in history (Acts of the Apostles) and in biographies (Gospels) in which followers of Jesus of Nazareth told of his life and the beginnings of Christianity. Writers of the next generation of early Christians – the apostolic fathers – added voices of comment, interpretation and explanation to the earlier material. From the early second century the Romans also took an interest in Christianity. The senator Pliny the Younger wrote about his contact with them in what is now Asia Minor. The historian Tacitus and biographer Suetonius noted events of the first century. For more discussion of these and other sources and some notes on how to pursue specific topics, see the Further Reading section at the end of the book. References to ancient sources are found in the Notes, keyed to the pages on which they appear.

People lived in a world of gods. Those of the Jewish tradition as well as polytheists worked diligently with those gods to make their lives successful. Any change in their relationship was daunting, even frightening. Yet a new relationship arose and spread during the first century AD and came to dominate the Western world. How and why did people make such a change? The explanation lies in their apprehension of the supernatural and in shared experiences across monotheism and polytheism.

2

POLYTHEISTS, JEWS AND
THE SUPERNATURAL

IN THE FIRST CENTURY AD some polytheist and Jewish people took up an approach to the supernatural found in the Jesus movement. A new, simple message appealed to traditions with many gods as well as a tradition focused on one. How could this be? How could the same message appeal to traditions the West usually sees as antithetical – many gods versus one god? It is true that the movement appealed to polytheists and to Jews in somewhat different ways. But before difference came sameness. Christianity was a vision of how the supernatural operates in human lives. Both polytheists and Jews lived in a world that shared a wide range of basic attitudes to the supernatural. These shared beliefs were the foundation for a new movement that could appeal to both.

Whether polytheist or Jewish, most people lived in a world that was at times orderly and predictable. There were many aspects of existence that came naturally, according to plan and according to known experiences. So, too, the underpinnings of social interaction among people followed predictable courses. No one offered a vow to the gods in order to preserve gravity or the family as the basic social unit, because there was no chance that such a basic arrangement would ever change. No theorising was needed, no deep questioning. Some things were just reliably there and always would be – predictable, controllable.

Another rich, active realm overlay, underlay and interlaced this everyday world. Unpredictable, powerful forces were always and everywhere at work. Everything had a sort of electrical charge that could power results in the natural world. Everything was pregnant with that power, waiting for the occasion to act. The constant interaction between the natural, or human, and supernatural, or superhuman, was normal, something to be dealt with, just like the variety of human interpersonal interactions.

For both polytheists and Jews, the supernatural could affect the predictable world in happy, healthy ways or in threatening, danger- ous ways. Although these forces manifested themselves in bewildering array, we often use the general term, 'gods', to capture them all. Poly- theists by definition had many gods. Jewish traditions also saw a world full of gods who engaged humans in different ways, but with Yahweh as their special protector. While that early tradition gradually gave way to a more universalised Yahweh, the tradition always accepted the exist- ence of a wide array of supernatural powers.

Both traditions understood that a person could know these forces and communicate with them, for the forces operated on the same prin- ciples as did humans. That is to say, they thought like humans, they had emotions like humans and they were, in general, in the shape of humans, or at least collections of human and animal parts rearranged. Even when a god declared he or she was not like humans, the conceptualisation remained analogous to how humans acted. For example, in the Jewish tradition Isaiah states: '"For my thoughts are not your thoughts, neither are your ways my ways,"' declares the Lord,' but the god in question still has 'thoughts' and 'ways', just as humans do. Because forces were like humans, they could be influenced as humans could be, by entreaty, wheedling, threats, bribes and deals. The difference lay in the unequal levels of power, for the supernatural forces were more powerful than humans, sometimes by a little, usually by a lot.

We are used to thinking of the natural world and the supernatural world as distinct although they interpenetrate at times. In the ancient world, people did not perceive things that way. Rather, the operational realms were not separate, sealed off from each other, with some commu- nication, but not a regular intertwining. Rather, they were a single entity. There was not a 'natural' sphere distinct from a 'super-' or 'supranatural' sphere. There was, however, despite their human-ness, a sense of other- ness with regard to the unnatural world. The powers that inhabited this sphere surpassed human capabilities, often defying human comprehension, and dwelt not only in the human sphere but in their own discrete realms inaccessible to humans.

Those dwellings of supernatural forces also mimicked human experience. They seemed to live in human-like places located geographically distinct from humanity. Places on earth closest to the realms above and below also had special interest for supernatural forces. So wells were a good place to throw a petition to underworld gods, while mountaintops such as Mount Olympus or Mount Sinai were special habitations for Zeus or Yahweh.

The adventurous interaction of human and supernatural beings was told in myths. The supernatural created the natural, as Jewish Yahweh created the universe from the void or the polytheist goddess Earth generated heavens and seas. The supernatural created human beings themselves, out of the soil by Yahweh or in Greek thinking by Prometheus. The supernatural supplied critical elements for human existence, as Prometheus gave humans fire or Yahweh allowed humans to know the difference between good and evil.

The animation of the relationships and the accounts of human benefits that myth provided is only part of the picture, however. Supernatural forces were not only human-like entities inhabiting a human-like (other) world. There was also continuous habitation of the human realm, forces that were constantly in the natural world, not just as visitors. These were beings such as the polytheist nymphs and powers such as Morpheus, the god of sleep and dreams; or Lilith, a demon spirit in the Jewish tradition. Supernatural forces were also immanent in natural-world objects. The animistic element that combined tangible, physical essence with an intangible, invisible power produced talking plants: as Moses was tending his father-in-law's flocks on Mount Sinai, the mountain's resident deity, Yahweh, spoke to him from a burning bush. Rivers had personalities. They could even participate in warfare: as Achilles was slaughtering his enemies near Troy, Scamander, the local river god, became angry and called out to him from a deep eddy, 'Achilles, come now, leave off.' What might look like a stone was not just a physical collection of minerals. It had a force within it that was accessible to humans and that could interact on its own. As the Hebrew patriarch Jacob slept, the stone he used as a pillow called up a dream of a stairway from earth to heaven; the next morning Jacob built a pillar, placed the stone on it and anointed it with oil. Jacob made the rock an object of worship, recognising its infusion with Yahweh's being. In similar fashion Pliny the Elder reported a tall stone found in Bactria that resembled hard limestone and which, when placed beneath one's head like a pillow, produced oracular dreams.

Managing the supernatural

The ways polytheists and Jews accessed supernatural resources varied greatly. These ways reflected the social and hierarchical structure of all settled groups – there was nothing like what we would think of as a truly egalitarian society in the ancient Mediterranean world. At the individual and family level the leading adults possessed the power and knowledge to act, whether in the technologies needed to farm or do business, in social knowledge to maintain stability, or in metaphysical knowledge to summon the assistance or ward off the evil of the supernatural forces. In a sense, leaders at all levels of the social hierarchy had a special relationship with those forces, so that, for example, at the family level sacrifice or prayer was needed from a father, not from a son or daughter. At the community level, leaders assumed responsibility for maintaining a good relationship with the supernatural on behalf of the entire group. On a macro level, leadership emerged that combined a social and political dominance with claims of superior access to the supernatural. Priests came more or less to monopolise important access points of the community to the supernatural through set liturgies and festivals. The rest of the people gained a sense of belonging and protection by participating in these festivals and sacrifices. The social template intertwining the natural and the supernatural world was heritable and stable.

But people also knew of others besides recognised social leaders who had the ability to work with the supernatural for benefits. Everyone knew of specially endowed prophets, magicians, seers or 'wise women' – all famously adept at curing diseases, physical and mental. All of these access points to the supernatural were additive. Arrangements by a community's religious leaders, family leaders and individual actors all played a role in helping people to deal with the supernatural in order to adapt their behaviour in ways meaningful to the contingencies of life.

The supernatural intertwined with Jewish and polytheist life in a variety of ways. Humans could, for example, request direct intervention. To prove Yahweh's superiority, Elijah successfully challenged prophets of their god, Baal, to a fire-lighting contest. He sought and gained direct intervention by Yahweh, who sent down fire and immolated not only the sacrifice, but also the stones, dirt and water around the altar. Chryses, the priest of Apollo, asked and gained Apollo's infliction of a plague on the Achaeans at the start of the Trojan War. King Croesus prayed to Apollo as well, seeking rain to put out the fire about to consume him and Apollo, like Yahweh, responded with rain 'out of a clear and calm sky'.

At other times, the gods intervened more or less on their own to favour a favourite. The Israelite judge Deborah did not request Yahweh's intervention on behalf of the Israelite army in its battle against Jabin, king of the Canaanites. She merely channelled Yahweh's instructions that led to victory. Thrasybulus, an Athenian general, encouraged his troops in 404 BC with the words, 'the gods ... are now manifestly fighting on our side. For in fair weather they send a storm, when it is to our advantage, and when we attack, they grant us, though we are few in number and our enemies are many, to set up trophies of victory.'

Humans took action to ward off harm at the hands of the gods, or to direct harm from the gods against their enemies. Diomedes, king of Argos and a major Greek hero in the Trojan War, asked Athena to help him kill his enemy Pandarus. Athena obliged. King Hezekiah of Judah sought Yahweh's aid in warding off harm when King Sennacherib, the fearsome ruler of the Assyrians who had recently destroyed the northern Kingdom of Israel, attacked Jerusalem. In about 701 BC Hezekiah's prayer went up: 'Now, Lord our God, deliver us from his hand, so that all the kingdoms of the earth may know that you alone, Lord, are God.' Yahweh heard him, and although the Assyrians besieged Jerusalem, they did not destroy it, rather settling for a huge ransom.

As these accounts show, polytheists as well as Jews took direct action to gain supernatural intervention. Prayers were offered, sacrifices made. It was possible to strike a quid pro quo deal with supernatural powers – a vow or a longer-range agreement for some human action in return for a god's support. Magical incantations and objects fell into this category, as they sought to bring a supernatural force to bear on a problem. But these attempts at provoking gods to specific actions often did not work; in fact, it was entirely unpredictable whether they would be effective or not. Despite all their efforts, ultimately humans were unable to control the supernatural forces, often buffeted seemingly at random by them in the uncertain and hence stressful natural environment they inhabited.

One might imagine that this situation – uncontrollable forces controlling life – would lead to despair, but this was not the case. Rather, people simply accepted the instability of their relationship to the supernatural and went on believing in their god or gods, giving them appropriate honour and seeking supernatural interventions in their lives. They adjusted and carried on – indeed, carrying on was foremost in their minds. At most they might invoke Fate, in polytheist parlance, or Providence, in Jewish, as a catch-all explanation for things going wrong (or right). A fable has Fate complain that humans 'charge me with responsibility for everything in one lump, including all the misfortunes and failures that come to a man by his own fault'. In the Jewish tradition, while Ecclesiastes in a polytheist way attributes all that happens to 'time and chance', most Jewish tradition puts Yahweh firmly in charge and responsible for whatever happens in the world, whether humans can figure it out or not.

In summary, then, polytheists and Jews believed that supernatural forces ('gods') existed; they were many; they could intervene in people's lives for good or for ill; their favour should be won and their disfavour placated through offerings and rituals, which differed according to specific contexts, desires and needs.

There were a multitude of worries in everyday life. One document from Egypt with a magical purpose gives a succinct list of possible evils. These words – things to be warded off – were written on a scrap of papyrus, rolled up and worn as an amulet to keep the evils at bay. The bad things were death, darkness, mental illness, grief, fear, illness, poverty, disturbance, rudeness, evil, the evil eye, debauchery, slavery, indecency, lamentation, troublesomeness, emptiness, malignancy, bitterness and arrogance. Polytheist and Jewish material such as dream interpretations, fables, proverbs, Greek and Latin inscriptions, magical formulas on papyri and biblical allusions reveal these and many other worries. Our sources make it crystal clear that people worried constantly about family issues, health issues, sex and love. Death was ever the unwanted visitor. More powerful persons were poised to take advantage. Enemies were everywhere, causing trouble. Verbal assaults, law suits, even violence were constant threats. Leviticus in the Old Testament speaks of people perverting justice, showing partiality to the mighty, judging unfairly, hating their fellows and seeking revenge or bearing a grudge. Economic woes were always just around the corner – a bad harvest, disaster on a business trip, robbery, trickery at the hands of rivals. Material well-being was very relative. Even if there was a modicum of success, this engendered worry about disasters. And, arching over all, a person had to be ever on the lookout to defend one's honour and the honour of one's family.

Polytheists and Jews lived in this unpredictable, non-rational, stressful environment, an environment that was potentially dangerous and disruptive. People dealt with all of these challenges, risks and contingencies as best they could. They engaged their own talents, but they invariably also engaged the supernatural.

As we have just seen, this environment created severe challenges in life as well as psychological stress. Then as now, although sometimes good things happened, it was the bad things that caused the most disruption in life. A matrix of personal and religious responses that allayed stress met those concerns. This is important because the containment of stress was fundamental. While stress was a natural reaction to physical and emotional situations, encouraging positive responses to solve problems, stress could also create dysfunctional responses that threatened at least personal, family and community well-being and, at the extremes, life itself. An ability to deal with the problematic world and not yield to despair or lash out in unproductive ways brought great personal rewards. Both polytheists and Jews developed what they saw as coherent responses that overcame a tendency to slump in the face of the meaninglessness and chaos of the world around them. Since there was no boundary between the natural and the supernatural, these responses developed in a seamless continuum of possibilities in both worlds.

A community's relationship with the supernatural is deeply entwined with group awareness and identity. The choice of deity or deities and the liturgies and festivals these involve create a network of recognisable and commonly held ideas and actions. Participation in this amalgam signals membership in the group. Rites of passage – birth, the transition from adolescence to adulthood, marriage, death – move individuals from one stage to another within the community. The rites and ceremonies also focus the entire group, promote solidarity and encourage the whole community to face issues together. Cultic actions increase the perception or reality of the community's unity. Since the leadership in the community cult(s) comes from the same socio-economic group as the one dominating society in other ways, the elite's position and the social hierarchy in general are strengthened and reaffirmed by their role in maintaining the community's central relationships with the supernatural.

Within but still part of the community, people experience the supernatural outside the cultic actions. They can take personal actions, for example travelling to consult an oracle. They can participate in extra-community experiences of the supernatural such as the mystery religions which offer direct, personal experience of the divine. But their identity is still as part of a community.

Because both community and individual relationships with the supernatural are so much a part of personal and group identity, challenge to the legitimacy of those relationships causes anxiety on both levels. Polytheists and Jews alike tend to react with hostility to such challenges.

On an individual level, the central issue in humankind's relationship with the supernatural was, 'Why do bad (and good) things happen?' Most people agreed that supernatural forces were responsible. Therefore, both polytheists and Jews had to relate to those forces to try to gain their help or ward off their evils. People thought of the gods in human terms, so they dealt with the supernatural beings in the same way they dealt with anyone else. If something bad happened it was because a spirit or power was wilfully angry. Or perhaps it was justifiably angry because an agreement between humans and superhumans had been broken. Or perhaps a group had failed to meet its obligations to a god. Fundamentally, the best way to stay on the right side of the supernatural was, as with powerful humans, overtly to recognise the superior's position. With gods, this was done by showing honour through ritual or other acts, through keeping one's side of a bargain by offering sacrifice or other actions and by seeing to it that the group as a whole also rendered appropriate attention and homage through prayer and ritual. A priest could act on behalf of the group. An individual could also determine the acts or words that would sway the supernatural. In addition, a person could try to allay a god's power by using divination to see the future, the better to try to avoid bad events, or, at least, the better to be prepared to deal with them. Throughout all of this, what the gods wanted in return for blessing a human always remained something of a guessing game. In response to such uncertainty, a whole array of experts was at hand in both polytheist and Jewish tradition to offer advice and in some cases to direct action.

There were two fundamentals in relating to supernatural forces. First, the belief that (the) god(s) could act. Although they might have been temporarily unavailable, or difficult to contact, or ill disposed, their innate ability to act was unquestioned. On humans' part, action brought reaction; by doing a particular thing humans could bring superhumans to their aid, or ward off their anger.

The power differential between humans and superhumans was immense. Not only that, the actions and motivations of superhumans often remained opaque to humans. A person could offer praise (prayer, hymns) and goods (sacrifice) to a god and hope to win that god over through obsequiousness. However, trying to intimidate superhumans usually was not a good idea. If a god was fed by sacrifices, it was possible to threaten to deny those sacrifices if the god did not produce. But, given the power differential, this was a risky business. A very common way to work in a power-differential relationship was to strike some sort of bargain: 'If I agree to do this, then you agree to do that.' In Latin this was called *do ut des* – I give in order that you might give in return.

Vows and votive offerings were the most common way in which this was done. These vows today provide us with an extraordinarily wide window onto people's concerns at the time. The normal form is the *do ut des* exchange already mentioned. There are thousands of inscriptions and dedicated objects noting vows. A bronze hand bears the Greek inscription, 'Zenon and Nikousa, who have made a vow, received satisfaction': the dedicators presumably promised this artefact to a god if the god healed a hand. Other examples are:

Araca Marcella freely fulfilled her vow to Peremusta the Great God in return for her safety and the safety of her loved ones.

Gaius Iulius Frontonianus, a veteran of the Fifth Faithful Macedonian Legion, gives thanks because following a vision his sight was restored. He freely and rightly fulfilled his vow to Aesculapius and Hygia and the other health-giving gods and goddesses of this place on his own behalf as well as on behalf of Carteia Maxima, his wife, and Iulia Frontina, his daughter.

Esuvius Modestus fulfilled his vow to Vacunae because his father's health was restored.

Quite naturally, not many people set up an inscription criticising a god for not carrying out his side of a bargain. Diogenes Laërtius noted Diogenes the Cynic's response to a person impressed with all the votives at Samothrace set up to the Great God for salvation at sea: 'There would have been many more if those who were not saved had made offerings!' And a wrenching epitaph from Capua (Italy) reminds us that vows were at times in vain:

Deeply grieving parents left this grave for Sylvinia Velleia, our very sweetest little girl. Our vows came to nothing. We were betrayed by time. Death mocked our sorrows. A life of worries is worthless.

The great historian of religion, Walter Burkert, captured the essence of many people's experience: 'Each of these [votive] objects, great or small, bears witness to a personal story, a story of anxiety, hope, prayer and fulfillment, to an act of personal religion. The intensity of religious feeling involved in this practice must not be underrated. There is the agonizing experience of distress, the search for some escape or help, the decision of faith …'

Personal vows were usually very practical, down to earth. It was also possible to create much more complex and far-reaching deals with gods. It might be quite vague, as Achilles said, 'Do the gods' will and they gladly hear when you pray.' It might be an action, a ritual or a sacrifice. It might include very specific, detailed obligations, as the lists of dos and don'ts in Deuteronomy and Leviticus. The principle was the same: adherence to the human side of the bargain would gain help from the superhuman side. If you tried to renege, beware, as Prepousa learned to her peril:

> Because Prepousa, the freedwoman of the priestess, had made a vow [to the god Men Axiottenos] for her son Philemon, that if he should become healthy without wasting money on doctors, she would write it on a stone, and although the vow had been fulfilled, she did not keep her promise, (therefore) the god demanded the vow now and punished the father Philemon; she fulfils her vow for her son and from now on she praises the god.

The point of interaction with the supernatural was to allay stress by resolving or at least seeming to resolve an issue at hand. Experience showed, however, that often, and in an unpredictable pattern, interaction failed to achieve the desired goal. The child died, or the husband failed to return from a voyage. Your prophets were defeated by the enemy's prophet, as in the case of Elijah and the priests of Baal. Your city fell to an opposing army, leaving you dead and your god carted off into another's power, along with your wives and children. Clinically, there was no technique or techniques available that would produce unerringly the desired effect in the supernatural world. Acknowledging this put a person back where he started, in a stressful state amidst the vagaries and dangers of the natural world. Neither polytheists nor Jews took that route. They offered a wide range of reasons for such failure: the wrong prayer, incantation or sacrifice was made, or made in the incorrect manner; a force or power did not receive the request at all; someone else had more influence with the god and was able to negate the request. Such explanations assumed that something mechanical had gone wrong. If the mechanics could be fixed, the appeal would be effective.

Another approach was to assume a grand bargain with the supernatural and then seek a reason for failure in the human not living up to his or her end of the bargain. This internalisation of fault effectively exculpated the force or power and put the onus of failure on the shoulders of the mortal. While humans could not reliably change a god's

actions, they could change their own and try thus to meet the requirements of the bargain in order to gain divine favour. But, as with the
mechanical explanations for failure, there remained no sure way to live
up to a bargain with a god, no action that would guarantee the outcome
a person desired.

Viewed from the outside, it is clear that religio-magical actions did
not have predictable and desirable outcomes, so their repetition might
seem puzzling, even irrational or absurd. However, a number of factors
made them much less so. First of all, anecdotal evidence from family
and/or their acquaintances was taken as proof of such actions' efficacy
– if not always reliably then sufficiently often to inspire some confidence
that, if done correctly, the sought-after result would follow. This and a
willingness to believe reports of successful outcomes at great remove of
time or distance combined to create a cogent body of confidence-inspir-
ing evidence. Contrariwise, experiences of failure could be explained
by citing incorrect practices, or even by making excuses for the god
invoked. The precarious lives of most people made them hesitant to
discount any action, supernaturally directed or otherwise, that was part
of the current repertoire; the mere fact that it was part of that repertoire
signified a long history of validation that would be ignored at one's
peril. A god's failure to satisfy a specific request did not, therefore, lead
to that god's rejection.

Why, then, would a polytheist or a Jew change a traditional relationship
with the supernatural? Change offered three possible outcomes: things
would stay the same, things would get worse, or things would get better.
Two of the three outcomes were negative. If things stayed the same, time
and energy had been wasted on change. If things got worse, this was
obviously a bad outcome. Of course, things might get better, but the risk
taken to find out was clear. In the face of obvious and complete failure,
say of prayers to a power to alleviate a drought, prayers to another power
might have been made. But usually try and try again was the operable
approach. Besides these more or less practical considerations, change in
any form introduced stress, the very thing people were trying to minimise through relationships with the supernatural. Changes in personal,
family, or community ways of doings things were truly frightening, and
therefore stressful. The hazards of change were just too great.

If this is so, what could alter relationships with the supernatural? Social change was one possibility. Intermingling of different approaches to the supernatural through cultural and social interaction presented new possibilities. The Israelites were constantly intermarrying with their neighbours and taking up their gods, much to the disgust of several prophets. Jeremiah lectured them, saying, 'You, Judah, have as many gods as you have towns; and the altars you have set up to burn incense to that shameful god Baal are as many as the streets of Jerusalem.' And Elijah railed against the influence of Jezebel, King Ahab's wife and a worshipper of Baal.

Geographical displacement could call for worship of powers of the new place, as when Ruth the Moabite went with Naomi back to Bethlehem and her Judaean god. Much as the settled Israelites did in Canaan, when settled in Egypt they took up various aspects of local Egyptian attitudes, for example by turning to a statue of Hathor (the 'golden calf') in Moses' absence on Mount Sinai. The increasing dominance of Hellenism after the conquests of Alexander the Great in the eastern Mediterranean made Greek culture as well as its approaches to the supernatural attractive to native peoples, including those of the Jewish tradition.

Enslavement often caused displacement and the concomitant exposure to new supernatural powers. While slaves might cling to some aspects of their original relationships, any based upon geographical connections were severed. A political reversal that resulted in submission was a powerful motivator because the superiority of the conqueror's gods was made manifest. The mere fact of enslavement in war was a strong indication that the gods of the conqueror were more powerful than those of the conquered, so their adoption might make some sense in the long run, if not immediately. Many Israelites took up worship of Baal, the chief god of their bitter and often successful enemies, the Canaanites.

On the polytheist side, the very open-endedness of responses to the supernatural made experience with change easier to consider. People could be inspired to try out a new relationship to the supernatural through listening to a religious spiel or talking with friends. Among the educated elite intellectual curiosity could lead to the amalgamation of various aspects of practice and belief, especially when wedded to philosophical speculation such as took place in Platonic thought. So

3 and 4. Alexander of Abonoteichus created a sensation with his oracle-giving and ailment-healing sacred snake, Glycon. The cult of Glycon survived for some time after Alexander's death.

while most people clung to their existing relationships, others experimented. Some polytheists even toyed with the concept of monotheism. The content and way of life of the traditions of Yahweh attracted one group, although we have no idea how large. These were called god-fearers (i.e. Yahweh-fearers). Some other men and women also turned to monotheistic worship of the Highest God (Zeus Hypsistos), a fairly mysterious deity especially popular in Asia Minor.

The most powerful motivator for change, however, was a demonstration that another supernatural force or power was stronger than the one(s) currently favoured. The 'show me' factor in personal decisions of this sort was paramount: if a supernatural power seemed effective, it became attractive, whether for the long term or just temporarily. Even such demonstrations did not always work. The Israelite prophet Elijah's experience showed this. He arranged a contest with the priests and prophets of the Canaanite god Baal, to see whether Baal or Yahweh was the more powerful. The contest was to see which god would ignite a wooden pyre. Baal's priests failed, but Yahweh answered Elijah's prayers by sending down fire. Despite this clear, miraculous proof of Yahweh's superior power, there is no indication that the Baal worshippers converted en masse to Yahweh worship.

Nevertheless, miracles definitely turned heads. In the second century AD a man named Alexander of Abonoteichus produced a large, human-headed snake he claimed to be a divine incarnation of the god Asclepius. People flocked to him, were (it was said) healed by him and changed their way of life to accord with his teachings. While conversion within polytheism was at least potentially much less wrenching than conversion to a monotheistic faith, Alexander and his snake are excellent examples of the role miracles played in changing people's minds about supernatural powers.

Polytheists and Jews shared deeply fundamental attitudes towards the supernatural. Each tradition lived its own life, and within each tradition many variations existed, but both shared a belief in the power, immanence, influence and dangers of supernatural forces – the gods. Both also took similar approaches to those gods to gain their favour or ward off their anger. People clung to traditional ways of dealing with the supernatural. These ways seemed validated by experience, even when they proved not particularly effective in a given situation. Change was generally considered unwelcome, even dangerous. Such change in personal orientation towards supernatural power did occur, even given the conservative outlook of most people. Motivation for change within any one individual must have been fairly idiosyncratic. But among other factors, the demonstrative power of miracles played a crucial role. The Western tradition has tended to emphasise the differences between polytheist and Jewish traditions. The appeal of Christianity to both ways of dealing with the supernatural rests, however, on their widely shared common ground.

3

ORDINARY JEWISH PEOPLE

PEOPLE OF THE JEWISH TRADITION shared a societal structure similar to that of other ancient Mediterranean peoples. The highest level is the elite, while the next level comprises artisans as well as small merchants and landowners. Poor farmers, often tenants, day labourers in the towns or in the fields and the destitute beggars make up the rest of the free population. Since most of our references to casual labour do not involve slaves, and archaeology confirms that large rural estates were rare if existent at all in the area, it is safe to say that in Judaea proper as well as further north in Galilee slavery, while it existed as part of the social fabric, was not a major institution. As was normal, the elite numbered perhaps 1 per cent of the population and the (ordinary) people accounted for the rest (assuming there were relatively few slaves).

People who lived by the Jewish traditions were the dominant population in Judaea and Galilee, an area I will usually refer to simply as Judaea. Despite the conquest of the area and later colonisation of some towns, the Hellenistic Greeks did not settle in large numbers in the area. The indigenous population had once been a mixture of Canaanites, Philistines and others, but during the ninth and eighth centuries BC the Hebrew Israelites came to dominate. However, the removal of many by the Assyrians in 722, followed a little over one hundred years later by the removal of still more, including the elite, by the Babylonians in the early sixth century left the population quite mixed. Gradually, after the exiles' return and the re-establishment of a kingdom, the area became increasingly Jewish once again. By the time of our concern, the first century AD, conquest and assimilation had produced a fairly homogeneous population following Jewish traditions.

During that century, the total population of Judaea was perhaps half a million souls with around 200,000 in Judaea proper and the rest in Galilee to the north and Idumea to the south. With few exceptions, the people were scattered in many small villages. Josephus says there were 204 villages or towns in Galilee alone. If the population in that area were around 150,000, then that would mean around 700 people per village, on average, small enough so that everyone could know everyone else. Archaeology indicates that villages were quite homogeneous. Aramaic was the everyday language. All this would encourage a close community.

The exact ethno-religious composition of the settlements varied, however. While towns along the Mediterranean tended to have more polytheistic influence, the people of the inland towns of Judaea have left an archaeology that is distinctly along the lines we would expect from a population following Jewish traditions. For example, there are many purificatory baths, both in homes and in shared environments. In the homes we find many examples of the stone dishes that were needed to prepare food in purity. Also, there is very little imported ware; simple, local, undecorated pieces predominate. Likewise, forbidden foods such as pigs leave few traces in the faunal remains, the typical village fare being bread dipped in sour wine or vinegar, soups, beans, lentils and stews (sometimes with red meat or chicken or, near the Sea of Galilee, fish). All of this is according to basic Jewish tradition. It is only in Jerusalem that we find extensive evidence of heavy Hellenistic and Roman cultural influence, and that only in the homes of the wealthy. In our time period, Judaea was definitely a Jewish environment.

Life for most people was, as everywhere in the ancient Mediterranean world, quite hard. Of course, it was easier for those with more resources. For the majority, though, life was at best an existence on the bright edge of want, always fearing the dark side.

Galilee was the area to the north of Judaea and separated from it by the land of the Samaritans. Close by Phoenicia and heavily influenced by

Egyptian culture to the south-west, the land held a large non-Jewish population down into the second century BC. Then those people were forcibly converted to the Jewish tradition by Hasmonean kings in the period 125–75 BC. Polytheistic populations melded with Jewish to form a single cultural unit.

The Romans took over the entire area after 63 BC. Herod Antipas, appointed as a client ruler by the Romans, managed Galilee's 150,000 inhabitants for more than thirty years from AD 6 to 39. Over the last decades some have claimed that Greek culture increasingly influenced the area from the middle of the second century BC onwards. Jesus's life and legacy have been explained within this supposedly Hellenising environment. But in fact Galilee lay outside the major polytheist settlement areas. There is no evidence of imperial cult or the stationing of Roman legions before the Great Revolt. In addition, its archaeological record and coinage circulation show little Hellenisation of local residents. As in Judaea to the south, its material culture indicates that the population consistently followed customs of the Jewish tradition. It is time to lay to rest the 'Myth of a Gentile Galilee', as it has been called, in order to understand the deeply Jewish background of Jesus's life.

Galilee remained relatively calm in the midst of the turmoil that often engulfed the area of Palestine during the first century AD. Its local ruler, Herod Antipas, waged only one brief war and there were no revolts, although his execution of John the Baptist about AD 30 did indicate a fear of unrest. After Antipas, the region experienced two decades of relative calm up until the beginnings of the Great Revolt in the 60s. Throughout there was a low level of violence, however, as bandits plagued the region.

The evidence of the Gospels and of Josephus indicates that Galilee was less troubled than Judaea. There the authorities did fear insurrection by the people. Josephus regularly claimed that bandits disrupted the land. But a careful examination of the evidence shows that even in Judaea relative calm was the rule in the first century AD, at least until the deposition of King Herod Agrippa I in 44 and mostly thereafter as well, up until the years just before the Great Revolt. Josephus painted a picture of unrest based upon a banditry linked organically to opposition to the Romans. But banditry was endemic in the ancient world; pillaging, theft and vandalism were hazards of life. It did not usually represent any sort of revolutionary class, much less religious conscious-ness, or an organised opposition to the existing order. It was in Jose-phus's narrative interest to make Judaea look as restless as possible in order to explain later Roman intervention. But until the Great Revolt there was little violent unrest that would have seemed out of place in the 'normal' ancient world. The absence of a Roman legion posted in Judaea until the time of the Great Revolt is clear proof that the Romans, at least, did not see the area as potentially or openly rebellious, despite the sporadic unrest Josephus recorded.

Women found their contribution to families through work in the home. The Mishnah summarises:

> These are works which the wife must perform for her husband: grinding flour and baking bread and washing clothes and cooking food and giving suck to her child and making ready his bed and working in wool. Even if she brought him in a hundred bond-women he should compel her to work in wool, for idleness leads to unchastity.

This rabbinical view was an idealised, patriarchal wish. The patriar-chal wish was modified in practice by the need for all hands to contrib-ute as much as possible and in all possible ways to the success of the household.

Within the Jewish tradition, women emerged as leaders. Their lives were much more active than the patriarchal stereotype. The judge Deborah and Huldah the prophet are well known. In the second book of Samuel a woman intervened to save her city. A rebel named Sheba had taken refuge in Abel Beth Maccah. Joab, King David's general, attacked the city to defeat him. The woman called to him from the city wall: 'Listen! Listen! Tell Joab to come here so I can speak to him.' He went towards her and she asked, 'Are you Joab?' 'I am,' he answered. She said, 'Listen to what your servant has to say.' 'I'm listening,' he said. She challenged his intention to destroy her city. Joab replied that if the traitor were handed over, he would spare her and her people. The woman promised to throw the rebel's head down to Joab. 'Then the woman went to all the people with her wise advice, and they cut off the head of

Sheba son of Bikri and threw it to Joab. So he sounded the trumpet, and his men dispersed from the city, each returning to his home.'

Among the people, a woman's contribution was greater than cooking and baking and spinning. Women took produce to the market or sold items from the front door; women staffed shops; women actively participated in the harvest of grain or olives, or in raising poultry or other livestock. Tobit's wife Anna both engaged in 'woman's work' and went out to deal in business:

> Then my wife Anna earned money at women's work. She used to send the product to the owners. Once when they paid her wages, they also gave her a kid; and when she returned to me it began to bleat. So I said to her, 'Where did you get the kid? It is not stolen, is it? Return it to the owners; for it is not right to eat what is stolen.' And she said, 'It was given to me as a gift in addition to my wages.'

Far from being stuck in her home, Anna went out by the road each day to wait for her son Tobias to return from Ecbatana. Women appeared in assemblies of the people, along with their children. In the first century AD, Paul came across Lydia, a merchant in purple dye, and other women gathered to pray outside of town, by a river; there were no men present.

Religious activities appealed to women. Those present in the synagogue were not, as far as archaeology can demonstrate, separated from men. We hear of female followers of charismatics such as Simon ben Giora and Simon the Magician. The writer Hippolytus notes that women were attracted to the Essene life, although they were not admitted, while the Therapeutae in Egypt had an active female contingent. Many polytheistic women in Antioch, Syria, were god-fearers and attended the synagogues there. Women followed Jesus and supported his movement, much as, on a richer level, the Hasmonean queen Alexandra had supported Pharisees in the first century BC, as had the unnamed wife of Pheroras, Herod the Great's younger brother, at a later date. Women had an active role in the early days of Pauline churches. Justin Martyr noted that they continued to play an important role in the Christian communities of his day, the second century AD. In that same century, Irenaeus mentioned Marcellina, a follower of the heretic Carpocrates and Tertullian complained that females played an active role in heretical

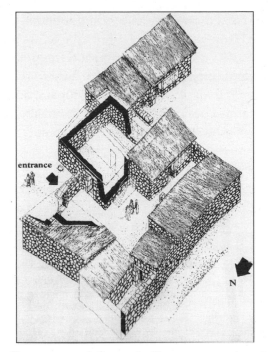

5. An ordinary person's house in Capernaum, 1st century AD.

sects: 'The very women of these heretics, how wanton they are! For they are bold enough to teach, to dispute, to enact exorcisms, to undertake cures – it may be even to baptise.'

Evidence simply does not support the notion that all women were home-bound and cloistered. Some at least could be mobile and active and could operate on their own initiative. Of course, this does not mean that they had the freedom of males. Note that Jesus, living out traditional Jewish habits, did not engage any woman in extensive conversation except the woman at the well – and then his disciples are astonished that he did so. But how about the men?

Sirach has, incidentally, a positive summary of everyday men's work. He notes the hard work of famers, ploughing and taking care of livestock; of artists and craftsmen 'who toil night and day engraving precious stones … and work far into the night to finish the task'; of blacksmiths who labour to complete their creations to perfection; the potter who kneads the clay 'with his feet until he can shape it with his hands; then he takes great pains to glaze it properly, and will work far into the night to clean out the kiln'. He continues:

> All of these people are skilled with their hands, each of them an expert at his own craft. Without such people there could be no cities; no one would live or visit where these services were not available. These people are not sought out to serve on the public councils, and they never attain positions of great importance. They do not serve as judges, and they do not understand legal matters. They have no education and are not known for their wisdom. You never hear them quoting proverbs. But the work they do holds this world together.

Sirach values the lives and work of ordinary men, but short-changes their potential for original thought. After all, Jesus was a *tekton*, a worker, yet he acquired the ability to speak and debate in the synagogues.

Jewish lives centred on the family. The important events of life occurred there: birth, circumcision, marriage and death rituals, and the observance of food and purity rules. There was prayer at sunrise and at sunset in the home. Religious instruction was based mostly on oral tradition handed down by fathers. In Exodus we learn that the father was responsible for passing on knowledge related to the Passover event. The historian Josephus, an educated person, still claimed that his father was important in his early training. The father led the Shabbat meal on the eve of the Sabbath. It was an important institution for religious instruction and the maintenance of cultural continuity.

The people of Galilee and Judaea suffered from the normal abuses of the elite in the Mediterranean world. The system of tenant farming and day labour kept rural workers at the edge of society. As archaeology has discovered, houses in both Capernaum and elsewhere were usually very modest affairs. The artisans or fishermen who inhabited them lived simply in cramped quarters with their families, a few animals, little furniture and locally made pots and dishes. They presumably eked out a living that was at best modest.

There is no evidence that the situation changed for the worse during our period but, even so, living conditions were fraught. The way of the elite was always to extract as much from people as possible, whether by

6. The Temple required taxes paid in silver shekels. This box contained nine minted in Tyre or Jerusalem during the first century AD.

manipulating markets or by tenancy agreements, or by paying as little as possible for labour. Taxes, whether paid to the temple or to client kings or directly to Romans, had always been a part of life. Trying to get more was like trying to get blood from a stone and, indeed, was counter-productive. There is reason to suppose that taxes in Judaea were heavier than elsewhere in the Roman Empire because of the additional revenue directed to the temple of Yahweh in Jerusalem, but since people were living either in or very close to poverty, any money taken in taxes was harmful and resented. There is no need to postulate increasing exploitation (for which there is no actual evidence) during the period. The existing exploitation was quite bad enough.

In Galilee, especially, the annual temple tax of a half-shekel was particularly irritating, as previously the tax had been paid once in a lifetime upon reaching adulthood. In general, collecting agents there, as elsewhere in the ancient world, were hardly loved. But there is no evidence that they became more resented than usual during our period. Jesus ate with tax collectors and had one as a disciple. He had only indirect chastisement for them as a group, with never a word about their supposed oppression of the people. John the Baptist hinted at their avariciousness, but urged tax compliance, asking only that tax collectors did not collect more than was owed, for even tax collectors came to be baptised: 'Teacher,' they asked him, 'what should we do?' 'Don't collect any more than you are required to,' he told them. Indeed, Jesus never complained about imperial taxation and urged people to pay. When he was asked if he, as a Jew, should pay the imperial tax, he replied, 'Why are you trying to trap me?' He continued, 'Bring me a denarius and let me look at it.' They brought him a denarius and he put the question to them, 'Whose image is this? And whose inscription?' 'Caesar's,' they replied. Then Jesus said to them, 'Give back to Caesar what is Caesar's and to God what is God's.'

Likewise, Jesus willingly paid the Jewish temple tax. Income from other sources such as taxes on trade and income from private estates may have provided as much or more than taxes on the people. This was scant consolation for most, even if they realised it, as existing taxes added to the general precariousness of their daily lives.

Life centred on making a living and being as successful as circumstances allowed. Naturally, part of the strategy was dealing with supernatural powers to help ensure those circumstances did not get worse. Beyond the family rites of the home, men and women gathered to understand and promote their relationship with their god, Yahweh. The gathering-place might be a home or a purpose-built building. It might be called a prayer house or a synagogue. The gathering was the important thing. Although few archaeological remains can be identified as having specific uses, hearing and talking about the scripture and praying together at the gathering on the Sabbath and on other days formed part of the cultural habit and could take place anywhere. Philo writes that people:

always meet together and sit down one with another, most of them in silence, except when it is customary to add a word of good omen to what is being read. But some priest who is present, or one of the old men, reads to them the holy laws, and explains each separately till nearly eventide: and after that they are allowed to depart with a knowledge of their holy laws, and with great improvement in piety.

General conversation would precede and follow gatherings like this. The combination of talking, reading and discussion produced a continuing knowledge of the basic ideas of the sacred writings, even if daily life left little time for introspection or more general education.

The Torah, or Pentateuch, was the five books of Moses, namely Genesis, Exodus, Leviticus, Numbers and Deuteronomy, and a document that could be copied and disseminated widely. It had become the central identity icon, the crucial symbol of Jewish tradition as well as a guide for the people. It provided mythical and cultural background as well as the basic rules of the covenant with Yahweh that had been forged by Moses in the crisis of the Israelites' escape from Egypt, a foundational act.

For those few who had time free from daily labour there was the possibility of studying the scriptures. As Sirach states, 'The wisdom of the scribe depends on the opportunity of leisure; and he who has little business may become wise. How can he become wise who handles the plough … ?' In the next passage he talks about the life of such a scholar:

He examines the wisdom of all the ancient writers and concerns himself with the prophecies. He memorises the sayings of famous men and is a skilled interpreter of parables. He studies the hidden meaning of proverbs and is able to discuss the obscure points of parables … Then, if the great Lord is willing, he will be filled with understanding. He will pour out a stream of wise sayings and give thanks to the Lord in prayer. He will have knowledge to share and good advice to give, as well as insight into the Lord's secrets.

While experts in the law forged varying opinions about the covenant and what Yahweh required in specific situations, only a few central theological ideas dominated the lives of the masses. They were mindful of the importance of purity, which meant, broadly, sticking to the commandments and rules of the covenant. Dietary laws and other rules on what and what not to do filled a good deal of the Pentateuch. We can doubt that many people were able or wanted to abide by all the rules, but the basic idea remained strong that purity was necessary in order to approach Yahweh and successfully gain his favour and assistance – and to avoid his anger and punishment. Atonement – confession, restitution (if required) and an atoning sacrifice – were crucial in making up for impious deeds and getting back into Yahweh's good graces, so that his supernatural power would continue to be available. The goal was a reunion with Yahweh after the separation caused by human action. A blood sacrifice was from the first used to accomplish this, but, of course, a person had to act sincerely for atonement to take place. As Philo wrote, 'Not without the sincerity of his repentance, not by words merely, but by works, the conviction of his soul which healed him from disease and restores him to good health.'

The central, and only, cult centre for Jewish people was the temple in Jerusalem. Travel there once in a while to attend a major festival generally satisfied specific religious requirements. At the temple, the priests conducted sacrifices and prayers according to the strict rules of the Torah. The procedures that took place in the temple and its role in the life of the Jewish people were highly contested, but most Jewish people certainly viewed the sacrificial system as fundamental to the worship of Yahweh. The temple was a powerful symbol of the covenantal agreement, even though it post-dated the covenant and was not included in the worship process of the Israelite people until the time of Solomon. Its desecration became a sign of degradation of the Jewish people. The centrality of the temple remained until its destruction in AD 70.

Jewish people probably joined their counterparts around the Mediterranean in believing that the sacrifices at the temple altar literally fed Yahweh, taking, for example, Leviticus 3:11 at its word: 'The priest shall burn [the sacrificed animals] on the altar as a food offering presented to the Lord.' Educated people moved beyond that, but still believed that sacrifices somehow 'fed' Yahweh and honoured him. Sacrifices took place daily and were especially potent during the most important festivals. People were spectators for the most part and did not worry very much about why the priests were doing what they did. It was the act of sacrifice itself that was powerful.

Festivals were an important part of the Jewish tradition. There were three main events, and in theory all men had to appear at them: the Festival of Unleavened Bread, the Festival of Weeks and the Festival of Tabernacles. Anyone attending all three might spend ten weeks of the year in travel and celebration. Even one festival lasting a week would cost a Galilean two weeks of travel, so three weeks altogether. Taking that much time away from work was not feasible for the majority – peasant, day labourer, artisan or petty merchant. So most did not attend every festival, or attend every year.

After Herod the Great expanded the temple compound in Jerusalem significantly at the end of the first century BC, it would hold many thousands of pilgrims. This might seem hard to believe, but a comparison helps. Pre-World War II Hajj pilgrims to the sacred mosque in Mecca numbered over 100,000; the mosque's footprint is 180,000 square metres, not a great deal more than Herod's temple at 144,000 square metres. Huge crowds could gather, and two or three groups were admitted serially during the great sacrifices of the Festival of the Unleavened Bread, so a figure of 200,000 or even more pilgrims seems possible. This many people, of course, filled Jerusalem to overflowing. Every room was let; families took in relatives and strangers; tented camps and worse sprang up in and around the city.

Such numbers made the authorities, Jewish or Roman, very nervous that things might turn ugly. Short of outright violence, control of a large, hostile mob was beyond the capabilities of ancient leaders. Once incited, rampage was very difficult to contain or stop without severe violence and bloodshed. With individual identity submerged in a crowd, the implicitly or even overtly threatening mob at times proved to be a very persuasive voice in turning the authorities towards a particular course of action. For example, popular opposition prevented the Roman governor Pontius Pilate from introducing effigies into Jerusalem. Cumanus, another Roman governor, was forced by the mob to punish a soldier who had destroyed a Torah. A crowd rushing to Samaria to avenge the murder of a Galilean was stopped only with difficulty by the governor. At all times authorities feared the mob. Although they could not prohibit gathering for the festivals, in other situations Roman and Jewish leaders tried to minimise opportunities for large crowds to assemble. At the major festivals, especially at Passover with its allusions to Israelite escape from the yoke of an imperial power (Egypt), authorities were on edge and eager to quickly prevent or short-circuit any disturbance.

Beyond personal devotion, communal gatherings and temple worship, people also had recourse to other means of enlisting the support or thwarting the evil of supernatural powers. Gideon Bohak, in his masterful treatment of Jewish magic, states that 'most Jews saw nothing wrong with an appeal to magical rituals and practices'. Although the written evidence for these practices during the Second Temple Period is surprisingly thin, given how much we have of this sort of material from later in antiquity, the footprints of magic appear. For example, amulets were a potent means of warding off evil. A tale from the Maccabean period illustrates well their widespread use among the people: after a battle, Judah Maccabeus had his men recover and bury the bodies of dead comrades. 'They found sacred charms, idols from Jamnia that the Law forbids Jews to wear, under the clothing of each of the dead.' Thus the soldiers wore protective amulets even though they were prohibited. The amulets found through archaeology provide further evidence of their popularity during this time, as before and after.

In addition, oral magic often negotiated the realm between prayer and incantation. Women now, as in all ages, had the reputation of being particularly adept. Misogynist rabbinic texts state that there were as many witches in a house as there were wives. This reputation presumably came from the important role of women as the keepers of home-medicinal knowledge and responsibility for cures including special prayers (incantations) and the preparation of amulets.

The diaspora

Not all Jewish people lived in Judaea. Ordinary Jewish people lived in towns in Babylonia and around the Mediterranean. Extensive scattering probably began with the displacements resulting from the capture of Jerusalem by the Babylonians in the early sixth century BC. Mostly elites were deported to Babylon, but some other people presumably were taken as well. Still others fled that fate and settled in Egypt and elsewhere. By the second century BC there were Jewish elements in

Alexandria and other Egyptian places as well as in Syria and Asia Minor, north of the homeland. Some at that time even made it as far as Rome. These people lived as coherent communities surrounded by polytheistic culture and people. Josephus in his *Antiquities of the Jews* chronicled their struggles for autonomy in regard to their traditions. Philo of Alexandria, also in the first century AD, wrote extensively about relations between Jewish people and polytheists in that large city. Although these communities kept in touch with the Judaean homeland, they developed Jewish traditions in some ways of their own. This was natural since there was never a centrally enforced manner in which the Jewish traditions had to be understood or carried out. Individuals and groups and communities were free to study the Torah and think their own thoughts about it. Nevertheless, the very existence of a document that all shared, both in Judaea and in the diaspora, provided a core of commonality and a loyalty to fairly consistent religious habits. The temple, too, provided a focal point for all. Those living in the diaspora made pilgrimages to Jerusalem and sent the temple tax back to the temple to support its priests and sacrifices. Even with these commonalities, Jewish people in the diaspora escaped some of the disruptive aspects of life in Judaea. They were not drawn into the intra-group squabbles that resulted from disagreements about the meaning of rigorous religious purity, the political direction of the government, or the exploitation by the elite of the majority.

People in the diaspora lived differently, perhaps, from peasants in Judaea, but as merchants or artisans they shared very similar lives. The family structures at home and abroad were the same. The influences of polytheistic culture around them made diaspora Jewish people more susceptible to adopting the ways of that culture. Certainly, Greek became the dominant language for them instead of the Hebrew or Aramaic of the homeland. At a fairly early date even the sacred scriptures were translated into Greek and used in religious services alongside or even instead of the original Hebrew documents. It should not be surprising that polytheistic learning penetrated contemporary opinion regarding Jewish traditions, the work of Philo of Alexandria being the best example. Through it all, however, the most important fact about Jewish people living scattered about the Mediterranean littoral is that they did in the main keep to their traditions and played an important role in the events that unfolded there.

The lives of Jewish people were thus in many ways quite unremarkable. Relations with the supernatural were a normal and important part of those lives. They had a well-defined tradition to follow, based upon a covenantal relationship with their god, Yahweh, and a body of writing on how this agreement should work out. Their dealings with the supernatural were consistent with the attitudes of their polytheist neighbours. In one important way, however, their attitude differed. That was in how they viewed Yahweh and how he affected their lives.

4

THE JUSTICE OF YAHWEH

You are always righteous, Lord,
when I bring a case before you.
Yet I would speak with you about your justice:
Why does the way of the wicked prosper?

THE COVENANT BETWEEN YAHWEH and his people supposed a
good outcome for a person if Yahweh were pleased. As a just god, he
would reward the good and punish the bad. Yet in the ups and downs
of individual lives, it is safe to assume that all too often such a good
result did not occur. On the political level, in the post-exilic period, it
became very evident that good things were not regularly happening to
the community, either. From the third century BC to the first century AD
the Jewish tradition worked out an explanation of how Yahweh was
just, even as overt experience seemed to show that he was not actively
favouring his people. This explanation, based on the people being
pious and righteous and Yahweh promising in response not immediate favour, but glorious vindication in an unspecified future, developed
slowly. The conviction that present righteousness would bring spectacular future reward appealed because it explained the contradiction
between Yahweh's promises to favour his people and his dereliction in
present circumstances. As the idea spread in various ways through the

tradition, the door opened to accepting change in people's relationship to Yahweh, for delayed response by a deity was novel. Once at the open door, a convincing presentation of an option for change could prove persuasive. The stage would be set for the approach to Yahweh that Christianity would offer.

Jewish people of the first century lived in a time of competing and clashing views of their supernatural world. The 'justice of Yahweh', the way Yahweh fulfilled his obligations under the covenant, was the fundamental theological issue among the elites. As a covenantal people, Israel gave obedience and reverence to Yahweh in return for Yahweh's protection and guidance. Experience showed that disaster regularly visited Israel. Why was their protector allowing this to happen? Where and what was his justice? Working out answers to this question affected the majority of people very directly.

The word 'prophet' meant someone who spoke as the voice of someone else. From earliest times in the Israelites' history the designation meant a person who channelled Yahweh's plans, promises, wishes and chastisements to his people. There was a wide array of prophets: Abraham, Moses, Aaron, Miriam, Deborah, Samuel and many more. Their inspired task was to speak out, to criticise religious deviance, as well as the social and political injustice of the priestly and secular elites with the goal of bringing everyone back into a right relationship with Yahweh and so avoid his wrath. Moses himself foresaw one such prophet when he spoke to his people:

> The Lord your God will raise up for you a prophet like me from among you, from your fellow Israelites … The Lord said to me: '…
> I will raise up for them a prophet like you from among their fellow Israelites, and I will put my words in his mouth. He will tell them everything I command him. I myself will call to account anyone who does not listen to my words that the prophet speaks in my name.'

Hosea in the eighth century BC is a good example of a prophet. He railed against idolatry and syncretistic cultic activity. He emphasised a personal relationship with Yahweh: 'For I desire steadfast love and not sacrifice, the knowledge of Yahweh rather than burnt offerings.' He criticised the priests and king. Returning to Yahweh was the only salvation: 'Return, Israel, to the Lord your God. Your sins have been your downfall! Take words with you and return to the Lord.' In like manner, the prophet Amos derided the secular elite: 'Woe to you who are complacent in Zion, and to you who feel secure on Mount Samaria, you notable men of the foremost nation, to whom the people of Israel come! ... You put off the day of disaster and bring near a reign of terror.'

Micah later also criticised the grasping elite: 'Woe to those who plan iniquity, to those who plot evil on their beds! At morning's light they carry it out because it is in their power to do it. They covet fields and seize them, and houses, and take them. They defraud people of their homes; they rob them of their inheritance.' He further included merchants in his critique of injustice: 'Shall I acquit someone with dishonest scales, with a bag of false weights?' Amos added further scorn on those 'skimping on the measure, boosting the price and cheating with dishonest scales, buying the poor with silver and the needy for a pair of sandals, selling even the sweepings with the wheat'. Prophetic utterances through the centuries had emphasised a similar message, the basis for which was that all Israel was equal under the covenant which meant there should be fair treatment of everyone. Prophets advocated just religious, economic, judicial and administrative behaviour because this was what Yahweh wanted in return for his favour.

The Israelites had a very hard time living up to their end of the bargain. Social injustice and neglect of worship were often rampant. This failure to live up to their covenant infuriated Yahweh, who rightfully measured out condign punishments of both individuals and the whole nation. The prophets' task was to turn the Israelites back to a proper covenantal relationship with Yahweh before he punished them (more), since Yahweh wanted the covenant to work and so was always willing to give people a 'second chance' (in fact, repeated second chances) if they returned to their due reverence for him.

The prophetic tradition deeply influenced people's relationship to Yahweh's covenant. Two elements were especially important. First, the prophetic tradition highlighted that direct communication with Yahweh was possible without intermediaries of the priesthood or the elite. Indeed, direct communication often alerted people to Yahweh's wishes that were contrary to earthly powers. While the classic prophets seemed exceptional in their unmediated relationship to Yahweh, it was a short step to thinking that a wide swath of people might enjoy that same relationship. The realisation that individuals could have a direct relationship was fundamentally important. Prophets undercut the cultic aspect of the people's relationship to Yahweh by promoting a direct relationship that bypassed priesthood and elite. As Amos put it:

> I hate, I despise your religious festivals; your assemblies are a stench to me. Even though you bring me burnt offerings and grain offerings, I will not accept them. Though you bring choice fellowship offerings, I will have no regard for them. Away with the noise of your songs! I will not listen to the music of your harps. But let justice roll on like a river, righteousness like a never-failing stream!

There is a direct connection between this realisation and the later pietist and charismatic activities that had popular appeal.

The covenant forged on Mount Sinai between Yahweh and the Israelites was the foundational event for the Hebrew people. The Israelites' deal with Yahweh promised to secure protection and success, both individually and as a community, in a very uncertain world. This relationship had many ups and downs, but the destruction of the northern kingdom of Israel by the Assyrians in 722 BC dealt a severe blow to the idea of Yahweh's protection. Then, in the early sixth century BC, the Babylonians repeated the trick: they captured Jerusalem, destroyed the temple and carried off into exile a portion of the inhabitants of the southern kingdom. Again the Israelite god's protection had failed. In the aftermath of two failures by Yahweh to save his covenanted people from secular destruction, the issue of Yahweh's justice becomes the centre of theological contention. The prophetic tradition of social justice came to clash with the priestly and elite views about what was central to maintaining a right relationship with Yahweh, and so his protection.

The catalytic element is the problem of theodicy. How could an all-powerful, all-knowing, beneficent god allow so much evil in the world? As the prophet Jeremiah lamented, 'You are always righteous Lord, when I bring a case before you. Yet I would speak with you about your justice: Why does the way of the wicked prosper?' The prophet Ezekiel introduced a radical solution to the problem of how to guarantee their god's blessings. Bad things were not Yahweh's breach of covenant, he said; rather it was the sins of the people that broke that agreement and brought evil into people's lives. Yahweh judged each person as an individual, not as a member of family, clan, or nation. Each person had a clear choice: he could be righteous and then rewarded; or he could be evil and be punished:

'Yet you say, "The way of the Lord is not just." Hear, you Israelites: Is my way unjust? Is it not your ways that are unjust? If a righteous person turns from their righteousness and commits sin, they will die for it; because of the sin they have committed they will die. But if a wicked person turns away from the wickedness they have committed and does what is just and right, they will save their life ... Yet the Israelites say, "The way of the Lord is not just." Are my ways unjust, people of Israel? Is it not your ways that are unjust? Therefore, you Israelites, I will judge each of you according to your own ways, declares the Sovereign Lord. Repent! Turn away from all your offences ... and get a new heart and a new spirit. Why will you die, people of Israel? For I take no pleasure in the death of anyone,' declares the Sovereign Lord. Repent and live!

The concept that personal righteousness could guarantee a right relationship to Yahweh becomes very important in the aftermath of the destruction of the temple in 587 BC. 'I the Lord search the heart and examine the mind, to reward each person according to their conduct, according to what their deeds deserve,' as Jeremiah put it.

The Exile was a pivotal time in the history of Israel's relationship to its god. The tradition of the Israelites before exile in 587 BC is different in significant ways from post-exilic tradition. For example, it is not clear that Passover or the Sukkot festivals were celebrated before the Exile, at which time Israel emphasised monolatry – the worship of one god without denying the existence and power of other gods. Monotheism, the idea that only one god existed, as opposed to monolatry, the idea that only one god should be worshipped, did not exist. Other pre-exilic traditions did continue over into the post-exilic period after the return of many Israelites to Judaea that began in 537 – the temple, circumcision, some food habits such as not eating pigs.

The most important gift of the exilic period and its immediate aftermath was the establishment of an authoritative Pentateuch, the Torah. Elements of written tradition had, of course, existed before the Exile, but the Torah as we know it coalesced only in the sixth century BC. In the absence of temple and king, the Torah writings became the anchor of the Jewish people's relationship to Yahweh. This situation had two major repercussions. First, the temple and a king, although they remained important, ceased to be the sine qua non for the faithful. Second, the centrality of the Torah and related sacred writings, especially of the prophets called Isaiah and the Psalms, allowed, even encouraged people to make their own decisions about how Yahweh wished them to act.

The centrality of the Torah meant that the covenant could continue not only in the absence of the temple (as it had during the Exile), but also in the absence of political independence: obedience to Yahweh did not require such independence. This was important because, except for brief periods in the second and first centuries BC, the Jewish people would not be an independent political unit free from imperial control during the entire ancient period and, indeed, over the next two thousand years. During our period Judaea was controlled first by the Persians until the end of the fourth century BC, then by the Seleucid successors to the conquests of Alexander the Great until the Romans arrived on the scene in the first century AD, and then by the Romans for over six hundred years.

Continuous subservience to one imperial power or another during our period gave rise to alternative interpretations of Yahweh's justice. One possibility was that Yahweh required loyalty in only religious matters, not in the political sphere. Pure cultic activity in the land through the temple priesthoods could and did continue even under political domination. The cultic leadership would predominate, steering an earthly local theocracy under the suzerainty, direct or indirect, of others. In this model, right relationship with Yahweh relied on two things: strict community adherence to cultic practice through the priests and individual relationship to Yahweh through ethically and socially approved action. Political action was not important. Righteousness involved supporting the community's cultic activity and only secondarily individual righteousness. If all were done exactly as required, Yahweh would reward the people with his support in the here and now. The temple priesthood advocated and represented this cultic model.

A second model envisioned the restoration of the pre-exilic situation in which a sacred element (the priesthood) and a secular element (the king) jointly ruled under Yahweh's guidance. In this vision, Yahweh would establish and protect a political Judaea complete with king and temple if the Jewish people were sufficiently pure in their obedience to him. This expectation led to the revolts against imperial powers under the leadership of the Maccabees, in the failed Great Revolt of the 60s AD and of the Bar Kochba revolt in the 130s. A combination of an angry population and ambitious priestly and secular elites hoping to gain or retain political power represented this priest and king model.

Finally an extra-temple, prophetic engagement with Yahweh arose that stressed individual obedience through purity as the key to winning Yahweh's approval and so help. This manner of relating to Yahweh descended directly from the prophetic element so prominent for so long in Jewish tradition. Purity came not primarily from proper cultic behaviour based on the temple. Rather, purity came from proper behaviour following the Torah first and temple cult second, if at all. Yahweh's reward for righteousness would come not in the here and now, but at a final judgement when the righteous would be rewarded and the unrighteous destroyed. This eschatology of delayed satisfaction developed what the prophets meant by a promise of victory for the righteous and punishment for the wicked. It declared that Yahweh would reward the faithful in a way that made current political subservience irrelevant. Early in the post-exilic period believers in this avenue to Yahweh's rewards became known as 'the pious ones' (Hasidim). This piety model introduced a wide range of approaches that came to exert a powerful influence on how Jewish people dealt with the problem of the justice of Yahweh.

All three possibilities – the priest-and-king model, the priestly model and the piety model – intermingled in different ways to create a complex situation. Their adherents were often in conflicts that reached into people's lives.

All agreed that Yahweh destroyed those who did not do his will and helped those who did. Their traditions about the earliest days of the world emphasised this: Adam's fall, the fate of Sodom and Gomorrah, the destruction of humanity and Noah's preservation and, of course, various and sundry military successes and disasters. The question was, how would this work out in present time?

By the priestly and priest-king account, Yahweh would take direct action in present time to reward and punish in accordance with the covenantal agreement. Yahwehan punishment of the entire community had a long history in the tradition. Betrayal of the covenant led to personal and community disaster. Hosea called Israel to account and Jeremiah railed repeatedly and horrifically against Jerusalem before the Babylonian conquest: '"Because you have not listened to my words, I will summon all the peoples of the north and my servant Nebuchadnezzar king of Babylon," declares the Lord. "This whole country will become a desolate wasteland and these nations will serve the king of Babylon seventy years."'

The converse was the conviction that Yahweh would bring success for the righteous, as for Joshua and later Deborah leading the fight against the Canaanites and King David defeating the Philistines. Righteousness was the key: correct personal and public rituals; adherence to monolatry; individual moral lives (or repentance and reform in the absence); and social justice.

This conception of the justice of Yahweh, that he would reward and punish the people in present time according to their adherence to the covenant, gradually fell out of favour with many after the return from exile in the sixth century BC. There is no sign of it when Pompey takes Jerusalem in 63 BC. However, there were some who resurrected the arguments of Hosea and Jeremiah at the time of the Great Revolt. Jesus, son of Ananias, issued a prophesy of doom for seven and a half years before the final fall of Jerusalem, although Josephus does not tell us that these were specifically accompanied by a call for repentance in order to avoid disaster. Indeed, it is interesting that a long list of portents that Josephus reports included no indication that anyone attributed the dire straits of Judaea to disobedience to Yahweh. In fact, during the Great Revolt the rebellious people clearly thought that Yahweh would stand by them. With the Romans once again threatening both the temple and Jerusalem, the direct-action model of Yahweh's justice was put to a severe test and, not for the first time, failed.

An alternative explanation of Yahweh's views and actions had arisen long before: that he would take indirect, delayed action if, despite the ugly lesson of destruction and exile at the hands of the Babylonians, some in the community continued in their failure to live up to his standards. The present would continue in its terrible state, but there would be a future redemption: the pious would be rewarded; their enemies would be destroyed.

In a view predominant in pre-exilic times, Yahweh punished the wicked directly, in present time, not in an undisclosed future. In individuals' lives, the obvious difficulty was that often the wicked quite clearly were not punished, as Jeremiah's quote at the beginning of this chapter indicates. The disaster of the destruction of the first temple and the Babylonian captivity underlined the inadequacy of the direct action model on the community level. In the post-exilic period it became more satisfactory to think that Yahweh punished and rewarded, but that this would take place either in a great upheaval at a time ordained by Yahweh, or in the afterlife, or both. With the community as with individuals, Yahweh would set things right, with the Jewish people victorious, but not until later, at a final judgement.

Jeremiah established a corollary principle that ended up playing an important role in Jewish life. As the Babylonians advanced on Jerusalem, he urged that submission to that secular power was required by Yahweh. He proclaimed that Yahweh himself would, in due time, champion the Jewish people:

> The God of Israel says: 'I will surely gather them from all the lands where I banish them in my furious anger and great wrath; I will bring them back to this place and let them live in safety. They will be my people, and I will be their God. I will give them singleness of heart and action, so that they will always fear me and that all will then go well for them and for their children after them.'

This attitude remained a strong strain in Jewish thought and action. Only four revolts are recorded in Judaea or the diaspora over three hundred years: the Maccabean, the Great Revolt, the diaspora revolt of AD 115–17 and Bar Kochba's uprising. Basically, accommodation to imperial powers, not confrontation, followed the tradition of Jeremiah's admonitions. On the other hand, many lost confidence in a present-time restoration of a faithful political community, although such an event had been predicted in Jeremiah and Isaiah.

The pre-exilic Hebrew people were a tribal society led by a king but ulti-mately influenced heavily by a priestly class. After the Kingdom of Israel was destroyed by the Assyrians and the Kingdom of Judah uprooted by the Babylonians, upon return from exile the tribes were no more and the people became a group of clans. Identity as a cultural entity rather than as a blood tribe came about; conversion – joining the 'citizenship' of Judae-ans – became possible. Pre-exilic religious life was temple and priest based and community and/or family group oriented. Post-exilic development saw more individualised activities such as Torah reading and comment, and an emphasis on individual piety, righteousness and prayer.

After the Exile, some advocated return to the theocratic, priestly, kingly community. Others emphasised that the righteousness Yahweh required came through personal piety, which made priests and kings much less important. Different interests promoted each response. Elites who sought political power subscribed to a return to kingship. Senti-ment calling for the direct rule of Yahweh through a king in present time was never far below the surface. Of course, the memory of King David and the successive kings of the land down through the centuries until the Babylonian conquest inspired this goal. In the time of the Exile and immediately after, Jeremiah and Isaiah both imagined a king leading the people in the times directly after the return from Babylonian exile:

> 'The days are coming,' declares the Lord, 'when I will raise up from David's line a righteous Branch, a King who will reign wisely and do what is just and right in the land. In his days Judah will be saved and Israel will live in safety.'

Subsequently a desire to re-establish an independent, righteous, theo-cratic kingdom could surface at any time. This can be seen in the Macc-abean revolt and in the numerous Judaeans who rose to claim kingship during the first century right up to the capture of Jerusalem in AD 70.

The priesthoods claimed the leadership in the cultic, theocratic model. Priests would be in charge of maintaining a right relationship with Yahweh. They would exert influence locally through the high priest and his minions at the temple in Jerusalem. They had great power and at times even total authority in Judaea, both religious and secular. Since their claim was ultimately religious, Judaea might be under the ultimate political control of an external power, while the priests still held great power in local matters. In this scenario, Judaea would be left alone as far as cult and local affairs were concerned, and in return the area would, under the priests, remain obedient politically to a secular overlord.

This arrangement allowed the personal and cultic piety people believed Yahweh valued. Although there was at best a figurehead king, the elite's interests were served by the emphasis on getting along with the current imperial power. The priests downplayed both social justice issues and personalised religious experience because these potentially undercut their pre-eminent and indispensable position as designated mediators between the people and Yahweh.

Emphasising cultic purity as sufficient to the covenantal deal with Yahweh thwarted tendencies to present-time political unrest. Therefore, an imperial power was usually willing to operate through that temple–priest and pliant elite framework to control the land and its Jewish people. The Persians created the high priesthood as a co-ruler with a king (both appointed by them). The royal family then disappeared and the high priest became the leading political figure. By the fourth century at the latest, the high priest was the recognised head of the Jewish people (not just of the temple) – civil and religious authority in one. For example, he was responsible for the collection of taxes for the imperial power. Therefore, imperial powers were willing to operate through the temple–priest framework. Control of the priesthood remained central to political machinations within the Judaean community throughout the Second Temple Period (c.537 BC–AD 70). But under the Romans its power was more limited as the civil authority was stripped away and given to a Roman governor or to a client king.

Under priestly rule cultic purity could continue within significant peripheral cultural changes. After Alexander's conquests and the imposition of Seleucid rule in the area, many began to see the advantages of adopting elements of Greek culture. At first the elite and then even some of the masses adopted Hellenistic habits such as the Greek language in everyday (but not cultic) life. Greek philosophical speculation came to influence elite thinking. Important ideas were influenced, if not caused, by that close contact with Hellenistic culture. But for the priests, the only thing that could alienate them from their ruling role was an outside threat to cultic purity.

7. Silver tetradrachm of King Antiochus IV Epiphanes who ruled the Seleucid Empire 175–164 BC. His actions in Judaea inspired the Maccabean Revolt in 167 BC.

Another group of people came to believe that they could best satisfy Yahweh's covenant by living pious, righteous lives. Obedience to Yahweh's laws as recorded by Moses claimed prime importance. At first these pious ones saw themselves as part and parcel of the general community and looked for Yahweh to reward the people for their faithfulness. They hoped Yahweh would protect in return for their righteousness. As Isaiah put it, 'Yahweh will conquer: the Lord will march out like a champion, like a warrior he will stir up his zeal; with a shout he will raise the battle cry and will triumph over his enemies.'

There were two aspects of life that might lead to political resistance. The elite and the pious ones might rise up, hoping to combine a desire for politically independent and pious lives and putting their trust in Yahweh. Then again, attempts to lessen or even eliminate their cultic independence might alienate the priesthood and so cause them to lead a revolt. These two strands of potential resistance, popular and cultic, to imperial rule came together in the early second century BC.

The clan of the Greek general Seleucus had taken over a large swathe of Alexander the Great's empire at his death in 323 BC. For reasons that remain mysterious, King Antiochus IV Epiphanes broke from the habit of his Persian and Greek predecessors. He viewed the high priests merely as another local elite to be manipulated and used. As a result he ignored the local tradition that they were divinely appointed by Yahweh and simply removed and appointed as his policy dictated, playing factions of elites and priests off against one another. This and the creeping Hellenisation he rewarded in loyal vassals led to the alienation of Jewish people who felt that the covenant with Yahweh left little room for overt conversion to Greek ways. The unacceptable chaos that ensued in Judaea as one high priest aspirant fought another led Antiochus to attack Jerusalem, pillage the temple, place an idol of Olympian Zeus on the main altar and conduct a campaign against the worship of Yahweh. One of the things he did was to proscribe possession of the Torah, which shows what an important place it had come to hold in the perpetuation of Yahweh worship.

A minor priestly clan from the Judaean village of Modein took up the banner of religious purity and political independence and led a revolt against the Greeks, fully in the tradition of anti-idolatry that had inspired radical action in earlier Israelite history. Mattathias of the Hasmonean clan led this revolt. At his death his son, Judah, nicknamed Maccabee ('the hammer'), took over, eventually defeated the Seleucids and re-established the traditional cult in the temple at Jerusalem. His brother Jonathan became high priest. But Jonathan did not assume the title of king, even at the death of Judah. At Jonathan's death another brother, Simon, was soon named not only high priest but also king. Despite the titles, however, Simon remained in control only by offering subservience to an imperial power, in this case the Seleucid kings yet again. Notwithstanding this reality, the ideal of a theocratic kingdom led by a king and a high priest (often one and the same person) remained strong in the leaders' and people's imagination long after the initial Maccabean uprising.

The Yahweh direct-rule mode, the re-establishment of an independent, righteous, theocratic kingdom in real time, was the dream of the likes of Jeremiah and Isaiah. But the model as it played out in real life had significant problems that troubled many people. Unfortunately, and contrary to the dream of the prophets, the actual enactment of king-and-priesthood-rule replicated what was bad from Israel's past: a theologically and politically corrupt leadership dominated, which was just what the Hebrew prophets of old had so strongly criticised. The establishment of Yahweh's kingdom assumed that Yahweh would reward and punish in present time according to his justice. Looking about them, many concluded that suffering in political and private life continued. They saw a current world in disorder and social dysfunction. Humans lived in thrall of pessimism and in fear of alienation from Yahweh. The symptoms were physical – earthquakes and other disasters – as well as social – injustice, immorality and apostasy among the faithful, persecution of the followers of the righteous. The earth seemed ruled by the wrong powers.

Humanity could not on its own rectify the dysfunctional situation, either interpersonally or in the physical world. It required the intervention of a supernatural power. Yahweh would seize control. He would hold those responsible for dysfunction to account. He would fulfil the promise of social justice explicit and implicit in the covenantal agreement by raising up righteous people and rewarding their personal piety. This would ultimately mean the destruction of the old world in conflagration or other disaster and to justification of the living righteous, resurrection and reward for the dead righteous, and a new creation into eternity. Yahweh's rule might be delayed, but it would be powerful when it came.

Everything was very volatile. Elites and priests struggled in various factions; outside imperial powers meddled. The whole stressful, tense structural situation seemed to boil down to one thing: the promise of the covenant and thē on-the-ground realities of internal strife, foreign domination and cultural challenge did not add up. Some people responded radically. The delayed-rule model conceived of an End of Time ruled by Yahweh's justice. It introduced an apocalyptic vision that provided both consolation and explanation in present suffering and exhortation and promise of a better, even vengeful, future. Thus, an apocalyptic belief in a delayed rule by Yahweh provided meaning for the present and hope for the future. It also inspired different courses of action. Some turned to armed resistance in the present to help bring about Yahweh's time more quickly. Others withdrew in expectation of the New Age, patiently awaiting in righteousness a judgement and reward in this life or post-mortem.

By the second century BC, the delayed-rule idea already had a long history in the people's traditions. Prophets of the Day of the Lord were long-standing. Isaiah had written: 'In that Day the Lord will punish the powers in the heavens above and the kings on the earth below.' While Joel added:

> Multitudes, multitudes in the valley of decision! For the Day of the Lord is near in the valley of decision. The sun and moon will be darkened, and the stars no longer shine. The Lord will roar from Zion and thunder from Jerusalem; the earth and the heavens will tremble … I will show wonders in the heavens and on the earth, blood and fire and billows of smoke. The sun will be turned to darkness and the moon to blood before the coming of the great and dreadful Day of the Lord. And everyone who calls on the name of the Lord will be saved.

The prophet Obadiah warned the oppressors, 'The Day of the Lord is near for all nations. As you have done, it will be done to you; your deeds will return upon your own head.' And Zephaniah reminded that only righteousness in the Lord offered hope, 'Seek the Lord, all you humble of the land, you who do what he commands. Seek righteousness, seek humility; perhaps you will be sheltered on the day of the Lord's anger.'

Focus on this idea that Yahweh would intervene violently, already present in the prophets, emerged in strength during the third century BC: the earth is a place of anti-Yahweh activity and injustice; the present age is evil, but it will be replaced by a heavenly age; a time of divine judgement will occur at the intersection of the two during which evil and injustice are punished and eliminated, while the righteous in Yahweh will flourish. Enoch (perhaps as early as 300 BC) had a clear and influential statement of this expectation. His inspired message was that Yahweh would come in might and the righteous would be rewarded:

With the righteous He will make peace and will protect the elect, and mercy shall be upon them … While the wicked godless will be punished: And behold! He comes with ten thousands of His holy ones to execute judgement upon all, and to destroy all the ungodly and to convict all flesh of all the works of their ungodliness which they have ungodly committed, and of all the hard things which ungodly sinners have spoken against Him.

This prediction of divine deliverance and retribution fitted a historical pattern of resistance common in the temple- and king-centred powers of the Near East. It also fitted with dire predictions of the later Hellenistic period. The Oracle of Hystaspes (second–first century BC) captured a polytheist take on the theme. A certain Hystaspes described the injustices of his time and said that the righteous, the pious and the faithful, would call upon Jupiter to set things right. 'And Jupiter will look upon the earth and hear the voices of the people and exterminate the godless ones.' In Egypt, the Oracle of the Potter (third century BC) touched on a similar theme, predicting that a righteous king would come, end present evil and establish a new age. Indeed, the blessings of that age would be so great that 'those who survive will pray that the people who have previously died will rise (from the dead) in order to share their blessings'.

In the Jewish tradition, the dead would be resurrected as part of reward and punishment in the afterlife. From an earlier day, Ezekiel's dry bones were now reinterpreted in the third century BC to refer to resurrection of the dead at the Day of Judgement. The Book of Daniel (early second century BC), clearly expressed a resurrection and judgement: 'Multitudes who sleep in the dust of the earth will awake: some to everlasting life, others to shame and everlasting contempt. Those who are wise will shine like the brightness of the heavens, and those who lead many to righteousness, like the stars for ever and ever.' And that resurrection would come with retribution for those guilty of oppressing others, as Enoch predicted:

I tell you, you sinners, you are content to eat and drink, and rob and sin, and strip men naked, and acquire wealth and see good days. Have you seen the righteous how their end falls out, that no manner of violence is found in them till their death? Nevertheless they perished and became as though they had not been, and their spirits descended into Sheol in tribulation.

The Yahweh-delayed model emphasised righteousness as the way to fulfil humans' side of the covenantal agreement. This emphasis, although not contrary to the cultic activities of the priesthood and the temple, decisively moves the focus from the temple activities to the people and to their ongoing way of living. While maintaining purity in following Yahweh's commandments was always one strain of the covenantal agreement, and one the prophets did not fail to emphasise, in the post-exilic period seeking purity became intensely personal because it was the way to righteousness and so reward at the final judgement. All the major approaches to fulfilling the covenant would from now on flow from this concern for purity and righteousness.

Varying conceptions of the justice of Yahweh occupied the minds and actions of the secular and priestly elites, who were often intricately interrelated. Would Yahweh perform his side of the bargain in the present time or in a future time? What righteousness did Yahweh require to bring rewards on a community and/or personal level? Who were the true interpreters of the covenant? In the struggles for power and prestige, the answers had important results among the Jewish people. At the political level, the effects were mostly related to being caught up as pawns in the confrontations of the elites. Recruited as solders in civil or external war; taxed to support temple and kings; caught in the crossfire as elites wrought vengeance on defeated civil populations; orchards and fields destroyed by competing armies; life could be tormenting at almost any time. In terms of daily survival, the traditional explanation that Yahweh rewarded and punished in real time in response to the righteousness (or lack thereof) on the part of a person or a person's ancestors lost much of its appeal. Yahweh had not and was not punishing his enemies; his justice was not evident. Projection of that justice to a future time removed this apparent contradiction between promise and deed. But waiting for the end of the world and suffering in the meantime was hardly more appealing. In the face of unjust suffering, Job had said to Yahweh: 'I know that you can do all things; no purpose of yours can be thwarted. You asked, "Who is this that obscures my plans without knowledge?" Surely I spoke of things I did not understand,

things too wonderful for me to know ...' Such a faith in an inscruta-
ble and unpredictable justice left daily crises unaddressed. The idea of
personal responsibility for righteousness combined with charismatics
preaching social justice and repentance appealed. In particular, the charismatic preachers and the sort of doctrine evident in the Essene movement could offer answers in present time and empower individuals to
think they could affect their own fates, winning the favour of Yahweh
in the process.

But also, in the face of disease, or a dangerous journey (and all jour-
neys tended to be dangerous), or childbirth, or failing crops, people
continued, as they had always done, to seek immediate reassurance
of supernatural aid and protection. Magic had the advantage of being
ready at hand, with practitioners who promised immediate results.
There was a long history of success. People simply ignored the contradictions with the official, theological responses to crisis. Magical actions
were compartmentalised, sealed off more or less effectively from more
generalised explanations and solutions the tradition offered, just as the
actions that embodied those explanations and solutions continued in a
person's world despite reliance on magic in specific situations.

The Jewish people struggled in an unjust world to come to terms with
Yahweh as a god of justice. That struggle opened up new ways to conceptualise both Yahweh's actions in the human world and people's relationship to Yahweh. While magic continued to be used as an ad hoc
means of dealing with contingencies in life, people were also attracted
by a longer-term conviction that Yahweh would vindicate their lives at
some future time if they were sufficiently righteous in the present. The
power of magic and the insistence of injustice in their lives made them
receptive to new approaches to Yahweh and his justice, and ultimately
opened some minds to Christianity's offering. Before we explore those
openings, it is necessary to look first to the polytheist experience.

POLYTHEISTS IN THEIR WORLD

POLYTHEISTS, LIKE THE JEWS, generally lived as members of a family and a community, worked hard to stay alive and improve their lot, and enjoyed pleasures such as children and religious festivals. They had a panoply of attitudes and approaches to the supernatural which the term 'polytheism' encapsulates. Their religious habits were conservative, closely tied to their identities in their families and communities. However, at times change entered the picture in interesting ways.

The common people's experiences were in some ways distinct from those of the elite. Only the elite had access to cultured learning: the study of philosophy, in particular, was the preserve of a tiny portion of the population. Elementary material was more widely known; perhaps 20 per cent of a given population, at least in the towns, was somewhat literate. At this level, school exercises, fables and maxims figured largely in teaching basic reading and writing. Instruction had the effect of emphasising simple, essential social values such as the acceptance of hierarchy and authority, and that the gods and Fate were in control of the learner and his world. So the divide was great between a highly educated 1 per cent or so and many of the rest. While the upper echelons of the general population aspired to at least some of the education normal among the high elite, others – petty artisans, merchants, workers, peasants, women, children and slaves – were at best semi-literate. Because of the great education gap, elite and non-elite sometimes had different ways of looking at the same supernatural powers – the latter character-istically straightforward and concerned with outcomes, the former more intellectual and concerned with inner well-being.

This cultural divide needs to be kept in mind when we look at evidence of religion and religious experience, but it is hard to tell just where the divide fell. Certainly, there were elites who did not believe in the traditional gods (the Epicureans, for example) and there were those, such as Lucian, who ridiculed popular concepts of the supernatural and their role in everyday life. In his *Meditations* the emperor Marcus Aurelius recalled thankfully that Diognetus taught him to ignore the claims of miracle-mongers and charlatans with their incantations to expel demons and the like – but he thanked his mother for teaching him piety. Like his mother, most elites would agree that gods existed, as Seneca and Cicero both insisted. The devil was in the detail. The range of thought and action was wide, although the situation was not quite 'quot homines, tot sententiae'. There were the scientifically minded, such as Pliny the Elder, who whenever he could sought non-supernatural explanations. There were etherealisers such as the Stoics and Platonists, who admitted a supernatural world, but one in tension with the way people conceived traditional gods. A good middle Platonist like Plutarch had respect for those gods while at the same time retaining some scepticism and criticism. On the other hand, an elite such as Aelius Aristides could be a completely committed believer in the traditional god Asclepius. Elite attitudes were more sophisticated but degrees of superstition and reverence for the traditional gods existed side by side with scepticism and disbelief.

The general public and elite thinkers, so different in their socio-economic and political stations, lived nonetheless in a common cultural community. The Oxford classicist Teresa Morgan has shown that popular morality and philosophical, moral thinking shared many principles and ideals. Although fables and proverbs do not use exactly the same terms as philosophy, they recognise concepts such as honesty, foolishness, wisdom, justice and rationality. If philosophy deals in values such as temperance, courage, justice and wisdom, so, the evidence suggests, do the people in everyday life. Both share an aversion to traits such as anger, greed and lust and praise those such as honour, friendship and piety. They agree on the importance of health, wealth and reputation.

This is not to say that philosophical discourse expresses the ways of everyday people – far from it – but we can see that certain values hold throughout the community. While we consider ordinary people's lives on their own terms, we can also note the influence philosophical inquiry could have on tenets held throughout the community.

Polytheism in Greece and Rome had no canon of literature, no priestly hierarchy, no centralising organisation. But despite a, to us, bewildering variety of gods, their religious experience shared basic elements: super-human powers existed; they were many; they lived in, entered and left the natural world at will; they could intervene in people's lives for good or ill; their favour could and should be won over through approved action, prayer, offerings and rituals; and Fate and Fortune ruled.

Gods tended to be, at least at the beginning, tied to local environments – peoples, geographical locations, towns and cities. Peoples who shared culture and language accepted the 'local' gods as a group and worshipped them in the same way. Once a group came to accept a body of gods, it was possible and often useful to conceptualise the body of gods of another group as being like theirs, and for one group to use the god-names of another similar group for their own gods. So polytheism readily assimilated various groups' conceptualisation of super-natural powers, for all shared the same fundamental approach to the supernatural.

The basic issue for polytheists as they navigated their lives was that something was out of whack with the world they lived in – there was suffering, unpredictability and injustice that distributed happiness haphazardly. Human beings lived in an unpredictable, irrational environment; it could be dangerous and disruptive. The human mind had evolved to expect cause and effect, to seek reasons for why things happened. A chaotic, causeless, irrational world created challenges in life and, with that, psychological stress. Although sometimes good things happened – and people certainly addressed the supernatural to obtain good results – it was the bad things that caused the most disruption.

The explanation for why bad things happened (aside from Fate and Fortune) was that a spirit or power was angry because of some alienation (intended or not). The polytheist's religion was directed towards controlling disruption individually or communally through winning back the supernatural powers' favour or warding off their anger. People did this by honouring the gods both at home and in sacred places (ritual), making deals (vows, sacrifice), beseeching (prayer) and divination (foretelling what was to happen in order better to deal with events). The variety of polytheist approaches came from how these elements combined in life. For example, if 'honouring the gods' was thought to require particular moral behaviour, that factor was included in thinking about the supernatural. If it required only specific sacrifices, then there was little overt moral content. However worked out, polytheistic relationships with the supernatural always retained their fundamental importance in people's lives and people viewed their relationships as worth cultivating.

The polytheist approach assumed that supernatural powers could intertwine with any event. Sometimes this presence was more metaphorical, but sometimes it was animistic. Pliny the Elder caught the power-imbued nature of the world around when he wrote, 'Once upon a time trees were the temples of the deities and in conformity with primitive ritual simple country places even now dedicate a tree of exceptional height to a god; nor do we pay greater worship to images shining with gold and ivory than to the forests and to the very silences that they contain.'

While philosophers worked hard to assess, order and explain the working of the supernatural (and natural) world, the majority of polytheists were content to use mythology as an avenue to understanding. In keeping with the bedrock belief of polytheism that the gods existed, the number and variety of religious acts was almost infinite and so too were the myths. But mythology hardly stood alone as entertaining stories. Rather, they were the grounding that made religious actions understandable; they existed in active conjunction with accepted habits of worship, sacrifice and so on. That said, many if not most acts must have been performed in the instant without much careful thinking about origins or colourful stories. But this did not mean that the myths were not there, to be beckoned when needed to understand or accentuate a particular rite or sacrifice.

The variety of supernatural powers may seem rather bewildering. We readily recognise the high gods that figure in the books of mythology, gods such as Jupiter/Zeus and Mars/Ares. Certainly these in their many local guises were an active part of people's religion. Likewise, those half-human figures such as Asclepius and Hercules, who because of their greatness the high gods allowed to become one of them. Hercules was the most famous, a hero famed for his concern for humanity, while Asclepius was a healing god also very concerned for the welfare of humans.

Daemons (not to be confused with the later Christian concept of 'demons') were supernatural forces above the human sphere and of but not exactly in the sphere of the high gods. They came in two active forms: an entity between humans and gods with specific powers and competences and a usually protective force often linked with an individual's destiny. Humans appealed to them – feared, reverenced and/or worshipped them.

The array of supernatural beings and powers was immediate to the polytheists, who believed they not only existed but also interacted tangibly with humans. It is not just Homeric gods aiding this or that hero. People were certain that gods could and did walk among them. A remarkable example of this is what happened to the early Christian missionaries Paul and Barnabas at Lystra in Asia Minor, where they were mistaken for Olympian gods. Paul was preaching in the town when he saw a man who had been crippled from birth listening intently. Paul fixed him in his gaze and, sensing his belief, said loudly, 'Stand upright on your feet.' The cripple, Acts tells, then got up and walked. The astonished Lystrians took Paul's miracle as a sign of divinity: 'The gods have come down to us in the likeness of men!' they shouted, deeming Barnabas to be Zeus and Paul to be Hermes. The local priest of Zeus prepared a public sacrifice to these gods-come-to-earth. Barnabas and Paul had some difficulty stifling popular enthusiasm for a Zeus sacrifice right then and there.

Polytheists learned in traditional ways about their relationships with the supernatural and how to deal with them. The elite intellectual Seneca sneered, 'The greater part of the people goes through their rituals not knowing why they do so.' But polytheists directed their attention to practical goals, not to understanding anything deeply theological or philosophical about what they were doing. Lore and tradition came through family and community. Devotion in the family setting was not controlled or guided from outside; the father was the specialist

8. A family Lar (protective deity) from a wall painting that
was part of a household shrine (*lararium*) in Pompeii.

who preserved the way to do and understand things. Celebrations of
festivals and entertainments with a religious tinge retained and passed
on attitudes, actions and relationships with the supernatural in the community. Since there were relatively few specific, written documents to
provide fixed guidance in this process, the oral and active culture of a
given community or family provided the parameters. The habits and
guidelines could vary, but the basics were efficiently passed along from
generation to generation.

We possess polytheists' prayers and hymns, incantations and other
material as well as, of course, myths, fables, gnomic utterances and proverbs. But these were not organised into a theology, much less a creed. It
is important to note that there was nothing, or at least nothing that we
possess today, that replicates the complexity and force represented by

the Torah writings in the Jewish tradition. Neither was there an organised, regular locus for systematic proclamation and discussion such as existed in the prayer houses and synagogues of the Jewish people. Nevertheless, the moral guidance that emerges from popular literature has many similarities to what is found in the Jewish tradition. Proverbs of Publilius Syrus offer examples of the golden rule ('As you treat a neighbour, expect another to treat you'); advocacy against infanticide ('Barbarous, not brave, is he who kills a child') and care for the less fortunate ('To do a kindness to the needy at once is to give twice'). What was lacking was a coherent, overall moral theology.

Polytheist worship

In the home, the polytheists, 'when they daily rise from their sleep, go in the morning to worship and minister to their idols; and before all their works and undertakings they go first and worship their idols'. Daily routine included a libation at meals and stopping at shrines or temples to make small offerings or prayer in the course of moving about, or to address a particular problem. People constantly used images as focus for worship, whether the family Lar (protective deity), an altar at a crossroads, a statue in a temple, or the home of a spirit such as a grove or stream. This focus on physical artefacts, often idols, as the point of worship separated polytheists from their Jewish counterparts. The basic theology of interacting with the supernatural was the same, however. The principle of *do ut des*, 'I give so that you might give in return,' drove polytheist relationships with the supernatural just as it did Jewish. Sometimes this was active – a worshipper sought help or advice, offered a recompense, and a god responded (or not). Sometimes it was passive – a worshipper expressed reverence without an explicit request with the understanding that this should generate a favourable treatment by the power. Gods could also intervene on their own in people's lives. They summoned people to worship them or sent them dreams, epiphanies, or oracles to guide their actions. In this, too, polytheists were like Jewish people.

Rituals and customs surrounded the transitional stages of life – birth, marriage and death. Prayer was an integral part of sacrificial worship. As Pliny the Elder put it, 'the sacrifice of victims without a prayer is supposed to be of no effect ...' The Greeks referred to the gods as *epekooi*, those who listen to prayers.

Prayer could also be for general help, as in the example:

Eternal Lord [dominus], Cascelia Elegans asks you through your mercy, on her behalf and that of all who are hers, as you have shown mercy to these created beings, I ask you, Eternal One, by earth and sea divine, by whatever good thing you have created, by salt and sacred seed, be merciful to me and mine, I beg, by your piety, your living law, your creatures, Eternal One, [I beg] you [to be] favouring, on behalf of my fellow slave and my daughter and my master Primus and Celia wife of my patron, Lord.

Prayer could be a physical act, as in this offering of a vow:

While I am unable to bear the dire pangs of body and spirit, wandering forever near the edges of death, I, Tychicus, by Mars' divine love, am saved. This little thanks-offering I dedicate in return for his great caring.

Or again, a prayer could be like an incantation: Pliny noted in his encyclopaedia that 'on walls, too, are written prayers to avert fires'.

Polytheism also knew purity regulations – foods that could not be eaten, sex that could not be had – and specific instructions as to dress. Such purity could be important to the efficacy of rituals. The healing god, Asclepius, was especially concerned with purity, as this dedication shows:

By command of the Lord Asclepius, Lucius Numisius Vitalis son of Lucius erects this podium at his own expense. Anyone wishing to ascend onto the podium should abstain for three days from women, pork, beans, barber, and city baths, and should not enter the balustrade wearing shoes.

Incubation (sleeping in a holy place and awaiting a dream with instructions), oracles and even graffiti were forms of worship. Pliny the Younger wrote that at the Clitumnus sanctuary near Hispellum in Italy, 'you can study the numerous inscriptions in honour of the spring and the god which many hands have written on every pillar and wall. Most of them you will admire, but some will make you laugh – though I know you are really too charitable to laugh at any of them.' Many inscriptions recorded a vision or an explicit commandment received from a god. One person offered a dedication to Mars Augustus as the result of an order 'from the very god himself'. Gaius Clodius paid a vow after a vision of the divine Fates. Rogatianus had a vision of Mercury, carried out the god's instructions and gained health for himself and his family. And in one case a certain Ianuarius was told in a vision to restore a public well, which he dutifully did.

On a daily basis, people had their favourite methods of turning aside harm. The elite and the masses shared many superstitious habits, as in the case of Julius Caesar, who, in response to a near-fatal chariot accident, always thereafter repeated three times a formulaic prayer for a safe journey when he seated himself – 'a thing we know that people do today', Pliny the Elder remarked.

Sacrifices, rituals and festivals formed an important part of a community's religious life. Plutarch included ordinary people in his description of community participation in such actions. He vividly captured the social release a grand celebration offered them. Everyone loved a festival!

The attitude towards God that we find in the ignorant but not greatly wicked majority of mankind contains no doubt along with the sense of reverence and honour an element of tremulous fear; but outweighing this a thousand times is the element of cheerful hope, of exultant joy, and whether in prayer or in thanksgiving of ascribing every furtherance of felicity to the gods. This is proved by the strongest kind of evidence: no visit delights us more than a visit to a temple; no occasion [more] than a holy day; no act or spectacle [more] than what we see and what we do ourselves in matters that involve the gods, whether we celebrate a ritual or take part in a choral dance or attend a sacrifice or ceremony of initiation ... Wherever the mind believes and conceives most firmly that the god is present, there more than anywhere else it puts away all feelings of pain, of fear and of worry, and gives itself up so far to pleasure that it indulges in a playful and merry inebriation … In processions and at sacrifices not only crone and gaffer, not only men without wealth or station, but even 'The grinder with her heavy legs, who pushes at her mill' and the servants of household and farm feel the lift of high spirits and a merry heart.

Communal religious experience helped mitigate the fears and worries of the everyday. Temple areas were swept, statues were cleaned and anointed, then wreathed with flowers or branches appropriate to the god. The entire area was sprinkled with holy water. Sacred ceremonies often included a meal: 'kitchens' and like spaces in temples were extremely common. The cult of Mithras had a sacred meal much like the Christian agape feast. Dance could also be a part of devotion. Lucian described reverential dancing: 'I must note that not a single ancient mystery cult can be found that is without dancing, since they were established, of course, by Orpheus and Musaeus, the best dancers of that time, who included it in their prescriptions as something exceptionally beautiful to be initiated with rhythm and dancing.'

Festivals such as one Plutarch imaged in the quotation above were particularly important to people. Holidays were celebrated with enthusiasm as well as devotion. The local festival of Artemis in Ephesus included a grand procession from the city to the temple that lay nearly a mile from the town:

> All the local girls had to march in procession, richly dressed, as well as all the young men … There was a great crowd of Ephesians and visitors alike to see the festival … So the procession filed past – first the sacred objects, the torches, the baskets and the incense; then horses, dogs, hunting equipment, some for war, most for peace … And when the procession was over, the whole crowd went into the temple for the sacrifice …

In Egypt the festivals in honour of the god Sarapis drew both reverence and wilder forms of celebration. Strabo recorded that temple visitors sought and found cures and oracles, but then somewhat disapprovingly added, 'But to balance all this is the crowd of revellers who go down from Alexandria by the canal to the public festivals; for every day and every night is crowded with people on the boats who play the flute and dance without restraint and with extreme licentiousness, both men and women.' The Christian Tertullian prejudicially but perhaps accurately criticised such festal activity and in doing so gave us another vivid picture of what might unfold as men set up braziers and benches street by street in the open air, making 'the city look like nothing but a tavern', enough wine spilled to make mud of the street and people rushing around 'in droves for outrage, impudence and the incitements to lust'. The very extensive description of the festival of Isis procession in Apuleius's *Metamorphoses* also shows how much public enthusiasm and participation a festival generated.

A festival meal usually followed a parade and public sacrifice. After the sacrifice, the people held a banquet to consume the sacrificial meat. There is evidence in many ancient authors of the excesses that went on during some festivals, such as those mentioned just above. Sometimes meals related to sacred ceremonies went on for days and days. The diners could include all citizens, or resident aliens, or some hierarchical selection. Women and children usually did not participate, although if they did, it was customarily at separate tables from the men. Along with spectacles such as theatrical events, the festivals were one of the few times when a large body gathered and felt itself to be a community. As a social event, the banquets that were held for the citizen population both were an expression of the social order and served to legitimate and reinforce that order. The combination of religious fervour, community affirmation and opportunity for excess meant that festivals remained essential and popular events in polytheists' lives throughout antiquity.

Sponsoring these extremely popular public feasts fell to the elite – none that I know of was tax supported. Elites organised, financed and managed everything. Their influence was ongoing and pervasive; it came as a result of their pre-eminent position in society. The beneficent activity of sponsoring festivals and the like confirmed their leadership and fed their image of noblesse oblige. Meat, bread and wine were typical of festival fare. For most people, eating lots of meat and drinking to excess remained exceptional; festivals were the time to do it, and the elite were to be thanked. But the festival celebrations also integrated with people's personal religious lives as their relationship with a divinity reaffirmed a god's importance in private votives and sacrifices, all under the umbrella of elite care.

Of course, elites did not send out missionaries or preachers, either on their own or as agents of a government. They and local priests (usually one and the same) did try to impress with parades, meals and handouts, but there was no overt pressure on individuals to take part. What elites did by way of honouring the gods did create visible and compelling evidence of their importance. Any basic change in people's approach to polytheism that minimised the elites' role would alienate the elite that relied so heavily on religious habits to confirm their leadership in a community.

I have said that polytheism lacked an overarching moral imperative, but don't want to overstate the case. People had guidance from their traditions and habits that informed their moral attitudes and responses. Although there was no all encompassing, established standard that could be referred to, daily life indeed confronted and dealt with moral issues in fairly consistent ways.

If we ask what the Justice of Jupiter/Zeus required, taking the high gods as a representative of the entire pantheon of polytheism, the answer is fairly similar, in principle, to what Yahweh required. That is to say, moral behaviour crops up continuously as a concern of the gods. There is no covenant between people and gods of the sort Moses took down from Sinai, but the basic expectations are, on a purely moral level, quite similar. We find these expectations expressed in common thought as seen in fables and proverbs. We find them expressed in votive prayers and sacrifices recorded on stone as epigraphy. They are an organic part of life. As far as we can tell, priests did not get involved in teaching morals, however. That became the realm of philosophers who came more and more to emphasise moral issues in the lives of people.

There was no doubt in ordinary people's minds that supernatural powers sought revenge when disrespected. Offending behaviour included the improper execution of ritual, or its neglect, and moral turpitude. The gods especially went after perjurers, but on a broader level they famously were supposed to punish the wicked. These expectations are expressed in an inscribed potsherd from Egypt:

9. A libation for the dead was often poured onto or into a grave. Here a gravestone has a hole and plug to make this offering easy.

Claudius Silvanus and his brothers to mistress Athena against Longinus Marcus. Since Longinus – against whom we have often appealed to you because he was after our lives while we did no wrong, poor as we are – while he wins nothing with this, he still continues to be malicious against us, we beg you to do justice. We have already asked Ammon for help as well.

And on a lead tablet from Britain:

Cenacus complains to the god Mercury about Vitalinus and Natalinus his son concerning the draught animal that was stolen. He begs the god Mercury that neither may have health unless they repay me promptly the animal they have stolen and repay to the god the devotion which he himself has demanded from them.

Supernatural powers wrought their vengeance in this life. While elite literature has some idea of reward and punishment after death, most people had little sense of punishment in a future life for failings in this one. That is not to say that people had no idea of life after death. It is true that some believed that death ended everything. A graffito from Pompeii expresses it well: 'Once you are dead, you are nothing.' The expression 'I did not exist, I existed, I don't exist now, I don't care' appears on numerous inscriptions. But archaeology and inscriptions clearly show that many, many people believed that the dear departed continued to exist not only in memory but also in a nebulous way. They regularly made offerings in acknowledgement of some sort of continuance. Justin Martyr pointed out that polytheists had many ways to connect with the dead. He mentioned dream interpretation, appeal to spirits, inspired demoniacs, famous oracles such as that at Delphi, and the experiences and opinions of various honoured authors such as Empedocles, Pythagoras, Plato, Socrates, Homer and the like. But whatever that post-life existence actually was, it did not usually include the possibility of being punished for deeds in the earthly life.

Fate and Fortune were the final explanations for unexpected occurrences. Sometimes it could be a cosmic ordering, a predestination that fixed events in life – Fate. Sometimes it could be more like Fortune – luck or accident – an unpredicted event or outcome. Both Fate and Fortune had to be considered because some things happened beyond the ken or power of humans in unpredictable ways. Careful planning and preparation did not work. Invocation of the usual supernatural powers did not work. Magical formulae did not work. Fate and Fortune worked in the ultimate black box: actions occurred in life and results occurred, but how the actions led to the results remained entirely mysterious.

Philosophers struggled with the concept of Fate: Stoics accepted it as ruling the cosmos, Epicureans denied its power, while Cynics – seeking fortification of self against Fate – responded with serenity to anything Fate or Fortune could come up with. People tried to control their own lives through decision making and dealing with the supernatural, but they also prayed to Fortune, made sacrifices to Fortune, tried to predict what Fate or Fortune was going to do. But nothing could work for certain. Randomness in much of human experience needed an explanation, and Fate along with Fortune was it. Knowing that 'Fate decreed it' was perhaps cold comfort, but some comfort nonetheless, for it asserted that the cosmos had order, even if humans could not discern it.

10. The Fates were very active in the lives of polytheists. One spun the thread of life, one measured it, and the third cut it.

In the home and the community, inspired individuals could play an important role in the lives of people. Wandering holy men (or their imposters) came and went through the towns, performing miracles (or deceptions) and preaching. Exorcisms were a particularly popular event. The storyteller Xenophon has a tale of diviners and priests being asked to expel an evil spirit from a girl. Apuleius in his *Golden Ass*, a work filled with magic and miracles, has one Zachlas, an Egyptian miracle worker, bring a corpse back to life. In another instance, priests of a Syrian goddess travelled about the countryside pretending to inspiration and accepting donations from the gullible. Apollonius of Tyana, a follower of Pythagorean lore, preached and performed miracles in Asia Minor and Syria during the latter years of the first century AD. His disciple, Alexander of Abonoteichus, followed him, endowed with a supposedly wondrous snake, Glycon; a cult of Glycon actually survived for some time.

Philosophers also had a special role in polytheism. This might seem counterintuitive since the earliest philosophers sought to discover the workings of a mechanical world without a guiding 'mind' or supernatural interventions. In the sixth century BC Anaximander offered non-supernatural, mechanical explanations for things like eclipses and lightning. Anaximenes sought the underlying order of the cosmos in the four elements of air, earth, fire and water interacting in various ways, while Empedocles advanced this quadripartite elemental explanation of the physical world to canonical heights. Democritus took the elemental approach further by introducing atoms as the make-up of the universe – chance collisions of atoms in the voids between them created the visible world. This explanatory science began a wider investigation, the understanding not only of the mechanics of the cosmos, but of humans – human actions, life and death.

In the early fifth century BC, Parmenides was the first to apply the new, scientific thinking to human actions. Late in that century Socrates, Plato's teacher, directed his thoughts exclusively to the nature of human existence. He tried to discover what the good life – one of excellence or 'virtue' – actually might be. Since Socrates admitted that he had no magic key to the human cosmos such as the physics of the pre-Socratics offered for the physical cosmos, he focused on inquiry in a dialectical format to arrive at probable but not certain answers. In Plato's hands, the Socratic dialectic became the basis for inquiry into the human world of morality and excellence. Nature, Plato said, had teleology – to embody the good. In the *Timaeus* Plato posited an artisan god who created at the ideal level an ordered and good cosmos. Mind and reason were the agents for understanding and so at least potentially able to guide humans towards doing and being good.

For all of ancient philosophy, reason remained the touchstone for investigations. While reason drove the pre-Socratic philosophers away from traditional concepts of the supernatural – Xenocrates had attacked the anthropomorphic Homeric gods – the drive to understand human actions moved thinking towards some form of knowing supernatural power that guided or at least inspired human striving for the good, however defined. Philosophical inquiry in the fourth century BC strove to understand both the physical and human cosmos. However, from the third century on, philosophers more and more often simply accepted the physics of their predecessors and focused on moral philosophy – what it meant to lead a good life. The answers were disparate, but all the mainstream thinkers – Platonists, Stoics and Epicureans – strove to discover truth, and with it understanding, and so how to live out a good life.

It was precisely such overarching moral thinking that polytheism in all its varied guises lacked. Some philosophers, especially the Epicureans, had little place for traditional gods in their thinking. But others made their peace with the old ways. True to the essentially sponge-like quality that underlay all their thought and action, polytheists could absorb moral guidance from philosophical teaching without giving up their sacrifices, festivals and so on.

Philosophy qua philosophy scarcely touched the general public. Elite scorn for such people pervades all schools of ancient philosophy from Plato on. Epicurus and Epicureanism alone had, some claim, appeal to the ordinary. Close inspection of the ancient evidence disproves even this. Epicurus himself stated, 'I was never anxious to please the common people. I had never learned the sort of thing they liked and the things I knew were far removed from their perception.' Widespread adherence to Epicureanism is a myth, based almost entirely on a single quotation from Cicero. Lucretius, the great purveyor of Epicureanism, noted that 'the common people shrink back' from the teachings.

Nevertheless, touches of philosophy could trickle down in various ways. Hawkers, public speakers and entertainers filled public spaces such as forums, street corners and city-gate areas with the din of competing messages. Paul spread his message in the marketplace. Cynics railed at passers-by. Hucksters proffered advice about astrology, magical cures and fortune telling. Covered porticos in central plazas offered a place for discourse protected from the elements. Indeed, Stoics took their moniker from the name of the place where their founder, Zeno, first taught, the Painted Stoa in the Athenian marketplace. Others with a message sought a hall and lectured: Paul once rented Tyrannus's lecture room when his message irritated those in the synagogue at Corinth. Homes served as venues. Philosophers at least since Plato had presented in homes and Paul another time moved his message to the home of Titius Justus when the synagogue assembly at Corinth responded to his message with hostility. Travelling purveyors of messages wheedled their way into people's homes and presented their offerings – the male-dominated literature regularly claims that women were especially susceptible to such presentations.

In Pompeii, the Tavern of the Seven Sages offers amazing, and amazingly humorous, evidence of the merging of the mundane and the philosophical. Wall paintings of the Seven Sages decorate the latrine. Above the toilet holes sages look down, graced with parodic allusion to their wisdom. Chilon of Sparta graces one wall with the annotation, 'Cunning Chilon taught how to fart without making noise.' Men defecating are painted on the wall below. There would be no humour without the confluence of popular and elite traditions about the Sages.

Philosophers used material from popular culture extensively – fables, gnomic utterances, stories of events – in illustrating and making their points. Early philosophers as well as later ones like Seneca, Plutarch and Maximus of Tyre used exempla and gnomic sayings, many of which were widely known. This indicates they were familiar with the common culture around them and that a body of knowledge and custom in that culture was relevant to all levels of society. It also means that high philosophy dealt with topics that were the common cultural possession of all levels of society. It could hardly be otherwise. Dealing with imaginary issues or issues that were culturally inconceivable would be ridiculous. Indeed, Aristotle forthrightly said in the *Nicomachean Ethics* that he begins his discussion of basic ethical ideas such as unrestraint versus self-restraint and self-indulgence versus endurance with an assessment of popular opinion about them.

By the first century BC philosophical moral thinking and traditional polytheist religious habits had reached a symbiotic alliance – perhaps more commonly among the educated elite, but philosophy as a way of life also penetrated more and more actively into the rest of the population. One aspect in particular deserves emphasis. Philosophy from the first century BC increasingly stressed the importance of their founders' sayings and teachings, rather than further independent inquiry in the traditional philosophic mode. Replication of a founder's life and teaching became very important. Biographies of famous philosophers proliferated; today we have a third-century AD example in Diogenes Laërtius's *Lives and Sayings of Eminent Philosophers*. When it came time to write a 'biography' of Jesus of Nazareth, the 'life of a philosopher' model provided the genre. Like a philosopher's, Jesus's message was told in tales and pithy sayings illustrating morals and virtues embedded in a non-chronological framework that included reference to such things as nationality, parentage, early life, education, death and burial. A polytheist hearing or reading a Gospel would have immediately thought of philosophers and their teaching habits.

Speculation about the best life to live threw up the most famous public philosophers of antiquity: the Cynics. Typical preaching by Cynics – so called because they yelped at passersby like dogs, *kunes* in Greek – included confrontational speech and direct, scathing repartee with interlocutors. They did not preach in extended, logical discourse or lectures before crowds, as many philosophers did. They took up any available venue and unabashedly advocated a countercultural simple life. Their speciality was puncturing the everyday assumptions and habits of people and elites alike. Appearance often identified them. Scruffily bearded, usually dressed in a simple cloak, often in rags, carrying only a staff and pouch, they sat at a temple's stairs or stood on a street corner and shouted their message. Their very theatricality attracted the attention of elite writers, and so we have descriptions of them by Lucian and Martial. For example, Martial describes Cosmus the Cynic:

> You often see him, Cosmus, in the recess of our temple to Athena and by the threshold of the New Temple, an old man with staff and pouch. His bristling hair is white and powdery, his unkempt beard falls on his chest, a threadbare cloak, spouse to his bare pallet, covers him, and the crowd that comes his way gives him the food he barks for.

Diogenes of Sinope in the fourth century BC was arguably the most famous Cynic. He and his followers through the centuries saw themselves not as part of an intellectual pursuit, but rather as advocates and practitioners of a way of life. They sought to live 'according to nature', which meant rejecting all 'unnatural' constraints laid on by culture and society. Conventionally acceptable values regarding fame, wealth, power and sexual behaviour were irrelevant and blocked a true life. Diogenes used unorthodox methods to shock people into abandoning false values. He sought to make them aware of the incoherencies of civilised life compared to the ideal life, the 'natural life'. Cynics preached, wandered and begged for a living in search of their goal.

It is possible (although not clearly demonstrable) that Cynics were numerous in the hustle and bustle of town forums and squares throughout the empire. How many there were depends on how we read our sources. Lucian, an almost hysterically anti-Cynic writer, left the impression that they were in every town and village, at least in the eastern Mediterranean. Dio Chrysostom left the same impression with regard to Alexandria in Egypt when he gave an unsympathetic description of the local Cynics. While admitting that their tenets 'comprise practically nothing spurious or ignoble', he blamed their most obnoxious habits on the fact that they had to make a living. They,

> posting themselves at street-corners, in alleyways and at temple-gates, pass round the hat and play upon the credulity of lads and sailors and crowds of that sort, stringing together rough jokes and much tittle-tattle and that low badinage that smacks of the market-place. Accordingly they achieve no good at all, but rather the worst possible harm, for they accustom thoughtless people to deride philosophers in general, just as one might accustom lads to scorn their teachers and, when they ought to knock the insolence out of their hearers, these Cynics merely increase it.

Nevertheless, it remains hard to know how many people witnessed the tirades of a Cynic. In addition, it is not at all clear how many actual followers these men had. Some scholars talk of a mass movement and state that almost everyone knew the sayings of Diogenes. But there is scant evidence for a positive response among the lower classes. After all, Cynics declared that poverty – rejection of possessions and living as simply as possible, by the generosity of others – was a high good. Known Cynics were wealthy men who then, some willy, some nilly, became poor. Most people, more or less poor to start with, surely were baffled by such an almost romantic view of being poor. Their main goals in life were, first, to stay alive and, second, to prosper. In addition, alienation from the foundational cultural institutions in the family and community would have left most without the network and support they needed to survive. Cynics' tirades against such religious activities as the mystery cults, prayer, dream interpretation and purification did not endear them to many. Their emphasis on self-sufficiency, escaping the constraints of society and keeping Fate at a distance through detachment from the world might not have appealed to many, either, since it was all quite anti-religious in a traditional sense. People were more likely to think of them as frauds (as did many of the elite, such as Seneca, Petronius and Martial), or fools than as models to be emulated. It is possible that Cynics appealed to some, but surely the way of life they offered with their harsh critique of society and harsh living situation would not have entranced the majority. There is no evidence that it did except in the way that preachers shouting on street corners attract a crowd of the curious.

Cynics represented the extreme of a general shift in philosophy as thinking and exposition aimed at life improvement became very important. This development took up a lack in the normal polytheist relationship to the supernatural, the lack of a theology of moral action. Although individual cults and traditions had a moral element – ideas of right and wrong with regard to human interactions and interactions with the supernatural – polytheism lacked a general moral vision. What humans asked of the gods and what the gods expected in terms of moral action had some general, shared qualities, but was shifting and often nebulous. Cynics' moral approach in general, as well as their belief that, according to their founder, Antisthenes, there were not many gods, but only one, showed in a spectacular and very public way the possibilities for thinking about a moral vision within polytheism. Although the Cynics offered a powerfully negative critique of traditional gods, their very methods provided the outline of how to insert clear and general moral principles into the variety of experiences that polytheism provided.

These Cynics have been compared to the charismatic preachers of the Jewish tradition. Great effort has been expended in finding parallels between Cynic sayings and habits, material in the Dead Sea Scrolls and the Jesus tradition. It is true that the Cynics as public preachers who chastised people for the way they led their lives bore some similarity to the prophets. At least some prophets were itinerant, lived a lifestyle of poverty (though they hardly recommended it on principle), criticised social norms (though to bring people back to a previous good state, not to recommend a radical change to something new) and advocated for a single god. Their public harangues approached the level of oral performance that the Cynics perfected. But the whole direction of prophetic declarations was entirely different from that of the Cynics. The similarities in expression and theme may have been there, but the goals were not the same. To think that the Jewish traditions as seen in the prophetic literature – the Dead Sea Scrolls and the life of Jesus – are Cynic results from a serious misunderstanding of the messages and messengers of the two traditions.

Although it would be wrong to draw too sharp a distinction, polytheistic approaches tended to separate activities of the individual participating in rites with fellow citizens – religious practice tied to a community and place – and individuals practising private rites outside the sphere of the community's gods. The most widespread phenomena of the latter sort were the mystery religions and the new religions arising from the Near East such as Jupiter Dolichenus, Isis, Mithras and Christianity. These approaches to the supernatural focused on an individual's experience in a defined setting not tied to a traditional local community. Often the experience was very emotional. Aelius Aristides, a devotee of the curing god Asclepius, likened his personal experience to that of an initiate into a mystery religion:

> For there was a feeling as if taking hold of him [the god Asclepius] and clearly perceiving that he himself had come, of being midway between sleeping and waking, of wanting to look, of struggling against his departure too soon; of having applied one's ears and of hearing some things as in a dream, some waking; hair stood straight, tears flowed in joy; the burden of understanding seemed light. What man is able to put these things into words? Yet if he is one of those who have undergone initiation, he knows and is familiar with them.

While elites joined the mystery religions, the best known being at Eleusis in Attica, few followed the personal religions until well into the high empire. The first Roman senator known to be a Christian appears only around the middle of the third century. The elites were tied to the community cults they led and which reinforced their position in society. The people felt less constrained in experimenting with new ways of thinking about and acting towards the supernatural. They could, in theory

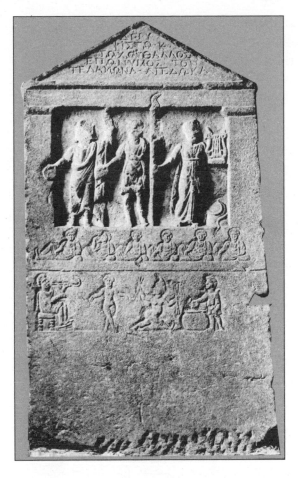

11. Many ordinary people worshipped Zeus Hypsistos (Zeus Most High). The cult was especially popular in Asia Minor. This stele, from Panormus (northwestern Asia Minor), shows the gods' association meeting and feasting.

at least, continue to participate in the community cults while pursuing whatever other satisfactions the cult of Isis or some other might offer them.

The people were open to new contacts with the supernatural, which is not to say they hankered after religious change. The idea that a general angst led people to embrace new religions – specifically, Christianity – derives from history as apology, history as the explanation of why Christianity 'won'. The sources, such as inscriptions, do not indicate among the people any seismic shift in religious sentiment or any abstract longing for a better spiritual life, much less dissatisfaction with their current gods. The new religions offered new things – different kinds of community and interpretations of which supernatural powers were effective – but the needs they met were the same as those that had been met for aeons in their old relationships with the supernatural. For some, however, the new options seem to have met them better.

Shared community outside the home and outside traditional religious activities formed an important element of many of the new approaches. From Greek tragedy to the Roman experience with new cults in the second century BC to the numerous mystery cults, the bonding in a shared religious experience outside the civic and family cults appealed to many people. In Egypt in the first century BC a group met devoted to Zeus Hypsistos (Zeus Most High). A papyrus recorded the rules of the community. It offers an interesting example of a new religious association gathered together. A president was chosen for one year; he was responsible for organising the monthly meetings-cum-drinking session. 'All are to obey the president and his assistant in matters concerning the fellowship and they are to be present at those occasions and meetings and assemblies and excursions which are enjoined upon them.' At each meeting the group made a libation and offered prayers for the king of Egypt. The meeting then turned into a social gathering. The rules anticipated rowdiness and tried to forestall it: 'No one is to ask questions at the drinking feast [sic] about the origins of another member, or to show contempt for him or gossip about him or to make accusations against him or reproach him, or to refuse his participation for the [current] year or place any obstacle in the way of the common drinking feasts ...' The rule probably also included prescriptions about paying dues and establishing membership. The problem of sub-groups forming and causing tension recalls Paul's similar problems with Christians assembling at Corinth.

The cult and associations related to Zeus Hypsistos illustrate how much we should appreciate the role of people's religious life in groups outside the family and civic community cults. The evidence for Hypsistos is largely epigraphic. It begins to appear in the last century BC and becomes widespread in the eastern part of the Roman Empire in the early centuries AD. Adherents were not from the high elite. Although they worshipped a 'Most High' (Hypsistos), singular god, their other fundamental beliefs remain unknown. Mere details are vouchsafed to us, such as their prayers at the rising of the sun and certain votive habits. The obvious guess is to associate these worshippers of one god with some sort of polytheistic accommodation with the approach to the supernatural of Jewish people, but that would be rash. From the fourth century BC onward inscriptions from the Near East indicate that popular religion in various cultures, including the Judaic, was moving towards monotheism. But there does seem often to be a close connection between the Hypsistos people and the Jewish communities in their area, perhaps sharing a common Near Eastern religious heritage.

Beyond the Near East, henotheism (focused worship of one god without denying the existence of others) was an active part of philosophical speculation during this same time. Philosophers lectured in halls and in theatres, surely to more than just the high elite. Apuleius in a speech asked, '"What form of entertainment is the theatre going to provide?" If it is a mime, you will laugh; if a rope-walker, you will tremble lest he fall; if a comedian, you will applaud him, while, if it be a philosopher, you will learn from him.'

Cynics preached in public as well. Percolation of purveyed philosophic ideas about henotheism, a common enough theme in philosophy's various guises, also had its effect. The cult (or cults – there is no indication that associations dedicated to Hypsistos were in communication with each other, or shared a set theology) remains enigmatic. However, its very existence among the people serves as remarkable evidence for the importance of religious experience that has only a very low profile in elite sources – similar, indeed, to the profile Christianity would have if we lacked the written material of that tradition.

Some polytheist associations were, like the Hypsistian, overtly god-focused. Another good example is the association honouring the god Dionysus in Philadelphia (Asia Minor). This group met to honour the god. Members were required to maintain a high level of moral and ritual purity. Failure to do so resulted in the wrath of that god: 'The gods will be gracious to those who obey and always give them all good things, whatever gods give to men whom they love. But should any transgress, they shall hate such people and inflict upon them great punishments.' This association was open to men and women, enslaved and free, and met in the house of the sponsor.

Christian associations – their communities (*ecclesiai* = 'churches') – combined the same functions and activities as polytheistic ones. The letter of James chastises some who act a bit too much like members of a polytheistic association, travelling to conduct business and make money rather than paying attention to their immortal souls. Pliny the Younger seems to have identified Christian communities as associations. He saw their agape meal as typical of meetings frowned upon by Roman authorities. Recognising this, the Christians he criticised immediately stopped assembling for the meal. In the later second century AD Tertullian assumes that Christian gatherings were like polytheistic associations when he writes, 'Should not this have been classed among tolerated associations, when it commits no such actions as are commonly feared from unlawful associations?' A polytheist with experience of a Christian gathering would have immediately thought of it as an association like others he had known.

Beyond assembling for a specific religious purpose, people joined groups that had more secular purposes, such as trade guilds and burial associations. These all had a religious component, but religious activity was not the central, day-to-day element. They offered an extra-familial opportunity to form common interest groups for fellowship (shared meals were always an important element) as well as networking.

All these associations, whether religious or secular, potentially posed a threat to the Roman authorities. This is because any meeting could be turned to a political purpose – agitation of the political status quo. The authorities did not have the resources or inclination to examine every association and deem it politically innocuous or otherwise. They just assumed that people getting together could mean trouble. The evidence shows that, despite this hostile attitude, an attitude that carried down the line from imperial to local bodies, both secular and religious associations were common throughout the empire at all times. There was little consistency: for example burial clubs of polytheists or the synagogues of the Jewish people were officially approved while a seemingly harmless fire brigade in a town in Asia Minor was prohibited. In the face of such inconsistent enforcement, the on-the-ground norm was to tolerate the wide range of associations that existed, despite official disapprobation. Nevertheless, the opposition in principle to the right of assembly made it possible to initiate a crackdown on Christians and other groups when it became expedient to the authorities to do so.

The elite focus on social structure, so dear to their own status in society, tends to subvert our understanding of how important mystery religions and other associations were in the lives of the common people. Plutarch as an elite may disparage their 'festivals and sacrifices, which may be compared with ill-omened and gloomy days, in which occur the eating of raw flesh, rending of victims, fasting and beating of breasts', as 'not performed for any god'. But the widespread popularity of these religions and associations proves how important was a sense of belonging, of acting with a group of like-minded persons in either a strictly or semi-religious context.

The public participated in religious activities that were conceived on an empire-wide basis. While emperors might introduce oddities into religion, such as Emperor Hadrian making his favourite, Antinous, a god, or Elagabalus elevating his favourite, the Syrian god Elagabal, there is no example of any long-lasting official religion based on a traditional god. However, the institution of the imperial cult can be thought of as an official religion. People did participate in this cult along with the feasting celebration that might attend it, just as they would other official gatherings. The imperial cult was meant to consolidate the Roman world on the model of how a local civic cult served as the focus of a community's identity. However, as important as the cult was to the elite, providing as it did a stage upon which to demonstrate loyalty to the empire, it was seldom an important part of people's daily religious lives. There are few votive dedications to the emperors, deified or living, that treat any as a god active in everyday life.

Occasionally, the religion of a people was used by the local elite as a focal point to rally the citizenry against an outside power. The use of the Egyptian religion in Egypt, Druidic religion in Gaul and the Judaean religion in Palestine are excellent examples. In general, however, religion did not have a political element. The tolerance within polytheism for other people's ways of dealing with the supernatural meant that local religious habits were usually left alone by the authorities. People could go about their way unhindered, so long as that way did not disrupt the peace.

Did polytheists try to persuade each other to change gods? There is little evidence of this. The usual approach to difference was one of live and let live. New approaches to the supernatural spread from one place to another, for example the worship of Isis from Egypt to Rome and other parts of the empire. This happened as people moved around or were exposed to new ideas and actions, but seldom through overt persuasion and never through compulsion.

Philosophers were the proselytisers of the day. They gave lectures and wrote treatises and preached on street corners to persuade others of their ideas. Presumably, some people actually changed their ways as a result and became in some sense followers. There was, again, no compulsion, and no penalty for not doing so. This was proselytising at a very calm level – except, perhaps, for the Cynics' tirades.

Some people did change their relationship with the supernatural. This was not easy for, as Eusebius well puts it, continuity with the past was basic to maintaining identity. Polytheists, he wrote 'have thoroughly persuaded themselves that they act rightly in honouring the deities … [and adhering to] the laws, which require everyone to reverence ancestral custom, *ta patria*, and not to disturb what should be inviolable, but to walk orderly in following the religion of our forefathers, and not to be meddlesome through love of innovation'. And Porphyry adds: 'The chief fruit of piety is to honour God according to ancestral custom.' However, quiet change must have taken place fairly widely as cults such as those of Isis and Mithras gained adherents in the first centuries AD.

Jewish prophets are constantly calling people back to Yahweh from the gods of neighbours, but there is no indication that their neighbours were proselytising Jews. Rather, motivations to change worked in some people's minds, as the normal interchange and interaction of people, including intermarriage, brought change in supernatural affiliations. The polytheistic approach to the supernatural was organic; it adjusted to changes in culture and customs, and even to political shifts. People were more susceptible to these changes than the elite who had such a strong vested interest in the status quo approaches. Sometimes, though, an immediate change took place. Lucius in Apuleius's novel the *Golden Ass* (*Metamorphoses*), rather spectacularly changed allegiance to Isis (although his previous allegiance is left unclear). His case points to the reason for quick change: Isis promised to miraculously change him back from his asinine shape into that of a man. He was literally converted from beast to human by the power of Isis. We do not have an account of Lucius then urging his friends and neighbours to take up with Isis because of her power to heal, but it could be readily imagined – readily, because people sought answers to their immediate problems. A witness to a successful approach to healing was a powerful inducement to try that in the case of one's own ailment.

In this practical world of the ordinary we should look with suspicion on wide-net explanations for religious change. The lives of people were pretty consistently uncertain through the ages; the point of their relations with the supernatural was to allay that uncertainty as much as possible. The ancient world after Alexander, and especially under the Romans, allowed a much freer flow of possibilities, at least in and between urban areas. New religious approaches centred in those areas except in the case of new military religions such as that of Jupiter Dolichenus, which followed the troops. Rural areas remained wedded to their traditional approaches, regardless of urban change. This picture of change driven by new approaches and their proof by demonstrations of supernatural power needs to be kept in mind as we look at polytheistic people changing relationships to the supernatural in their daily lives.

PATHS TO CHANGE

IN THE CENTURY FOLLOWING the Israelite year 3761 from creation, the year 754 from the foundation of Rome and the year 324 from the death of Alexander the Great – year AD 1 in an as then yet unknown chronology – the potentialities for religious change described in the last two chapters grew and blossomed. A number of options sowed in the Jewish tradition coalesced around covenantal fundamentals of purity and righteousness and a hope for relief in a last judgement. Under the influence of popular philosophy, some polytheists inched towards a moral and religious outlook that had a good deal in common with many basic precepts of the Jewish tradition. People in both traditions continued to value overt displays of power in both magic and miracles as touchstones of supernatural efficacy, an efficacy they sought to access as they faced the contingencies of life.

In AD 1 the people of Judaea had been independent for only the briefest of periods through the previous six hundred years. Most recently, they had lived through almost two hundred years of turmoil, a time that had seen Seleucid domination, brief independence, lengthy quasi-independence and, finally, domination by the Romans – many years filled with political intrigue and violence without Yahweh rescuing his covenanted people. In this environment that encouraged questions about the justice of Yahweh, seeds of radical change in the people's religious outlook took root and flourished. The tradition of a covenant with

Yahweh continued to stand at the centre of their existence. However, disagreement about exactly what that meant in personal lives prevailed. Possession of and reverence for a written tradition of that relationship with Yahweh allowed specific, long-running, threaded discussion of exactly what that relationship meant. Unlike their polytheist neighbours, their possession of detailed written instructions, with illustrative historical and devotional material, meant that there could be consistent arguments about a commonly agreed upon core of material, arguments that led to various ways of fulfilling the covenant with Yahweh.

As has been noted before, the intellectual, cultural, religious and political elements of survival under the domination, direct or indirect, of major imperial powers moulded responses to the essential question of how such bad things could be happening to a people beloved of an all-powerful, all-knowing and benevolent Yahweh. Although the most visible aspects of this struggle involved primarily the secular and religious aristocracy of the area, such turmoil necessarily affected the people as they were buffeted by the influence and aims of their leaders.

That secular aristocracy was a small group of landed elite. Their wealth and subservience to imperial powers assured their position. They tended to drift towards Hellenising ways under the influence of their masters. Priestly families made up the religious aristocracy. The Zadokites traced their pedigree back to Eleazar, the third son of Aaron, Moses' brother. Zadok himself was King David's high priest. Ezekiel described the sons of Zadok as the only ones suitable to perform the rites in the temple: 'The Levitical priests, who are descendants of Zadok and who guarded my sanctuary when the Israelites went astray from me, are to come near to minister before me; they are to stand before me to offer sacrifices of fat and blood, declares the Sovereign Lord.'

These men controlled the high priesthood until the time of the Maccabees. Their number later became known as the Sadducees. This priestly class, led by the high priest, were willing to cooperate with imperial powers so long as their cultic work under the covenant and their position of power in the state were not disrupted. They enjoyed a more or less happy economic situation. However, economic and social eminence was not everything. The traditions of the covenant with Yahweh remained strong. The potential and real conflict between their position of prominence under imperial powers and the requirements of the covenant for obedience to Yahweh directly affected their attitudes and actions. Their actions had to be able to be spun as according with that obedience, or serious repercussions from rivals and from the people would arise.

The people gained nothing from their position as subject to either an imperial power or to their own elites, or to both. While the elites could feather their secular nests by running things either directly or, at least, for so long as they met the demands of higher authorities, the people provided the labour they needed. As the elite's position improved, the economic conditions of the people worsened. The covenant, however, with its combination of religious conservatism and prophetic social justice, had enough force in everyday lives to keep the society together.

Jewish identity could be maintained only in a non-political way. Political authority derived from overlords. Their political dominance pushed people to interact with non-Jewish ways. People chose whether to seek identity in the larger milieu by cultural accommodation, or resist it. Religion – Yahweh's people as documented in the Torah – not political independence, became the focus of identity. The synagogue and Torah became central avenues to maintain that covenantal identity. The Torah was the focal point for worship and discussion. The synagogue was a place to do it.

Of course, this dialectic between Hellenising and maintaining Jewish identity was a continuum, not an 'either–or' situation, nor a situation that normally required immediate action or response on the part of the people. But the dynamic of political subservience and religious identity produced a range of cultural responses, often mutually antagonistic, within the Jewish communities in Judaea and in the diaspora.

One response was rebellion. The Maccabees are the best example of this option. Their clan, the Hasmoneans, appears to have been a peripherally powerful family based in Modein, a town in north-western Judaea. Mattathias was the patriarch; his sons, Judah, Simon and Jonathan all played important roles. Nothing is known of them until they took advantage of a period of disorder brought on by the Seleucid king Antiochus IV Epiphanes, trying to tighten his grip on Judaea, one of his territories. Religiously, they were fundamentally Torah and temple people, and some Hasidim (pious ones) followed them at first. After Mattathias's death, the Maccabee brothers played fast and loose with some aspects of the tradition, such as becoming high priest without Zadokite lineage and king without Davidic ancestry. The Maccabees did not seek to extirpate Hellenistic influences altogether. They retained a balance between local exclusivism in religion and wider integration into the Hellenistic Greek political environment. They focused on the temple and cultic ritual as the primary emblem of religious identity while they condoned cultural adjustments in other areas of life. The later Hasmoneans, although claiming kingship, fell back under the sway of first Greek and then Roman overlords.

Under the Maccabees and all other suzerains the basic question for the people of Judaea was, why Yahweh allowed the political and attempted religious subjugation of his people. As I have indicated, the answer shifted from punishment for being bad people (pre-exilic) to a belief in an End-of-Days reversal of the disasters. This answer focused the people on the Torah as the primary emblem of religious identity to find the answer. The spectrum of interpretation of what this meant tended towards more and more rigorous opinions. The eschatological thinking encouraged rigour in purity, preparation for the final judgement and revenge.

Like the Torah's interpretation, the management of the temple was contested. Rival sects claimed the right and ability to cleanse and manage it and some rejected it altogether. Although the temple was controlled by the priests, it could also become a focal point of unrest and, as such, the imperial power in authority at any given time watched activities carefully. The Great Revolt began in the temple in AD 66.

The elite, both priestly and secular, struggled to find appropriate responses to the politically dependent situation. Accommodation was the pragmatic path. Resistance was dangerous and might be suicidal. For the elite, two things were at stake: their authority and power within the community and the survival of that community's identity. These high stakes provoked violent disagreements and power struggles. King Alexander Jannaeus, who ruled from 104 to 76 BC, was a particularly vicious example of these struggles. He killed literally thousands of fellow Jews as he sought to keep control of his throne. Herod the Great (king 37–4 BC) likewise engaged in extensive bloodletting in his numerous efforts to shore up his political position.

On the religious front, various groups emerged dedicated to

particular visions of righteousness within the covenant. The disagreements were very important, for the debate was over how best to be righteous and so gain and retain Yahweh's favour for the people. The period from 164 BC to AD 70 is known as the Age of Sects. Judaeans were involved in many groups: the groups represented in the Dead Sea Scrolls, Christians, Essenes, Pharisees, Sadducees, Sicarii, Zealots – perhaps others. The Talmud, a body of writing expressing the later rabbinic Jewish tradition, speaks of twenty-four sects during the first century AD. This proliferation seems to be a response to the churning of ideas about what Jewishness meant in everyday life. The confrontation was not between assimilationists, who wanted to jettison Jewish traditions or change them radically by reinterpreting them in a Hellenistic mode, and the traditionalists, who wanted to keep everything completely as of old. Rather, the primary fields of polemic were the interpretation of the Mosaic Law in everyday life, the relevance of other scripture and the role of the temple. Especially vexed were confrontations over the observance of the Sabbath and traditional festivals; the functioning of the temple; and marriage laws. The most radical critique came from the Essenes and the followers of charismatic leaders such as John the Baptist and Jesus of Nazareth, who withdrew from the political scene, focused on purity and righteousness and strongly criticised the socio-economic and political abuses of the priests, the temple and the secular elite.

Throughout the history of the Jewish people there had been a pull between pious observance of what was needed to fulfil the covenant with Yahweh and a tendency to spin off into the habits of neighbouring peoples, neglecting Israel's special relationship with Yahweh. Priests took action to thwart this tendency. Phineas, son of Eleazar, son of Aaron, killed worshippers of Baal Peor and so stopped a plague on the people. As a result, he is singled out as an archetype of protest and action. Later, prophets regularly railed against the anti-covenantal tendencies. Elijah might be called the patron saint of this situation. During the ninth century BC, he spoke against Jezebel and the cult of Baal, towards which many Israelites were tending. He then used miracles and violence to make his point, that loyalty to the covenant was pre-eminently important. But he was persecuted and found himself almost alone in piety. He complained to Yahweh about how few pious people remained in the land: 'I [Elijah] have been very zealous [*zelos*] for the Lord God Almighty. The Israelites have rejected your covenant, torn down your altars and put your prophets to death with the sword. I am the only one left, and now they are trying to kill me too.' But, believing himself to be under Yahweh's guidance, he persevered in punishing the ungodly with words and violence down to the day of his assumption in a chariot of fire.

If we imagine that there was a remnant of Jewish people in the land who tried to keep the covenant despite the Hellenistic temptations around them, the terms 'pious ones' or 'zealous ones' would be an appropriate description of their relationship to the worship of Yahweh. Various psalms praised the 'pious people' of Yahweh. Psalms were especially eloquent about the reward for the pious and righteous and about punishment for the wicked: 'For the Lord loves the just and will not forsake his faithful ones. Wrongdoers will be completely destroyed; the offspring of the wicked will perish. The righteous will inherit the land and dwell in it for ever.'

Obedience to the Mosaic Law was at the heart of any concept of piety. Zeal for living out the covenant inspired the Maccabean revolt. Mattathias began the uprising when he objected to the Seleucid king's demand that Jews sacrifice to a polytheist god:

> Even if all the nations that live under the king's rule obey him and have chosen to follow his orders, departing from their ancestral religion, my sons and brothers and I will continue to live according to our ancestors' covenant. We will never abandon the Law and its commands! We won't obey the king's orders by turning aside from our religion to either the right or the left.

Then a Jew came forward, ready to offer sacrifice according to the king's demand. 'When Mattathias saw this action, he burned with zeal and his spirit was stirred up. He gave way to his righteous anger and he ran over and killed the man on the altar. He also killed the king's officer who was overseeing the sacrifice at that time and he tore down the altar. He burned with zeal for the Law.' Then Mattathias shouted loudly in the town, 'Everyone who is zealous for the Law and supports the covenant should come with me!' Mattathias and his sons fled into the hills, leaving behind everything and stirred up revolt.

Mattathias is described as zealous to defend Yahweh's covenant, as Elijah was. Deeply pious Jews, the Hasidim, followed him. However, they did not make a particularly good showing. First, in their intense purity, they refused to fight on the Sabbath and Greek forces slaughtered them. Then they believed lies by the high priest Alcimus, in league with the Greeks, and were again slaughtered. Yet, the author of 2 Maccabees asserted that Hasidim were the core of Judah Maccabeus's army. It is clear that people who thought of themselves as pious and zealous for Yahweh were willing to engage in military action, however unsuccessful, to protect the covenant among the people.

During this same period another group began to take action according to their understanding of what being pious and zealous meant. The area where the Qumran scrolls were discovered during the mid-twentieth century lies near the Dead Sea, hence the common term, Dead Sea Scrolls. The settlement that produced the scrolls was inhabited from around 140 BC, towards the beginning of the Maccabean period, until its destruction by the Romans in AD 68 during the Great Revolt.

Sometime early in the period a man in the tradition of the prophets arose preaching piety and a justice of Yahweh that called for punishment of the wicked at a final judgement. He was a prophetic figure who spoke Yahweh's words. He received special knowledge from Yahweh and offered a new covenant to the true faithful. He claimed a similarity to Moses. He promised a final judgement in which he would be Yahweh's instrument for cleansing the Jewish people. This man, called the Teacher of Righteousness, was an Elijah-like figure who advocated return to a proper relationship with Yahweh. He positioned himself in opposition to a man known only as the Wicked High Priest. This priest is usually identified as Jonathan, a brother of Judah Maccabeus, who became high priest in 152 BC. Although of a priestly family, Jonathan was not a Zadokite – a descendent of a son of Aaron and member of the group that traditionally held the high priesthood. Enraged at this breach of purity in the worship of Yahweh, the Teacher protested, was driven into exile and eventually died. His followers believed he would return, like Elijah, when it was time for Yahweh to intervene in history and assert his right to reward the pious and punish the wicked. Therefore, they withdrew from the common life of the Jewish people, set up their distinct community and lived a life apart as the true, pious remnant of the People of Israel, focused on doing Yahweh's will according to the covenant. In maximum purity they awaited the return of the Teacher and the last judgement that would accompany that return.

The scrolls are not as a whole doctrinally coherent with regard to the Teacher's message, but certain ideas and actions regularly occur in the main documents (Manual of Discipline, Damascus or Zadokite Document, Temple Scroll, Psalms of Thanksgiving and War Rule). These include living a communal life physically apart, strict admissions procedures, strict commitment to following a new covenant in honouring the traditional covenant with Yahweh and punishments for deviation from the rules of that new covenant. The basic goal was a life of purity before Yahweh according to the rules of the Torah. The community saw themselves living in a cosmos, with the 'children of light', who followed Yahweh's ways, pitted against the 'children of darkness', sponsored by supernatural forces allied against Yahweh himself. The 'children of darkness' were not just polytheists, but also Jewish people who failed to follow their way. The community's apocalyptic vision held that in the last days Yahweh would intervene in history to produce victory and reward for the righteous, defeat and punishment for the wicked.

Essenes, Therapeutae, Pharisees, Sadducees

This community the Teacher established is most commonly and probably correctly identified with the Essenes. The name, Essene, is a Hellenisation of the Hebrew Hasidim, a generic term describing those especially pious and zealous. It represents those Jewish people who made a point of their adherence to the covenant, as, in principle, all should have done. The most likely scenario is that some of the Hasidim, the pious or zealous ones, decided, perhaps in response to the various fiascos of the Maccabean political movement, to seek obedience to Yahweh and his covenant in a different mode under the guidance of the Teacher of Righteousness. As we will see, other pious or zealous ones chose different paths to purity.

We know a good deal about the Essene sect from ancient accounts in Philo, Josephus, Pliny the Elder and Hippolytus (a Christian writer

of the late second century AD). Neither the Essenes nor any other sect
was ever very numerous. Josephus is fond of giving numbers, some
of which might even be more than guesstimates. He says there were
4,000 Essenes. This was in a Judaean-Galilean population of perhaps
500,000 and certainly no more than one million. Some Essenes lived
in communities. We know of only one such, that on the shores of the
Dead Sea at Qumran. They also lived in cells in the towns and villages.
Probably the rule they followed was the same in either location. Membership was limited to celibate males. A president was in charge of each
cell. The group controlled its membership closely; there was a period
of probation and initiation lasting two to three years. Once admitted, a
member could be expelled for breaking the community's rules. Hippolytus has the interesting remark that though women might be attracted
to the community's life, the Essenes refused to admit them. Members
lived communally and supported themselves through agriculture and
some industry. All private property was forfeited to the community as
well as any earnings members might gain. They ate together twice a
day in an atmosphere of rigorous purity. Social justice reigned. Slavery
was forbidden and there was a commitment to support the poor with
the community's resources. There was no political involvement, nor
was the temple cult with its animal sacrifice a part of their lives. There
may have been some alternative form of sacrifice among themselves,
but purity was the sacrifice that guaranteed Yahweh's blessing. As the
Psalm stated: 'You do not delight in sacrifice, or I would bring it; you
do not take pleasure in burnt offerings. My sacrifice, O God, is a broken
spirit; a broken and contrite heart you, God, will not despise.'

Purity came from a strict adherence to the Torah and its laws. Each
Sabbath Essenes obeyed rigorous rules. They frequently bathed as
a purifying ritual. They convened in a synagogue for the study and
veneration of the scriptures (mainly the Pentateuch, Isaiah and the
Psalms). During the meeting a member read and then a leader taught.
Even within this very ordered way of life, there were disparities. For
example, Josephus tells us that some Essenes did, in fact, allow marriage, but for the purpose of procreation only. Theologically, Essenes
lived out the Torah as strictly as they knew how. They also held that Fate
ruled everything, by which they presumably meant the Providence of
Yahweh. Because Yahweh was just, he would end the human world in

a great conflagration and judgement during which the righteous would be rewarded and the wicked punished. However, they did not seem to have believed in bodily resurrection at that end of time. The Essenes we know by name number just four, two called prophets, one a dream interpreter and one a military leader in the Great Revolt.

The Therapeutae ('attendants of the god') were a group of pious ones similar to the Essenes, but who followed a slightly different path to righteousness. They were the only Jewish sect known from the diaspora. Philo tells us that their communities were widespread, but especially near Alexandria as well as elsewhere in Egypt. Unlike the Essenes they included women, were vegetarians, did not own property communally and lacked a faith in the last days. However, they shared the same commitment to a life of celibacy and extreme obedience to the Torah's dictates, piety and purity. No author besides Philo mentions them and some scholars have even claimed that his work is fiction, written by later Christians to provide an early example of the monastic life. If Therapeutae were real, they do represent another strain of the pious and righteous within the life of the Jewish people. They were distinctive in that they gave women an active role in communal religious life.

The Pharisees also claimed piety and purity as their main focus. Their name means 'separatists', but they were not separated like the Essenes and Therapeutae were, by withdrawing into a dedicated community. Rather they kept themselves separated from impurity while at the same time remaining in normal daily life. Josephus says there were six thousand in the time of Herod the Great. The source of their piety and righteousness was strict obedience to the Torah. Their methodology was discussing and pinning down as many of the details of that obedience as possible. They believed that, in addition to the written traditions left by Moses, he and the later prophets had left oral traditions of how the people should relate to Yahweh. These were an important supplement to the written commandments of the Torah. Pharisees shared their concern for the details of the covenantal law with another non-priestly group, the Scribes. Who Scribes were and exactly what they did is murky, but they and the Pharisees believed that the study of the Torah, the mastery of its details and the interpretation of those details in daily living were crucial. Abiding by both the written and oral Torah produced the desired purity, a purity that would guarantee any who were pious a place among the favoured of Yahweh at the last judgement.

Josephus provides the first notice of Pharisees. They appeared as a sect during the Maccabean times of the mid-second century BC. Their dedication to proper observance of purity and the Torah made them models for common people to follow as best they could. Josephus claims that their general popularity with the people came from their exemplary piety and theological positions, namely, strong belief in the Providence of Yahweh and in his (deferred) justice, 'for they taught that the soul survives death and is rewarded (or punished) in the underworld according to what happened during life'. Thus, reinforcing their interpretation of Yahweh's justice, they believed in resurrection and a final judgement of living and dead in the final days, and the rule by Yahweh over the righteous at that time. Because of their concern for the general piety of the people, they became deeply embroiled in the political life of the day. This was necessary because the central act of obedience, the cultic practice of the temple, was at play as part of the contest to control political life. Part of their expertise was knowledge in tiny particulars of how the cult should be carried out.

We know of only twelve Pharisees by name – more than the number of Essenes, but still a very small number. After the destruction of the temple, the Pharisaic tradition gradually developed into what became the rabbinic faith. Unfortunately, however, rabbinic tradition retains very few mentions of Pharisees specifically, nor did that tradition retain any document that can be shown certainly to date from before the temple's destruction.

The working out of piety, righteousness and correct relationships to the covenant drove the thinking and action of the pious and zealous. These efforts were open, in theory at least, to any devotee of Yahweh. The emphasis was on the people as individuals in relationship to Yahweh. To most people, the temple cult was extremely important in that relationship. Unlike personal piety and righteousness, the worship of Yahweh in his home on earth, the temple, required the service of experts. In Mosaic times Moses' brother, Aaron of the tribe of Levi, took charge of cult ritual affairs. His descendants, as well as others of the tribe not directly descended from him, continued this service in the temple in Jerusalem. Zadok was descended from Eleazar, son of Aaron;

he was the first high priest in the temple newly built by King Solomon. In turn, descendants of Zadok continued to hold the important priestly offices in the temple, while other Levites performed lesser duties related to the cult. High priests came from the Zadokite descendants. The elite class that emphasised proper temple worship, supplied the priests and maintained high prestige in the culture, called themselves Sadducees after the original Zadok. In brief, Sadducees saw the temple cult as the crucial focus of Israel's fulfilment of the covenant with Yahweh, while the Pharisees emphasised the piety of the Jewish people as individuals. Sadducees were few, according to Josephus, but their influence was great. During the years from the Maccabean revolt to the Great Revolt, Sadducees and Pharisees were often in conflict over ritual, practice and influence in the secular political sphere. But although they disagreed on some purely religious topics, they could also at times work cooperatively, especially with regard to the details of temple practices, in which the Pharisees were the recognised experts, while the Sadducees were the practitioners.

In the political realm the Sadducees felt that the high priest representing the whole people should be the effective ruler in a theocratic, centralised nation, while the Pharisees felt that the people themselves as a whole were the essence of Yahweh's nation. For Jewish people this meant an option between a custom based on cultic temple worship, or on individual piety in daily life. Of course these options were not mutually exclusive. But the flexibility and emphasis on the individual allowed by the Pharisaic approach opened the door to the appeal of charismatic leaders I will mention below.

For most people the Sadducean attitude towards the justice of Yahweh was significant as well. Sadducees believed that Yahweh applied his justice in the present world, not in a future time. This approach had a long and illustrious history in the Jewish people's traditions. Punishment in present time, whether community-wide in the case of Assyrians or Babylonians, or personal, resulted from failure to adhere to Yahweh's covenant. If the wicked were not punished immediately, then Yahweh was just reserving punishment to a future generation – the sins of the father would be visited upon the children. In line with a present-time view of justice, Sadducees denied a life after death and the survival of the soul or physical body after death. They also believed that people possessed free will and were entirely responsible for their choices between good and evil; Fate did not play a role. The widespread popularity of eschatological approaches to justice shows how unattractive among the people was this traditional explanation of why bad things happen to good people and vice-versa. Once the temple was destroyed in AD 70 the Sadducees' reason for existence disappeared and so did they. Before that their role had been important.

The groups just mentioned represent the main lines of thought and action that the leaders of the Jewish people took. However, there were more opinions and ways of reacting to the covenantal responsibilities, to the secular stresses of the time and to the politically precarious condition of the community. Almost any outstanding person might gain a following that lasted, at least for a while. For example, Simon son of Boethus, a high priest under Herod the Great who was removed by him, seems to have left a Boethian sect that followed precepts close to those held by the Sadducees. Hegesippus in the second century AD names, in addition to Essenes, Pharisees and Sadducees, the Galileans, Hemerobaptists, Masbotheans and Samaritans. The Talmud tradition held that there were even more. This multiplicity is important to recognise because it clearly illustrates how many different strains of ideas and recommended actions were percolating. The people were not divided among Essenes, Pharisees and Sadducees – or any other fixed constellation of actors. Rather, they went about their lives in the presence of their fellows who held, and tried to convince others of, a wide range of possible approaches to the covenant. All that we know of were in the context of maintaining the identity of the people as Yahweh's favoured ones. Beyond that, almost anything went.

The religious life of the Jewish people had many possibilities. Two aspects of that life particularly facilitated the penetration of differing ideas to the wider population. One was the celebration of festivals, especially the three major festivals of Sukkot (Booths), Passover (Unleavened Bread) and Pentecost (Weeks). Even before Herod the Great reconstructed the temple complex in grandeur, thousands of Jewish people – men, women and children – gathered in Jerusalem for the requisite cultic acts. It was a time to renew family connections, discuss problems in agriculture and trade, complain about taxes and politics and enjoy some special foods and fellowship. The chance to interact and exchange with others was also an opportunity to talk about topics such as possible and appropriate piety, Yahweh's requirements for a good life and the prospect of justice in the face of everyday injustices great and small. Some already had a perspective on life that they were eager to share; some came specifically to hear teachers and preachers of various ideas. Some could not have cared less, wishing only to perform their cultic obligations. But the general environment encouraged the spread of ideas both secular and religious in an everyday context that was not controlled by the elite because, in reality, it could not be.

People meeting regularly to hear the scriptures (at this time primarily the Pentateuch, the Psalms and Isaiah) provided another opportunity for exposure to and reflection on the welter of ideas and approaches around them. The Sabbath as a holy day remained central to the life of the Jewish people. The family celebrated on the evening of the Sabbath. Then, on the day, people gathered to hear the scripture read and explicated. The history of the synagogue or prayer house in this period remains somewhat unclear. What is clear is that gatherings occurred on a regular basis and that during those meetings people were exposed to the covenantal texts and, most importantly, to interpretations of them. In this environment, a person could expound an opinion to his neighbours and expect reaction. Even if most of the assembled simply listened to a teacher or leader, the talk before and after meetings of this sort touched on aspects of daily life, including approaches to scriptural examples and commandments. It was an opportunity to engage new as well as traditional lines of thought.

This environment of advocacy, interpretation and discussion produced an overall atmosphere of thought and action that could focus men on particular actions without adhering to a particular sect. Quite specifically, the emphasis of all the Hasidim-type sects on purity, piety and righteousness leading to covenantal reward from Yahweh opened people's minds to the more specific message of an inspired person, or to an inspired idea for action.

The conviction that there should be no master but Yahweh was fundamental to the covenantal agreement. A prophet writing under the name of Isaiah channelled Yahweh's message:

Listen to me, you descendants of Jacob, all the remnant of the people of Israel, you whom I have upheld since your birth, and have carried since you were born. Even to your old age and grey hairs I am he, I am he who will sustain you. I have made you and I will carry you; I will sustain you and I will rescue you.

In Yahweh's name, he emphasised the centrality of monotheism: 'This is what the Lord says – Israel's King and Redeemer, the Lord Almighty: I am the first and I am the last; apart from me there is no God.' From the Maccabean period on we see many examples of people who are willing to fight and die to defend their view of this principle – Yahweh would stand by them, as Jeremiah implored: 'Let my persecutors be put to shame, but keep me from shame; let them be terrified, but keep me from terror. Bring on them the day of disaster; destroy them with double destruction.'

Reward in a future afterlife might be all well and good, but surely Yahweh was in favour of action in the present to protect his people and their worship of him. This very simple idea did not require an elaborate morality or theology. It flowed easily and directly from the entire tradition of the Jewish people. Josephus spoke of a Fourth Philosophy existing alongside the other three 'philosophies' (i.e. sects) he mentions – the Essenes, Pharisees and Sadducees. Even he admitted, however, that this Fourth Philosophy had no special theological or daily life approach of its own to offer. Rather its adherents agreed with what the Pharisees taught, with one addition: that they must 'avoid calling any man master'. This was no new thought: that the Jewish people had only one ruler and that was Yahweh was a commonplace of the tradition. As Samuel lectured the Israelites: 'If you fear the Lord and serve and obey him and do not rebel against his commands, and if both you and the king who reigns over you follow the Lord your God – good! But if you do not obey the Lord and if you rebel against his commands, his hand will be against you, as it was against your ancestors.'

This conviction made some men fearless in their active opposition to rule by non-Jews or Jews who were deemed not to be genuine in their covenantal purity. The first leader of this group was a violent man named Judas the Galilean. From Josephus we can surmise that Judas and his men were not mere pillagers and destroyers. They were committed to establishing an independent, territorial, covenantal state based in Judaea and Galilee, or were willing to die trying. They believed that Yahweh's justice meant his direct intervention to help their righteous enterprise: 'Heaven would be their zealous helper to no lesser end than the furthering of their enterprise until it succeeded.' Judas preached in the prophetic tradition of social justice that the common welfare of the people depended upon his success. He also preached the direct-action model of Yahweh's justice: Yahweh would in present time defeat his enemies and bring triumph to his devoted. Josephus went on to say that the people 'responded gladly' to Judas's enterprise for, far from advocating the 'innovation and reform in ancestral traditions' that Josephus accuses him of, he was simply tapping into a long-standing zeal for theocratic independence that Mattathias and Judah Maccabeus had tapped into a hundred and fifty years before and that, clearly, had not died out in the interim. Judas attracted 'an abundance of devotees' and waged war with his band against those who disagreed with his approach, whether they were the elite of Jewish society or Roman forces.

A succession of men who took up Judas's mantle appear in Judaea in the period up to and even after the collapse of the Great Revolt. Josephus detailed the deeds of many, derogating their motivations and methods and labelling them 'bandits'. In the last years before that revolt new names attach to these violent people: Zealots and Sicarii.

To be 'zealous' in defence of the covenantal relationship was no vice; moderation was no virtue. Phineas, grandson of Aaron, the brother of Moses, was the prototype as he killed a backsliding Israelite and his non-Hebrew lover, satisfying Yahweh: 'Phineas son of Eleazar, the son of Aaron, the priest, has turned my anger away from the Israelites. Since he was as zealous for my honour among them as I am, I did not put an end to them in my zeal.'

Elijah was another model of zeal for Yahweh. The name 'Zealots' is merely a specific application to one group of the general ideal of zealotry in fulfilling Yahweh's covenantal relationship with the Jewish people.

Another violent band, the Sicarii, is different. A *sica* is a curved dagger. It is a Latin word well known from classical sources, as is *sicarii* in its meaning of 'murderers' and, more specifically, 'assassins'. Why was a Latin word used to brand violent Jews with a term from Roman law and custom? Latin was not the lingua franca in Judaea; Greek or Aramaic was. There is no similar Greek or Aramaic root that might produce the word *sicarii*.

These Jews – *Sicarii* – took their lead from an event during King David's reign. Then, Joab murdered one of David's enemies, Amasa, with his dagger. Sicarii likewise specialised in using a dagger to assassinate enemies, including in one instance a high priest. These Judaeans, like Joab, showed their willingness to kill fellow Jews who betrayed their cause. Roman authorities must have purposefully used a label familiar to them from their own laws against assassins (*sicarii*), and it stuck. We do not know what these 'dagger men' called themselves, but in ideology they closely resembled other fighters such as the Zealots.

Eleazar, a grandson of Judas the Galilean, led at least some of them. Josephus states that

> the Sicarii clubbed together against those who consented to submit to Rome and in every way treated them as their enemies, plundering their property, rounding up their cattle and setting fire to their habitations; protesting that such persons were no other than aliens, who so ignobly sacrificed the highly prized liberty of the Judaeans and admitted their preference for the Roman yoke.

Although also active in the countryside, they specialised in urban murders, appearing at festivals and stabbing designated collaborators.

Young men zealous for Yahweh were attracted to this group and other similar bands. They represented a violent alternative to the less aggressive approaches of Essenes and Pharisees in seeking to work out the justice of Yahweh in present time.

In discussing how Jewish traditions changed in the three centuries from around 200 BC I've been referring mainly to the people of Judaea, where most of the sources are. Many Jews lived in cities and towns scattered around the Mediterranean and in Babylonia. There is little information about the sects in these areas except for the Therapeutae in Egypt. These were strikingly like, if not quite the same as, the Judaean Essenes, which suggests there was an exclusivist, pietist streak in the diaspora more generally.

Does this mean that in the synagogues and prayer houses of the diaspora discussions of actions and doctrine were different than in Judaea? Sadducees were tied to the temple. Their concerns would not resonate much and their personnel not at all. In fact, detailed temple issues in general would not be to the fore. The Essenes were geographically limited, so irrelevant except as their ideas might be shared by groups such as the Therapeutae. Only the Pharisaic tradition, focused as it was on interpretation of the Torah – the central document for Jewish people everywhere – was easily transportable abroad. Issues of ancestral tradition, purity and intermarriage readily found fertile ground for people living in a world of polytheists. As we will see, the experience of Christian teachers and preachers in the synagogues of the diaspora are excellent evidence of the thriving inquiry, intellectual curiosity and religious searching that was going on in the Pharisaic tradition, a tradition that had already begun to attract some polytheists.

The Israelite relationship with Yahweh was a covenant between him and the twelve tribes of Israel, clans descended from the twelve sons of the patriarch Jacob (Israel), who in turn was the grandson of Abraham, the man with whom Yahweh first began a personal relationship. Although the idea of covenant went back to Abraham, the definitive form came from Yahweh via Moses, Jacob's great-great grandson. At some point, however, the tradition inserted the idea that Yahweh had promised Abraham, Jacob's grandfather, a broader mandate that included all the peoples of the earth. As recorded in Genesis, Yahweh spoke to Abraham: 'I will make you into a great nation, and I will bless you; I will make your name great, and you will be a blessing. I will bless those who bless you, and whoever curses you I will curse; and all peoples on earth will be blessed through you.' And to Abraham's son, Isaac, Yahweh reiterated: 'Stay in this land for a while and I will be with you and will bless you. For to you and your descendants I will give all these lands and will confirm the oath I swore to your father Abraham. I will make your descendants as numerous as the stars in the sky and will give them all these lands and through your offspring all nations on earth will be blessed.'

Under the name of Isaiah, a sixth-to-fifth century BC prophet emphasised the potentially wide reach of Yahweh's covenant:

'And I, because of what they have planned and done, am about to come and gather the people of all nations and languages, and they will come and see my glory. I will set a sign among them, and I will send some of those who survive to the nations ... They will proclaim my glory among the nations. And they will bring all your people, from all the nations, to my holy mountain in Jerusalem ...' says the Lord.

And:

'Foreigners who bind themselves to the Lord to minister to him, to love the name of the Lord, and to be his servants, all who keep the Sabbath without desecrating it and who hold fast to my covenant – these I will bring to my holy mountain and give them joy in my house of prayer. Their burnt offerings and sacrifices will be accepted on my altar; for my house will be called a house of prayer for all nations.'

The story of Naaman the Syrian is part of the universalising of Yahweh. The book of Jonah (third to second century BC) centres on the theme of Yahweh accepting and caring for non-Jews who repent and are obedient to him. As late as the Book of Enoch (second century) there was talk of 'the children of the whole earth' who would join with Jews in accepting correct teachings of the divine blessing.

'God-fearer' is the name that eventually attached to polytheists attracted to the traditions of the Jewish people. The term itself appears only in the first centuries AD – the New Testament uses it and it is attested later epigraphically in the synagogue at Aphrodisias in Asia Minor and at another at Panticapaeum in the Crimean region; god-fearers are also mentioned in donor lists from synagogues in Sardis, Tralleis and Philadelphia in Asia Minor. In the first century AD, it is a little curious that Philo did not mention even one person who was a god-fearer among the Jewish community in Alexandria. They do appear in the book of Acts, however. The centurion Cornelius is a good example. He was righteous and feared Yahweh, but was not a Jew; Peter got into trouble for eating with him, a non-Jew, because of the possibility of consuming impure food. Josephus used the term, but applied it to both polytheists and to

Jews, so it is not specifically directed at polytheists who accept many aspects of the Jewish tradition. He noticed many in Syrian towns and especially among women in Antioch. He also attested to the presence of a large number of polytheists at the Jerusalem Passover in AD 63 or 65 – surely these were god-fearers and not just tourists in town for the festival.

Following the guidelines supposedly from Noah's times, these non-Jews could access the Jewish traditions in a way that was less than fully committed. Most specifically, circumcision was not required. Rejection of idolatry as blasphemous to Yahweh was crucial. 'Anyone who denies idolatry acknowledges the entire Torah,' as the saying went. Denial of polytheism was the key element when a polytheist took up the traditions of Yahweh.

Polytheists could also completely convert to those traditions. Philo in his *Special Laws* talked about welcoming proselytes; he seems to give them equal rank in the community. Converting significantly disrupted a polytheist's social life. Philo urged Jews to make proselytes feel at home because they had left their country, friends, relatives and religious orientation. Indeed, Tacitus, from the polytheist point of view, made the same point about converts alienating themselves when he wrote of their separating from their (polytheistic) gods, homeland, parents, children and siblings. In the Jewish fictional romance of *Joseph and Asenath* the polytheistic Asenath destroyed her idols, renounced polytheism and chose to serve Yahweh.

Mention of proselytes by name seems to be very rare. Outside the Acts, the only reference in the New Testament is Matthew 23:15. Josephus has only one example: a Jewish merchant who converts the royal house of Adiabene. Philo mentions no proselyte by name. Full conversion involved not only rejecting worship of other supernatural powers besides Yahweh but also, if a male, undergoing circumcision. A convert had to follow the covenant as described in the Torah (the law), integrating into the Jewish community. This all seems very clear and straightforward but the multiple threads of the Jewish tradition include, not surprisingly, some that question the need for physical circumcision. From the time of the prophets, advocates for Yahweh held that the physical act of circumcision was an outward sign of an internal commitment to Yahweh's covenant. Following Deuteronomy 10:16 ('Circumcise your hearts, therefore, and do not be stiff-necked any longer') Jeremiah explicitly urged his people to follow suit. By this he meant that a life obedient to Yahweh had to follow the physical act of circumcision. He went on to say that Yahweh would punish Israelites who were circumcised in the flesh only and not in the heart. Ezekiel also emphasised the need to be circumcised both in the flesh and in the heart.

Josephus provides an excellent example of the disagreement about the necessity of converts undergoing physical circumcision. Ananias, a Jewish merchant, instructed the king of Adiabene and his family in Jewish ways. He insisted that circumcision was not necessary: 'The king could, he said, worship God even without being circumcised if indeed he had fully decided to be a devoted adherent of Judaism, for it was this that counted more than circumcision.' But then there came from Galilee another Jew, named Eleazar, 'who had a reputation for being extremely strict when it came to ancestral laws'. This man told the king that circumcision was, indeed, needed to complete conversion.

Eleazar clearly represents the prophet Isaiah's opinion that only the circumcised are the true Israel. The majority opinion among the Jewish people was that physical circumcision was necessary for complete conversion. People generally agreed that 'unclean' meant 'uncircumcised'. We do not know of any specific Jewish group in antiquity that accepted uncircumcised proselytes. That said, we know very little about many details of most strands of the tradition and the Josephus story indicates that some, at least, thought that physical circumcision was unnecessary. Philo referred to circumcision of the heart when he wrote that 'the proselyte is one who circumcises not his uncircumcision but his desires and sensual pleasures and the other passions of the soul'. These experience 'alienation from belief in many gods and gain familiarity with honouring the one God and Father of all'. He went on to call 'newcomers' those who 'have run to the truth'. The survival in rabbinic writings of 'Proselytes of the Gate', that is uncircumcised proselytes, indicates that the issue continued well past our time period.

So Jewish traditions attracted some polytheists. Those traditions to some extent accommodated that attraction by accepting interested but not fully committed polytheists (god-fearers) as well as actual converts. There was little or no active proselytising of polytheists, however. The later Hasmonean kings did forcibly convert non-Jewish peoples living in parts of their kingdom, but this was an aberration, and forced conversion is hardly proselytising. Jewish traditions lay passively open to interested polytheists. How many responded remains unknown.

As we will see presently, the approach to the supernatural that one Jew, Jesus of Nazareth, inspired also found enthusiasts among polytheists. Whereas the main strand in the rope that was Judaism of the first century AD accepted sympathetic polytheists into their number, early Christianity quickly developed a strand of its own that more actively sought polytheist adherents alongside Jewish people in Judaea or the diaspora who were interested in the new movement.

Both Philo and Josephus express general sentiments that can only be described as 'philanthropia', a positive attitude towards other human beings, regardless of their tradition. We do not have a clear idea how widely this attitude extended beyond a theoretical stance. Among pious Jewish people, at least, there was a clear concern for pollution that might result from contact with polytheists and, especially, with their food that might have been offered in sacrifice to their gods. Peter's mistake in meeting with the centurion Cornelius was eating with him because some of the food might have experienced an idolatrous use prior to human consumption. Different threads of the tradition acted at different levels of intensity. Some argued that just touching a polytheist produced impurity – although all seem to have agreed that this would be minor, at worst. Everyone agreed that non-Jews could not advance beyond the Court of the Gentiles in the temple.

Polytheists as oppressors brought out less milk of human kindness. From Maccabean times on, Jewish people saw such polytheists, whether Greek or Roman or Egyptian, more and more as intrinsically threatening to Jewish traditions. The Torah and its admonitions had long been the focal point for the identity of the tight-knit community. A feeling of separateness and specialness came easily from the knowledge of a covenant with Yahweh and the history of the people from Abraham to their present day. But an especially broadly held and intense feeling arose from the second century BC onwards, starting with the Maccabees. Perhaps the spectacularly ill-timed attempts by Antiochus IV to subvert the Torah's ways provided a focus for tradition's rays, starting a fire that was difficult to put out. The identity-protective mania was deep seated and widely shared in all classes, even, when pressed sufficiently, among the elites complicit in the political control of the people. Economic and political factors of discontent could come into play, but the flashpoint was always the interpretation of an event as threatening the identity of the community. This could not help but build an anti-polytheist mood in the minds of some, one that was easily accommodated within the ideas of cultic, devotional and daily purity that increasingly became the touchstone of a correct relationship to Yahweh. The ills of the people could be cured by exorcising the infecting spirit; for some this meant that polytheists had to go.

During the last centuries BC and the first AD, when the Jewish people underwent significant shifts in their relationship with the supernatural, the polytheists were also opening up to new possibilities. We have seen how Greek and later Roman philosophy became increasingly detached from its roots in close logical analysis of the physical as well as the metaphysical world and came to focus more exclusively on being a guide to life. Ethics and morality, never absent from inquiry and teaching, became the most important expressions of philosophy. As A. A. Long puts it, 'All of the Hellenistic philosophical schools emphasised the question, first posed by Plato and Aristotle: "What is happiness or well-being and how does a man achieve it?"' Often this inquiry could very conveniently take place without severe impact on polytheists' relationship to supernatural powers. That relationship did not lack moral and ethical aspects, but it did lack any centralised expression or theorisation about those things – a lack that philosophy could satisfy.

Some philosophical schools such as the Epicureans were hostile to the traditional supernatural powers. However, all the major ones except Epicureanism accepted them as an effective part of the cosmos. Epicureans advocated as a purely practical measure going along with polytheist practices, even while they denied their actual truth or relevance in theory. But philosophical schools in general provided at least the intelligentsia moral and ethical frameworks, with or without devotion to their gods. Their teachings nearly approach what we today think of as religion.

It is symptomatic that Philo and Josephus labelled distinct Jewish groups 'philosophies'. Josephus discussed the Sadducees, Pharisees and Essenes thus, and we have noted already his Fourth Philosophy – a group whose thinking differed on not much more than terror campaigns against the Jewish and Roman authorities. Philo described synagogue or prayer-house activity as devotion to philosophy. Jewish traditions seemed like a philosophy to some educated polytheists because of its basis in what they could understand as a philosophical document, the Pentateuch, its emphasis on a moral life and its devotion to an organising and ruling principle in Yahweh. As early as the second century AD, Christian thinkers (and converted polytheists) such as Justin and Tertullian were fitting their theology into polytheist philosophical categories and engaging with polytheists on a philosophical level. Such men were increasingly influenced and influential as philosophical approaches took over as the guide to understanding early Christianity.

How much did philosophical thought affect how people dealt with their lives? In cities and towns, at least, philosophers held forth in public venues. Perhaps in a theatre, perhaps in a rented hall, perhaps on a street corner men proffered their philosophical wares. A Greek inscription from Lyon in France describes a popular polytheist philosopher-preacher named Julius Eutecnius. He was a native of Laodicea, a prominent city in Syria.

> When he addressed the Gauls, persuasion flowed from his tongue. He circulated among various races; he knew many peoples and afforded training to the soul among them. He entrusted himself constantly to waves and seas, bringing to the Gauls and to the land of the West all the gifts that god ordered the fruitful land of the East to bear – for god loved mortal man.

Cynics were the most famous preachers. Their brash message of cultural criticism hardly inspired large numbers to change their ways, but the idea that commonly accepted rules and beliefs could be challenged helped open minds to new ideas.

Middle Platonism (a modern term for a combination of Platonic, Aristotelian and Stoic thought) offered a picture of the cosmos that approximated that of the Jewish people at this time. The basic idea was that there were intermediary divinities between humans and the ultimate supernatural reality. These intermediaries could feel emotions, be good or evil and affect directly human lives. This construct is very close to the angel- and demonology popularly accepted among Jewish people. Although Yahweh was unmistakably omnipotent, omniscient and beneficent, the agent of the covenant with his chosen people, this 'monotheism' never excluded the existence of other supernatural beings such as good angels and bad angels, i.e. demons. Likewise, polytheists certainly agreed that there were many supernatural powers working in the cosmos, with some benefit, and some harm, for humans. For Jews and polytheists alike, these intermediary powers explained a lot about the evil that happened in the world. For both groups the organising principles of Middle Platonism would be easily understandable. While philosophic ideas did not form the basis for most people's moral thinking, the educated among them were exposed in at least rudimentary form. Discussions in synagogues as well as in some polytheist associations provided a venue for exploring new ideas that had been heard on the street or in presentations.

Beyond the educated, polytheism lay open to new gods and beliefs by its very multifaceted nature. Most people never changed their traditional approaches to the supernatural, but the very traditional base of their habits left open the possibility of change. That base was a belief that the supernatural manifested its power in direct action. That could be intervention in human life (healing, cursing, saving, destroying) or in the physical world (earthquakes, storms, the need for rain). Proof of power turned heads. Thus, without any sophisticated philosophy about a singular, transcendent divinity, without a theology that explained layers of supernatural powers between humans and the ultimate divine, without any detailed reasoning, people usually defined a god's power by what he or she could accomplish. An outstanding accomplishment addressing human or physical world problems meant the god deserved attention. The primary path to change for polytheists was 'show me the power'.

A broad range of ideas and approaches to the supernatural and its devotees was circulating in the first century AD. No single, uncontested view dominated in either the Jewish or polytheist ranks. There were strong reasons for both to cling to traditional views and beliefs. But there was enough seepage into the traditional thought and actions of Jews to allow once-marginal ideas to take centre stage under the right circumstances.

For educated polytheists, evolving ideas of an overarching supernatural power combined with a religio-philosophical emphasis on way-of-life issues provided an opportunity for thinking about change towards monotheism. For other polytheists, the hesitancy to abandon traditional ways and all the socio-cultural importance they embodied stood in the way of change. But they were always ready to embrace demonstrated supernatural power. Enough power, and minds could be open to a new approach.

CHARISMATICS AND MESSIAHS

DEMONSTRATED ACCESS TO THE SUPERNATURAL powers has throughout human history been the stock in trade of popular religious leaders. A reputation for being able to interact with the supernatural brought attention and belief from the earliest shamans to the prophets of Judaic tradition and miracle workers of polytheist life. Charisma is a supernaturally infused personal essence that embodies the connection between a human and the supernatural. Once the connection is demonstrated, a charismatic leader can inspire action and change that might otherwise be unacceptable to people. Jesus of Nazareth came out of the Jewish tradition, but as an inspired person in the charismatic mould, his life, deeds and teachings also resonated with polytheists.

Josephus followed one of his descriptions of the Sicarii with discussion of another body of villains with purer intentions but more destructive ends, who no less than the assassins ruined the peace of Jerusalem. 'Deceivers and impostors, under the pretence of divine inspiration fostering revolutionary changes, they persuaded the multitude to act like madmen and led them out into the desert under the belief that Yahweh would there give them tokens of deliverance.'

Here he described another phenomenon directly linked to the passion for covenantal purity that was in the air. This was the emergence of the charismatic leaders in the prophetic tradition who claimed to know the way through righteous purity into Yahweh's good graces and thence into great rewards either in the present or at the day of final judgement.

Josephus had personal experience with one such person. He wrote that when he was sixteen years old, so in about AD 53, he decided that he wanted to gain personal experience of the sects within the traditions of the Jewish people at that time. He had already studied in the mode of the Pharisees; he further pursued knowledge of the Sadducean and Essene teachings. But he recognised that there was a fourth option he needed to explore, the tradition of the charismatic ascetic leader. To do this, he became a 'devoted disciple', as he said, of a man named Bannus. This charismatic lived in the wilderness (the rugged desert in the area of the Dead Sea), wore 'only clothing material that grew on trees and fed on such things as grew naturally'. Bannus preached radical purification and so Josephus underwent 'frequent ablutions of cold water, by day and night, for purity's sake'. He does not tell us the prophetic message that Bannus brought, nor does he say that Bannus had a large following there in the wilderness. But clearly he was an impressive person.

Bannus urged frequent ritual purification. In the sectarian squabbles of the time, Pharisees criticised men such as Bannus for emphasising outward rather than inward purity: 'The morning bathers said to the Pharisees: "We charge you with doing wrong in pronouncing the Name in the morning without having taken the ritual bath"; whereupon the Pharisees said: "We charge you with wrong-doing in pronouncing the Name with a body impure within."' People following the way of radical baptism were later called Hemerobaptists, which means 'daily baptisers'. Remnants survived in Judaea into the third century AD. Early Christians included John the Baptist in this group, but this is wrong as John did not engage his followers with daily baptism.

The charismatics in the wilderness represented an important element of popular religion in first-century AD Judaea. Such men called the people to repentance and promised Yahweh's blessing and help either in the present or at the last days, or both. Josephus offers a parade of such figures, one honoured, the rest carefully impugned.

The most famous of these prophets was John, known as 'The Baptiser'. Josephus called John a 'good man'. Perhaps he mentioned John in a positive light because John reminded him of his own mentor, Bannus. John operated in the wilderness beyond the Jordan, just as so many charismatics did. John apparently thought of himself as the prophet Elijah, mimicking his dress. Josephus stated that John's following came from his effective preaching, but Josephus did not go into much detail about his message. Apparently, he called on all people to lead righteous lives, to be just towards one and all and to be pious. Once a pious life was achieved, then baptism followed, not as a means of gaining pardon for past transgressions, but as an affirmation of the start of a new life of right behaviour. His message is elaborated in the Gospels. Even Pharisees and Sadducees came to him, but he rejected them as hypocrites. He preached righteousness in preparation for the Day of Judgement by the hand of Yahweh. In the usual apocalyptic tradition, he saw himself as a messenger proclaiming Yahweh's personal intervention in history at the last days. For him, righteousness encompassed social justice and honesty; he lectured on the need to share with the poor, for soldiers to behave themselves, for tax collectors to take no more than their due. This message is similar to that of the messenger promised by the prophet Malachi:

'I will send my messenger, who will prepare the way before me ... But who can endure the day of his coming? Who can stand when he appears? ... So I will come to put you on trial. I will be quick to testify against sorcerers, adulterers and perjurers, against those who defraud labourers of their wages, who oppress the widows and the fatherless, and deprive the foreigners among you of justice, but do not fear me,' says the Lord Almighty.

People considered John a prophet of great power. He had disciples during his lifetime. Andrew, one of the disciples of Jesus, began as a disciple of John, as Jesus himself probably did. John was killed by Herod Antipas, ruler of Galilee, in about 30. The crowds he attracted made Antipas nervous – crowds always made authorities nervous. John raised albeit indirectly the spectre of insurrection; hence, Antipas's pre-emptory strike to get rid of him. Unlike the false prophets to be mentioned, John's group of disciples, which included men who would become followers of another charismatic, Jesus, continued to propagate his message long after his death. In Ephesus Paul found his rival, Apollos, who knew only the 'baptism of John'. Also in Ephesus,

Paul encountered no fewer than twelve other disciples of the 'baptism of John'. They carried on John's message that Yahweh would soon intervene in history, so people had best repent, become pure and prepare. His followers did not proclaim that he was a forerunner to a human 'Son of God', but rather saw a prophet announcing the intervention of Yahweh himself. A small community in Iraq maintains the cultic importance of John up to the present day.

John was far from the only charismatic active in the middle of the first century AD. In 36 a man of Samaria, conventionally referred to as 'the Samaritan', convinced a throng that they should go with him to Mount Gerizim, the holy place of Samaria, and uncover sacred objects that Moses had buried there. Apparently there was a tradition that a Samaritan Restorer would appear, find these objects and re-establish Samaritan sovereignty. At any rate, Pilate, the Roman governor, felt threatened, sent troops and killed or scattered the multitude that had assembled to ascend Mount Gerizim.

Theudas claimed to be a prophet. In AD 45–6 he persuaded a multitude (Acts says 400, if this is the same Theudas) to take up their possessions and follow him into the wilderness. He promised to part the River Jordan so the people could cross. Clearly, he was claiming to be like Joshua, Elijah and Elisha who had all done this. Fadus, the Roman governor, sent cavalry that wiped out the following and delivered Theudas's head to the authorities in Jerusalem.

'The Egyptian', a prophet from, where else, Egypt, around AD 52–60 allegedly convinced thirty thousand common people (a more reasonable four thousand per Acts) to follow him into the desert, thence back to the Mount of Olives outside Jerusalem. He echoed the prophet Zechariah:

> The Lord will go out and fight against those nations, as he fights on a day of battle. On that day his feet will stand on the Mount of Olives, east of Jerusalem, and the Mount of Olives will be split in two from east to west, forming a great valley, with half of the mountain moving north and half moving south … Then the Lord my God will come, and all the holy ones with him.

The Egyptian proclaimed that from that vantage point he would command the walls of Jerusalem to fall down. The crowd would then rush through, overpower the garrison and, presumably, reclaim Jerusalem as Yahweh's holy seat with himself as ruler. Felix, the Roman governor, took the threat seriously, cut him off and slaughtered his followers.

Also in the time of Felix, false prophets 'called upon the multitude to follow them into the desert'. These men promised signs and wonders as certain proof that they were true speakers of Yahweh's designs. Sometimes Felix simply attacked and killed them and their followers. Other times, the charismatics were hauled before Felix and he punished them. Felix was clearly suspicious of these holy men, thinking that they were a cover for outright insurrection.

Finally, it is clear that many prophetic men came forward during the Great Revolt who did not bother with the wilderness experience. Many predicted that Yahweh would help those besieged in Jerusalem. Another man, Jesus ben Ananias, began in AD 62 to issue prophecies of doom from the city itself, in the tradition of Jeremiah. He persisted in this, despite attempts by both Albinus, the Roman governor, and by the priests to stop him. He was eventually killed during the siege itself some years later.

In modern writings on the first century, 'messiah' is often loosely used for 'charismatic'. They are not the same, however. Charismatics were frequently on the scene, but a thorough consideration reveals that, while the expectation of a messiah existed in some circles, it was not widespread. In the conceptualisation of the Judaic tradition, charismatics are prophets, not 'messiahs'. All messiahs would be charismatics, but few charismatics would claim to be a messiah.

Messiah meant 'an anointed one'. He (it is always *he*) was an agent of Yahweh. The anointing represented recognition of that agency. The close relationship of god and people meant that a people relied on their god for help and protection. The covenant of Yahweh and the Jewish people embodied just such a relationship. When gods did personally act in the world, they needed an agent to speak and act on their behalf. In the Israelite tradition, the process of anointing gave Yahweh's sign of agency. Whoever the person, that anointed one acted as Yahweh's agent.

In the overall history of the Jewish people, three types of persons were anointed: priests, prophets and kings. In the olden days, priests and kings were regularly anointed. Even a non-Jew could be an anointed agent of Yahweh. Isaiah praised Cyrus, King of the Persians,

12. Cyrus the Great stele at Pasargadae. Cyrus allowed all the Judaeans who wished, to return to Judaea and Jerusalem from Babylon. For this he was hailed as an anointed one of Yahweh.

as his (metaphorically) anointed and promised him earthly rewards because he returned exiles from Babylon to Judaea and reauthorised the king-and-priest theocracy in the land. The habit of regularly anointing kings and priests seems to have died out with the Exile. Later, from time to time, men claimed kingship openly or implicitly on the basis of Yahweh's authority, as for example Judah Maccabeus and his brother Jonathan, kings during the Maccabean rule, but they were never called messiahs, nor indeed do they seem to have been anointed. Judas, son of Hezekiah, Simon of Peraea and a shepherd named Athronges all claimed kingship during the uncertainty at the death of Herod the Great in 4 BC. None, as far as we know, claimed anointment. Priests, including the High Priest in Jerusalem, do not seem to have been anointed at this time.

Prophets followed the same historical trajectory. They could actually be anointed (as Elijah did for Elisha) or metaphorically so, as Isaiah: 'The Spirit of the Sovereign Lord is on me, because the Lord has anointed me to proclaim good news to the poor. He has sent me to bind up the broken-hearted, to proclaim freedom for the captives and release from darkness for the prisoners.' Their task as agent was to call the people back to a right relationship with Yahweh. But later, men we would call prophets, such as John the Baptist, apparently were not anointed. Our sources, including the Dead Sea Scrolls, did not call anyone an anointed prophet, not even the Teacher of Righteousness. Jesus of Nazareth was never anointed.

Thus, somewhat unexpectedly, anointed agents of Yahweh, fairly common in the pre-exilic period, disappear in the post-exilic period. The people remain the same – priests, kings, men we would call prophets – but none is said to be an anointed agent of Yahweh. Then, towards the end of the third century and the beginning of the second century BC, the idea of a future anointed one began to take hold. 1 Enoch and Daniel both foresaw Yahweh encouraging the people's righteousness and bringing judgement against their enemies. A messiah was not, however, yet an agent in this enterprise. The people of the Dead Sea Scrolls did emphasise just such an agent. The fragment called 'Messianic Apocalypse' (4Q521) mentions a messiah who in this life will re-establish the traditional Jewish social contract preached by the prophets and then will after the final days see the resurrection of the dead and will rule in heaven and on earth. Then, in the first century BC, a work called Psalms of Solomon mentioned a specifically political messiah in the mould of King David. This would be a messiah who was descended from David and who would re-establish the Jewish kingdom. A messiah announcing the final judgement of Yahweh also appeared in those psalms. That concept was applied not to a political messiah, but to a prophetic or priestly messiah.

If we did not have the Dead Sea Scrolls and the New Testament, we would thus have virtually no idea of a future messiah from the house of King David who would appear to carry out Yahweh's wishes for the Jewish nation. It is almost only in those sources that 'the anointed one' arises as an idealised future prophet, or priest, or king – one who would call the people to righteousness and, in the last days, see Yahweh reward the pious and punish the wicked, ushering in a time ruled directly by Yahweh.

The Dead Sea Scrolls represent the fullest development of this approach. The people of Qumran and those who thought as they did saw a final judgement when Yahweh would punish and reward. It was these people who brought to the fore a prophetic and priestly messiah who would act, probably through sacrifices, to atone for the sins of the people. He would also be Yahweh's agent in teaching the people the ways of piety and righteousness. As one scroll states: 'He will atone for the children of his generation, and he will be sent to all the children of his people. His word is like a word of heaven, and his teaching conforms to the will of God. His eternal sun will shine, and his fire will blaze in all the corners of the earth. Then darkness will disappear from the earth and obscurity from the dry land.' He will aid Yahweh at the End Time. But at the same time the scrolls anticipated a Davidic kingly messiah who would defeat the worldly enemies of righteousness ('sons of darkness'), both among the Jewish people and among the foreign nations. This king would be subservient to the prophet or priestly messiah.

These types of messiahs – prophet or priest and king – continue to evolve in the minds and actions of the Jewish people. The proliferation of kingly claimants bears witness to the lively ideal of a kingly leader, blessed by Yahweh, even though in the sources no claimant actually seems to be anointed, or claims messiahship outright. These 'kings' focused on a present world restoration of a Jewish kingdom.

The so-called 'Son of God' Dead Sea Scroll described a probably Davidic messianic war leader:

> He shall be called the Son of God; they will call him Son of the Most High ... He will judge the earth in righteousness ... and every nation will bow down to him ... with (Yahweh's) help he will make war, and ... [Yahweh] will give all the peoples into his power.

The same scroll highlights the peace that will come:

> And also his son will be called great and be designated by his name. He will be called the Son of God, they will call him the son of the Most High ... Their kingdom will be an eternal kingdom, and all their paths will be righteous. They will judge the land justly, and all nations will make peace. Warfare will cease from the land, and all the nations shall do homage to them. The great God will be their help. He Himself will fight for them, putting peoples into their power, overthrowing all before them. God's rule will be an eternal rule and all the depths of [the earth are his].

The array of charismatic men who claimed to lead the people to righteousness and position them well at a last judgement shows the liveliness of the charismatic prophetic ideal. Although this could become entangled with actual political establishment of a Judaean kingdom, its primary focus was next-worldly – preparation while still in the present for the world to come. For the people of the scrolls, the most important messiah was the one who would lead the people in social justice and preparation of righteousness to a successful place in the Kingdom of Yahweh. The 'Messianic Apocalypse' text speaks of a messiah whom earth and heaven obey:

> [The hea]vens and the earth will listen to His Messiah ... Over the poor His spirit will hover and will renew the faithful with His power. And He will glorify the pious on the throne of the eternal Kingdom, He who liberates the captives, restores sight to the blind, straightens the b[ent] ... For He will heal the wounded, and revive the dead and bring good news to the poor.

What the scrolls do not present is any suffering or dying messiah. The Teacher of Righteousness (who never claimed to be a messiah, nor was claimed to be one by others) was banished by his enemies and died in exile. He lived on only in his teachings.

Jesus of Nazareth

Describing Jesus of Nazareth is like trying to seize Proteus. The shape keeps changing, defying any purchase tried. Although all problems in ancient history are bedevilled by our lack of sources, as well as their often conflicting nature, we try to put together what we have in a coherent way. The problem of source evaluation in the case of Jesus presents probably the most vexed situation in all of ancient history. If we did not have material written by partisans of his life and message, we would know practically nothing about him. In fact, without that material we would know more about John the Baptist than about Jesus. There is no notice contemporary with his life. Josephus, writing perhaps in the 90s, mentioned him in a famous passage, but many historians think that later Christian editors either inserted it, or seriously massaged what Josephus actually had written. Pliny the Younger gives us the first certain notice. His letter to Emperor Trajan in about 112 certainly referred to Jesus and his followers, called Christians. Earlier notices by the historian Tacitus and by the biographer Suetonius refer to Christians in the context of the reigns of the emperors Claudius (49) and Nero (64). But this material was actually composed in the 120s, after Pliny's first notice. None of these sources helps us understand Jesus's message, why his disciples continued after his death, or how interest in his teachings and life spread.

In addition, the partisan nature of the sources we do possess does not mean that they agree. On the contrary, that material is biased in various ways, elusive, incomplete and often contradictory. Once we turn to it, we still have no biography by anyone who actually knew Jesus and had participated in his ministry. Jesus's contemporaries Matthew, Mark and John did not actually write the Gospels attributed to them. Other men used those names to claim legitimacy for their biographies, although those authors did draw on eyewitness accounts. Luke never saw Jesus in the flesh. We are left, then, with sources written by persons with only at best indirect knowledge of the man and his deeds. The traditional assumption is that 'Q' (= *Quelle* = Source), a putative basis for the Gospels of Matthew and Luke, goes back to a collection of sayings and tales from the earliest days. But there is no way to be sure the material is from witnesses of the life of Jesus, or, if so, that facts and quotations are truly representative of historical events. Some claim that the *Gospel of Thomas*, a collection of sayings of Jesus, pre-dates the four canonical Gospels; others claim it as a second-century Gnostic text. About 40 per cent of its sayings do not occur in the Gospels. There is no way to tell with certainty if they go back to a witness to the life of Jesus.

We are on better footing when it comes to material helping us understand the movement that survived him. Some actual participants left writings, most importantly the genuine epistles of Paul. These are: First Thessalonians (c.50), Galatians (c.53), First Corinthians (c.53–4), Philippians (c.55), Philemon (c.55), Second Corinthians (c.55–6) and Romans (c.57). The many other Pauline letters are pseudoepigraphic – written by others using his name to increase the prestige and authority of the piece. Luke, the first historian of early Christianity, may have accompanied Paul and so is another eyewitness to the period he writes about in Acts. But even that book dates from after the destruction of the temple in Jerusalem in 70, as do all the life accounts (Gospels) that we possess. This hodgepodge of material by a number of different hands is inconsistent at best, conflicting at worst. Each has his own interpretation about who Jesus had been, what his message was and how the movement came about, proceeded and grew. A wise scholar of Greek history once said that any answer to a conundrum that reconciles all available sources is undoubtedly wrong. Yet, the tendency to try to reconcile all the different strands of information about Jesus and his movement is practically irresistible, given the stakes in a culture so deeply influenced by Christianity. The wide variety of possibilities that our sources and the ingenuity of scholars, clerics and lay people alike have raised over the millennia requires that we be clear about our approach to Jesus and the movement that grew up after his death.

My treatment aims to capture how the people of the day viewed Jesus and, subsequently, those preaching his message. To do so means accepting details of his life, death and resurrection, because many people of his day did, whether or not they meet the threshold of what modern historians would like to think of as facts. People would not have been troubled by inconsistencies ferreted out by later experts, nor by events that some now might reject as mythical, fabulous, or impossible. In the next chapter I will lay out what I think attracted everyday people. But for now, it is important to form an idea of the Jesus that people in his day would have encountered. The material we have is consistent enough in broad outline to do this, despite the fact that delving into details enters a labyrinth with no exit.

As is evident by my placement of Jesus among the charismatic prophets of the first century, I am confident that people would have seen him as such. Other examples of the time – a shepherd here, a peasant there – indicate that people could find themselves inspired to take up an active life defending some aspect of the covenant with Yahweh as they understood it. Everything in the tradition as we have it in the Gospels emphasises that Jesus saw himself as a person awakened by the preaching of John the Baptist to the importance of an active life of righteousness according to the Torah. Just as many followed charismatics into the wilderness, Jesus was there with John. After his baptism, Jesus stayed in order to meditate and gain focus for his personal message. He emerged from the wilderness as a charismatic leader in his own right. At that time, John was arrested by Herod Antipas and executed.

Taking up the message of John, Jesus preached the need for social justice, repentance and a life according to the Torah. He seems to have developed his own interpretation of exactly what that meant, for he avoided a number of usual topics in prophetic utterance. He did not preach explicitly against apostasy or idolatry, he did not emphasise ritual cleanliness, nor did he criticise people for sexual immorality of various sorts, including intermarriage with non-Judaeans. In addition, he did not baptise as John did, or bathe for purity daily as Bannus advocated. His idea of righteousness was living according to the Torah; the Mosaic Law was central to living out the covenant it embodied. He followed the Pharisaic tradition of interpreting, even parsing the scriptures, but he drew broader conclusions, focusing on the Shema ('Hear, O Israel: The Lord our God, the Lord is one') and a personal, rather than a cultic act as central to righteousness: 'Love the Lord your God with all your heart and with all your soul and with all your mind and with all your strength ... Love your neighbour as yourself. There is no commandment greater than these.' These words came directly from the Torah.

All of this was perfectly normal within the bounds of the religious experience of the first-century Jewish people. The most revolutionary turn Jesus took was to claim that his message was not 'prophetic', i.e. he was not a mere agent channelling Yahweh, which was the traditional role of the prophets, including the likes of John. Rather, he claimed oneness with Yahweh. He claimed that his pronouncements were authoritative in and of themselves, not just as a dummy with Yahweh the ventriloquist. This clearly could have confused people, who quite logically thought of him as another John the Baptist, Jeremiah or Elijah, in other words as in the mould of a traditional prophet. The distinction between spokesmanship and authority was crucial to his role as a to-be-revealed messiah. But his biographers treated it as hidden knowledge, in the manner of the Qumran community or the Essenes keeping important material secret. Not worrying overmuch about categories of inspired leaders, the people revered the authority of prophet-like charismatics, especially those who demonstrated the ability to direct the power of Yahweh at will. Miracles were part and parcel of a prophet's repertoire, the proof of a share of Yahweh's power and so legitimisation as his spokesman. Jesus was adept at miracles and so all the more convincing.

Unlike the prophets in the wilderness, Jesus took his message to the villages of Galilee, a hotbed of eschatological fervour. He lived an ascetic life, moving as Elijah had from place to place. He had minimal clothing and equipment and lived on the largesse of others. Although he preached to mass gatherings (as many as five thousand by one account), many of his encounters were in or just outside homes. He associated with people who were considered unclean in Pharisaic and other circles. His commitment to social justice, again following John and earlier prophets, overrode the strict purity rules of these practitioners and emphasised purity of intent over external actions, again following earlier prophets. He emphasised that purity and righteousness was compromised by an individual's actions, not by ritual transgressions, as when he said: 'What comes out of a person is what defiles them. For it is from within, out of a person's heart, that evil thoughts come – sexual immorality, theft, murder, adultery, greed, malice, deceit, lewdness, envy, slander, arrogance and folly. All these evils come from inside and defile a person.'

He shared this attitude with others who saw a broad definition of right-eousness and purity.

Jesus's eschatology was standard fare for his time. He saw Yahweh intervening at the last days to judge the righteous and the wicked, visit-ing condign rewards and punishments and setting up a true theocracy, the Kingdom of Heaven, i.e. of Yahweh. It is common today to link Jesus with the political aims and even violence that some other charismat-ics of his day espoused. Jesus as a Zealot (a group first attested thirty years after the crucifixion) is particularly popular. I find no convincing evidence of this. Unlike some charismatics of his time, there is little hint in the tradition that he was, like The Egyptian, for instance, involved in action to hasten Yahweh's rule in present time. Unlike the Sicarii, he did not combine an ideology of violence with one of social justice. In fact, he never called for violent action to redress broad social justice issues – the trashing of the money changers in the temple, arguably his only recorded act of aggression, was highly symbolic, but hardly earth-shak-ing. Rather, he was typical of calmer charismatics who left it to Yahweh to bring about a time of triumph for the righteous, the establishment of a godly order and a scene of vengeance and retribution on his enemies. Only working from a prior conviction of Jesus as political agitator can produce Jesus as a revolutionary from the evidence we have.

The great popularity of Jesus's resonant eschatological message com-bined with his remarkable claim to direct relationship with Yahweh and the ability to validate that message through miracles explains his prob-lems with elite leaders. The consistent theme in Josephus's accounts of the fates of charismatics is that the authorities, whether Roman or Jewish, feared not their message per se. Surely prophets real and imag-ined were ranting on street corners and in marketplaces daily, while Pharisees and Sadducees just as certainly confronted each other and charismatics in debates short of violence. Rather the authorities feared their deepest fear, the potentially unruly or even insurrectionary crowds that gathered around charismatics.

The crucifixion of Jesus, mentioned by Paul, perhaps by Josephus and Tacitus, is as certain as any of the facts of his life can be. To almost everyone at the time, Jesus's execution by the Romans was just another example of a charismatic with a large following failing to bring about the rule of Yahweh they all claimed to be able to effect, but in the end could not. The tradition held that the Roman overlords executed Jesus because they feared him as a proclaimed messiah. The ridiculing plaque, 'King of the Jews', that is said to have been placed at the top of his cross witnessed this fear. While anything is possible, it is much more likely that Pilate saw nothing particularly special about Jesus. To Pilate, Jesus, like the other charismatics, was a threat to public order. The action against Jesus was brought on by Pilate's concern for eliminating people who could rally crowds, especially at a major festival with tens of thousands of people crowding the streets of Jerusalem. Later, he treated the threat of the Samaritan Restorer in the same way. Other Romans and their Jewish surrogates consistently acted likewise: Herod Antipas in Galilee had John executed for just these reasons. Regardless of the message that created the rallying, the rallying itself had to be controlled. Maintaining public order was sufficient reason for executing Jesus.

The evidence that Jesus called himself a messiah is mixed at best. In the Gospel tradition he referred to himself by this term only a few times, twice with the admonition to his disciples to keep it a secret. Jesus avoided the designation, at least publicly, until the interrogation before the crucifixion. For early Christians, Jesus's messiahship was not a central element of his message: outside the Gospels and Acts, written about forty years after the crucifixion, there are but four mentions of Jesus as the Messiah in the New Testament. Paul's only mention occurs in the letter to the Christian community in Rome. Jesus as Messiah evidently was not central to his message. Whatever the reason for the Gospel writers to accentuate Jesus's messiahship, it may well be an emphasis that did not go back to Jesus himself.

The Dead Sea Scrolls and some other Jewish writings also show some people panting for an anointed prophet and/or king. In addition, some passages from Isaiah could support such an expectation. But Josephus never used the term for the men such as Theudas – men we would think of as having obvious messianic pretensions. Other sources almost entirely lack mention of a messiah by that name; indeed, expectation of one was probably limited to sects such as at Qumran. It is notable that most documentation of an expected messiah comes from the Dead Sea Scrolls communities or the New Testament material itself. Few people ever identified Jesus as a messiah – most guessed, appropriately from their experience, that he was a particularly gifted prophet. The evidence that Jesus called himself a messiah is mixed at best. Jesus's followers fixed on messiahship as the defining descriptor of his life only after his resurrection, the ultimate miracle. The Gospels, Acts, and the letters of Paul all focus on Jesus as Christ, that is, the anointed one, the Messiah. His followers came to be known as Christians, 'Christ' being the Greek translation of the Aramaic 'messiah'. But the central importance of Jesus's messiahship developed only with those early Christians. As it took centre stage in the first century, it is not surprising that the story of Jesus as told ex post facto in the Gospels not only mentioned messiahship, but also made it seem that everyone was waiting for a messiah, an expectation fulfilled by their leader's appearance.

In the Jewish tradition, charismatic leaders played a recognised, traditional role in urging the people to observance of their covenant with Yahweh. Whether called prophet or messiah, the fundamental role was the same. Outside that tradition, polytheists also accepted the concept of an inspired, miracle-working person. However, the idea of a charismatic who performed the ultimate miracle, rising from the dead to defeat death itself, stretched credulity in both traditions. But some Jews and polytheists were ready to listen and, if the proof were strong enough, to believe.

CHRISTIANITY IN THE JEWISH AND POLYTHEISTIC WORLD

THERE IS NO REASON to question the basic elements of Luke's description of the first days after the crucifixion. The disciples did not disperse, any more than did the disciples of John at his death. The Twelve minus the traitor Judas Iscariot gathered: Peter, John, James, Andrew, Philip, Thomas, Bartholomew, Matthew, James son of Alphaeus, Simon and Judas – not Iscariot, but a person who was somehow related to one of the disciples named James. With them were some of the female followers of Jesus, including Mary, Jesus's mother. Jesus's brothers (James, Joseph and yet another Judas), were also on hand. Fifteen persons or so. Peter rose to the leadership from among the disciples. John and Philip are the only others of the Twelve who were afterwards mentioned by Luke in the early days. The mantle of leadership also fell to Jesus's (probably oldest) blood relation, his brother James. In fact, Jesus's family long continued to hold an important, if largely undocumented, role in the leadership. The last surviving blood relatives of Jesus, two grand-nephews, grandsons of his brother Judas, were still alive and well known in the early second century.

The disciples and the family seem to have remained in Judaea or Galilee, forming a core of the leadership there. In Luke's account, none ever travelled far beyond the homeland of the movement. Mary and the other women, except Mary the mother of John, simply drop out of the picture. A council of elders is mentioned, as are two non-disciples, non-blood leaders, Judas Barsabbas and Silas. Early Christianity, therefore, organised itself around the original followers of Jesus and his family.

The oddity is the emergence of Paul as a leader. He was called as a prophet of the new faith through the time-honoured process of Yahweh or, in this case, Jesus as his son, sending a very clear and miraculous message. Just as in the case of other prophets, he was to channel the message of the supernatural, in Paul's case to both the Jewish people and polytheists (gentiles). The leadership in Jerusalem was at first suspicious of his credentials, then because of his supernatural experience they accepted him as a true representative, an apostle (literally, someone who is sent out). The pattern was set that would allow a very flexible increase in leadership, for Paul's experience meant that anyone who was judged to have had a revelation could enter the leadership circle, not just blood relatives of disciples and of Jesus, nor only those that existing leaders chose to accept.

The adherents of early Christianity met in individuals' homes. Gatherings of like-minded people were an important part of life for Jews and polytheists alike. People met in groups defined by ethnicity or occupation or cult, sometimes even based upon factional preferences in entertainments like chariot racing. They met as friends getting together for a good time and support in burial expenses, or as workers seeking mutual support, or as devotees of a cult, or even as utilitarian groups such as volunteer fire-fighters. Groups could become almost an extended household or family. They were an important socially intermediate experience between the family unit and the community as a whole. As we have seen, they also could be, and usually were suspected of being, at least potentially political. This might be in a fairly benign manner, such as supporting candidates for office as in ancient Pompeii, or dangerous to the elites as hotbeds of mob organisation and action. Authorities saw them mostly as dangerous, as did Flaccus, a Roman governor in Egypt in Philo's time:

He forbade promiscuous mobs of men from all quarters to assemble together, and prohibited all associations and meetings which were continually feasting together under pretence of sacrifices, making a

13. Election graffito from Pompeii: 'The apple mongers association urges the election of M. Holconius Priscus to the position of chief magistrate.'

drunken mockery of public business, treating with great vigour and severity all who resisted his commands.

There are a vast number of parties in the city whose association is founded in no one good principle, but who are united by wine, and drunkenness, and revelry, and the offspring of those indulgencies, insolence; and their meetings are called synods and couches by the natives … Whenever it was determined to do some mischief, at one signal they all went forth in a body, and did and said whatever they were told.

Roman law and imperial decrees had a long history of attempting to throttle such associations. As the *Digest of Roman Law* put it: 'Unlawful assemblies must not be attempted, even by veteran soldiers, under the pretext of religion, or that of performing a vow.' The ban extended even to the bedrock of imperial control, the soldiery: 'By the Decrees of the Emperors, the Governors of provinces are directed to forbid the organisation of corporate associations and not even to permit soldiers to form them in camps.'

The Jews seem not to have run afoul of these rules when they gathered on the Sabbath and at other times in their synagogues or prayer houses. According to Philo, Emperor Augustus sent a letter

to the governors of the provinces in Asia, as he had learned that the sacred first-fruits were treated with disrespect. He ordered that

the Jews alone should be permitted by them to assemble in synagogues. These gatherings, he said, were not based on drunkenness
and carousing to promote conspiracy and so to do grave injury to the
cause of peace, but were schools of temperance and justice.

Josephus reports a Roman decree authorising similar gatherings in
Parium, in Asia Minor.

Although the Latin term for association, *collegium*, is never actually
applied to Jewish gatherings, the rhetoric defending them makes it clear
that they were considered by polytheists as cultic associations. With no
central authority to enforce a standard, Jewish people were free to meet
where they wished and with whom they wished to hold their religious
gatherings. Leadership sprang from the local people, while visiting
authorities such as a Pharisee or priest passing through could lead the
reading and discussion of scripture. Early meetings of adherents to early
Christianity mimicked the synagogue or prayer house meetings of their
fellows. Advocates of early Christianity regularly visited established
synagogues to take part in the lively discussions of scripture in the hope
of convincing fellow Jewish people that Jesus was the Messiah, the Son
of God. But they also met in their own gatherings.

Adherents thought of themselves as members of a large household,
the household of their god. A household meal formed the centrepiece of
gatherings. Tertullian in the late second century still saw the gathering's
event as a communal meal, presided over by a president, as was usual
for a *collegium*. About fifty years into the second century, a Christian
letter described how these groups meeting in various cities and towns
throughout the empire remained integrated into their local environments while at the same time standing apart because of their beliefs:

> For Christians are not distinguished from the rest of mankind either
> in locality or in speech or in customs. For they dwell not somewhere
> in cities of their own, neither do they use some different language, nor
> practise an extraordinary kind of life ... [T]hey dwell in cities of Greeks
> and barbarians as the lot of each is cast, and follow the native customs
> in dress and food and the other arrangements of life ... They dwell in
> their own countries, but only as sojourners; they bear their share in all
> things as citizens, and they endure all hardships as strangers.

Tertullian seconded this: '[We are] people who are living among you, eating the same food, wearing the same attire, having the same habits, under the same necessities of existence.' The early Christian 'assemblies' ('churches') were part of living alongside polytheists.

Within a group dedicated to the movement a distinctive hierarchy of authority and activities developed that gave individuals a place and status. Membership was easy and fluid. There was no elaborate initiation or long waiting period to join. Confession of the core belief in Jesus as the Son of God brought one into the fold. At the same time, members did not reject the deep cultural ties that the entire Jewish tradition offered. This meant that, although they could be criticised, those who wanted to could go about without a total disruption of their daily Jewish habits. They could follow the law, worship in the cultic activities of the temple, circumcise their children, observe food restrictions and so on.

Early Christianity carried its message – what they called the baptism of the Holy Spirit – beyond the Jewish homeland in Judaea. In keeping with its Jewish roots, adherents there were Jews or polytheists with an inclination to accept the Jewish people's traditions. That tradition had a place for proselytising, converts and sympathisers, the so-called 'god-fearers'. Although there is evidence of reaching out to the public world in general, for example Paul in Athens and activities elsewhere, the basic location for Christian preaching early on was the Jewish community in their synagogues spread across the eastern Mediterranean. The goal was to convince fellow Jews that a new understanding of Yahweh's covenant was at hand through the person of his son, Jesus the anointed one.

Jewish non-adherents called adherents 'followers of the one from Nazareth', i.e. Nazarenes. Polytheist opponents called them 'followers of the anointed one', Christians. Acts states that this name was first used in Antioch. There were many Jews, converts and god-fearers in Antioch and the general citizenry hated them, at least by AD 67. Antioch was a Greek-speaking city in Syria and the construction '-ianus' to mean 'adherent of a group', a 'follower', as in Caesarianus, a follower of Caesar, or Herodianus, a member of the Herodian party in Judaea, is purely Latin transliterated into Greek. There is no similar Greek construction. Like the name Sicarii, the name must have originated on a

Latin tongue. By the early second century it became the one-word identification of an adherent. Probably local citizens of Antioch complained
to the Roman authorities about the disturbance that Agabus, a prophet
in the Christian movement, was causing by preaching the coming disaster of a famine during the reign of the emperor Claudius, presumably
as a punishment from God. In complaining about the Jew, Agabus, his
enemies would have used a Latin construction to indicate to Roman
officials that he was a follower of one claimed to be a kingly and therefore potentially disruptive, anointed one, or messiah – Christ. The designation then stuck as a disparagement and so the name was not used
as a means of self-designation but by others. The early Christians called
each other such things as brethren, the faithful, the saints, believers and
the elect. In the 120s the writer of Peter's first letter tried to turn aside
the disparagement: 'However, if you suffer as a Christian, do not be
ashamed, but praise God that you bear that name.' By the mid-second
century, Christians were regularly calling themselves 'Christians'.

The early Christian movement was deeply embedded in the traditions
of the Jewish people. It presented itself as the correct interpretation of
those traditions or, as their leaders chose to put it, they were the fulfilment of the promises of the Torah and of the Israelite prophets. Time and
again Paul is presented as arguing this point in a synagogue environment by using texts from the scriptures as proof of his points. Indeed,
the heavy use of such texts by him and other early writers shows that
the target audience was Jewish people and god-fearers, for no one else
would have cared in the least about proofs from those esoteric scriptures.

Debates over the interpretation of scripture were a basic part of
the Jewish religious life. Other groups before the Christians had used
scripture to prove their way and actions correct in Yahweh's eyes. The
Qumran community had the road to righteousness laid out, including
an eschatological moment during the last days that would prove them
right in the judgements of Yahweh. In their paradigm, backed by scripture, the Teacher of Righteousness would return, like Elijah, at the End
Time and participate.

Analysis of the scriptural citations in the Dead Sea Scrolls shows
that the people of the scrolls classed scripture as being the five books
of Moses (the Pentateuch), the Prophets and the Psalms. That limited

selection from the entire Tanakh also formed the focus for the Essenes of the Qumran community. This was the core of Jewish scripture. The works cited by early Christians corresponded to that body of scripture as well: '[Jesus] said to them, "This is what I told you while I was still with you: Everything must be fulfilled that is written about me in the Law of Moses, the Prophets and the Psalms."' Over three hundred of the approximately four hundred citations of scripture in the New Testament are from just those works. In the Gospels, 120 of 127 Old Testament citations or references are to those bodies of scripture. Those of the Pharisaic persuasion, or the Sadducees, or any splinter group would focus on scriptural texts in exactly the same way. When it came to scriptural duelling, early Christians and their more traditional Jewish fellows used the same weapons.

All Jewish people shared a belief in the worship of a single deity, in their case, Yahweh. They also were convinced that there were many other supernatural powers and beings besides the one they worshipped centrally. There were the angels, messengers of Yahweh. There were the demons that caused disease. There was the arch-demon, Satan himself, most powerful competitor of Yahweh and the probable cause of much of the evil in the world. In fact the most powerful argument used against Jesus was that Satan (Beelzebul, as he was often called) powered Jesus's miracles as well as those of his followers. The innovation of early Christianity was to proclaim that there were two active aspects of Yahweh that were previously unavailable, the person of his son and the projected power that was the Holy Spirit. This innovation diluted Jewish monotheism in a way that many found intolerable, but others accepted. Either way, it was proclaimed within the context of existing Jewish traditions and beliefs.

The Law of Moses as recorded in the Torah was the foundation of the Jewish people's covenant with Yahweh. Jesus was fully compliant during his lifetime and never advocated the abrogation of the law. He seems to have made judgements based not only on the writings, but also on oral traditions (as the Pharisees did) and on the spirit rather than the letter of the law. His speaking with authority, not just offering opinions for discussion, did not sit well with the proclaimed experts in the interpretation of the law, Pharisees and Scribes and, to a lesser extent, priests.

Jesus announced a new covenant. The original covenant with

Yahweh had a long history. The first instance, between Adam and Yahweh, was broken by the human side, then renewed to Noah after the Flood. Yahweh confirmed the covenant with the patriarchs Abraham, Isaac, and Jacob. Then he did this once again using Moses as his agent. In this instance, the difference between 'renewal' and 'new' is blurred. Moses went through an elaborate public ceremony to emphasise the covenant with Yahweh: 'Then [Moses] took the blood [from a sacrificed animal], sprinkled it on the people and said, "This is the blood of the covenant that the Lord has made with you in accordance with all these words."' Jesus metaphorically replicated this pouring out of blood as a sign of a covenant with Yahweh. At the Last Supper, after the meal, he lifted a cup and said, 'This cup is the new covenant in my blood, which is poured out for you.' The Mosaic action has more the appearance of a new beginning for the covenant than a renewal of the old, but the continuing rhetoric of the Old Testament sources speak of a seamless covenant, especially from Abraham onwards.

The idea of a new covenant emerged clearly only in the chaos of the Babylonian capture of Jerusalem, the destruction of the first temple and the subsequent Exile. Jeremiah declared that Yahweh's people had so reneged on their part of the covenant that Yahweh would punish them harshly. But far from abandoning his wayward people, the prophet announced that Yahweh would then establish a new agreement going forward: '"The days are coming," declares the Lord, "when I will make a new covenant with the people of Israel and with the people of Judah ... This is the covenant I will make with the people of Israel ... I will put my law in their minds and write it on their hearts. I will be their God and they will be my people."'

The post-exilic Isaiah took up the promise: 'For I, the Lord, love justice; I hate robbery and wrongdoing. In my faithfulness I will reward my people and make an everlasting covenant with them.' These prophets' new covenant from Yahweh emphasised an internalisation of the law and a new beginning complete with forgiveness of past iniquity. The Qumran people took up this theme. Their Teacher of Righteousness proclaimed a new covenant that applied not to all of Israel, as the one with Moses had, but only to the remnant of 'true Israel' that would be saved through their righteousness at the last judgement.

Circumcision of males was a central act of identity within the covenanted people. The term 'uncircumcised' was regularly used throughout the Old Testament as meaning 'not Jewish'. The rite went back to Abraham: 'This is my covenant with you and your descendants after you, the covenant you are to keep: Every male among you shall be circumcised,' Yahweh declared. Jesus was circumcised according to the law. The act was mentioned only once again in the Gospels, and that in an example of Sabbath activity.

Although circumcision had a long Old Testament pedigree, it was only in the post-exilic period, and especially from the Maccabean times on, that circumcision came to the fore, along with observation of the Sabbath and of food rules, as required to be a faithful Jew. But in their efforts to reform the people, prophets had been busy altering the straightforward nature of a physical act. Scripture proclaimed the need for, indeed the superiority of, a 'circumcision of the heart' as an expansion on the physical procedure. Jeremiah set the tone for the post-exilic period when he pronounced, 'Circumcise yourselves to the Lord, circumcise your hearts, you people of Judah and inhabitants of Jerusalem, or my wrath will flare up and burn like fire because of the evil you have done – burn with no one to quench it.' And he emphasised, '"The days are coming," declares the Lord, "when I will punish all who are circumcised only in the flesh."'

It was a short step to the acceptance of *only* the 'circumcision of the heart' as true circumcision; the physical was unnecessary. No known Jewish sect besides the Christians went as far; even for them, the canonical Gospels left it unmentioned. But the apostle Paul did take the step. He wrote, 'So then, if those who are not circumcised keep the law's requirements, will they not be regarded as though they were circumcised?' And, 'For in Christ Jesus neither circumcision nor uncircumcision has any value. The only thing that counts is faith expressing itself through love.' The *Gospel of Thomas* read the leap back to Jesus himself: 'His disciples said to Jesus, "Is circumcision beneficial or not?" He said to them, "If it were beneficial, their father would beget them already circumcised from their mother. Rather, the true circumcision in spirit has become completely profitable."' So Christianity retained the important place of circumcision in determining a correct relationship with Yahweh, but early Christians spiritualise the process, expanding on an existing Jewish trope. This interpretation also eliminated a painful operation, the major stumbling block to interested polytheist males converting to Jewish traditions.

Keeping the Sabbath also came to the fore as a touchstone of Judaic tradition after the Exile. Some adherents of early Christianity celebrated the Sabbath, some did not. They might also celebrate both the Jewish traditional day, Saturday, and the Lord's Day, that is Sunday, the day of the Resurrection. Justin Martyr, writing around 150 described a Sunday meeting:

> [O]n the day called Sunday, all who live in cities or in the country gather together to one place, and the memoirs of the apostles or the writings of the prophets are read, as long as time permits; then, when the reader has ceased, the president verbally instructs, and exhorts to the imitation of these good things. Then we all rise together and pray, and, as we before said, when our prayer is ended, bread and wine and water are brought, and the president in like manner offers prayers and thanksgivings, according to his ability, and the people assent, saying Amen; and there is a distribution to each, and a participation of that over which thanks have been given, and to those who are absent a portion is sent by the deacons. And they who are well to do, and willing, give what each thinks fit; and what is collected is deposited with the president, who succours the orphans and widows and those who, through sickness or any other cause, are in want, and those who are in bonds and the strangers sojourning among us, and in a word takes care of all who are in need. But Sunday is the day on which we all hold our common assembly, because it is the first day on which God, having wrought a change in the darkness and matter, made the world; and Jesus Christ our Saviour on the same day rose from the dead.

A first-century Jew would recognise much of this ritual since it combined elements of a Jewish meal and a synagogue meeting.

The dietary rules in the Torah were contested by early Christians and became a major point of controversy with the Jewish tradition. Still, in the beginning some adherents kept to them. Many also participated in major Jewish festivals – Passover, Pentecost and the Day of Atonement. Finally, it is important to note that the temple continued to play an active role in the life of adherents who lived in Jerusalem.

There were many similarities as well between the theological thinking of early Christians and Jews. For example, both emphasised the power of Yahweh to forgive transgressions if the transgressor was honestly repentant. Confession was central: 'Then David said to Nathan, "I have sinned against the Lord." Nathan replied, "The Lord has taken away your sin. You are not going to die."' The idea of personal resurrection at the last judgement also held widespread favour in both milieux. As we have seen, all major groups believed this, except for the Sadducees. Many scriptural references could be cited. Ezekiel's dry bones could be taken literally, not just as a metaphorical reference to the return of Israel. The prophet Daniel in the second century BC expressed what became the general belief among the people:

> At that time Michael, the great prince who protects your people, will arise. There will be a time of distress such as has not happened from the beginning of nations until then. But at that time your people – everyone whose name is found written in the book – will be delivered. Multitudes who sleep in the dust of the earth will awake: some to everlasting life, others to shame and everlasting contempt. Those who are wise will shine like the brightness of the heavens, and those who lead many to righteousness, like the stars for ever and ever.

The apocalyptic tradition, that Yahweh would intervene at the end of time, with or without a subsidiary agent to help him, was also widespread.

The idea that a faithful servant of Yahweh could be taken up to heaven was exemplified in the case of Enoch and Elijah. The tradition of Elijah emphasised that such a person might return to earth. People were ready to accept the return of dead prophets, especially Jeremiah, Elijah or Moses.

The miracles and magic that appeared in the activities of Jesus and adherents of early Christianity find many parallels in the experience of the Jewish people down through the ages, including the miracle of bringing the dead back to life. The early Christian martyrs, for example Stephen and James, Jesus's brother, followed in the footsteps of other martyrs of the Jewish people. In social justice, too, early Christianity followed clear precedents among the Jewish people, especially in its concern for the disadvantaged such as the poor, widows and orphans. I have already traced this message in the prophets. Philo, in his *Apology for the Jews*, showed the tradition was alive and well in the diaspora, as it was among those of the Qumran community. The Gospels, the *Didache* (an instructional manual for early Christian teachers dating from early in the second century AD), and Pauline corpus all echoed the message. Even as late as the letter of James (early second century), leaders were focused still on social justice:

> Now listen, you rich people, weep and wail because of the misery that is coming on you. Your wealth has rotted and moths have eaten your clothes. Your gold and silver are corroded. Their corrosion will testify against you and eat your flesh like fire. You have hoarded wealth in the last days. Look! The wages you failed to pay the workers who mowed your fields are crying out against you. The cries of the harvesters have reached the ears of the Lord Almighty. You have lived on earth in luxury and self-indulgence. You have fattened yourselves in the day of slaughter. You have condemned and murdered the innocent one, who was not opposing you.

Social attitudes of early Christians were similar to traditional Jewish ways. For example, they subscribed to the usual views about the relationship of wives to husbands. Relationships to polytheists also echoed some Jewish attitudes, although the emphasis placed upon finding converts to the Christian movement among polytheists reached an importance probably unheard of before.

The methods used to advertise the importance of Jesus mimicked those familiar to Jewish people. Preaching such as that of John the Baptist had many practitioners proclaiming in the tradition of the prophets. Teaching in parables also had a long tradition. The geography of many important events in Jesus's life were familiar to Jews, places such as the River Jordan and the Judaean wilderness, the Mount of Olives and the temple Mount, not to mention Jerusalem itself and many towns in Judaea and Galilee.

Finally, Jewish history frequently saw the persecution of one group by another. The followers of the Teacher of Righteousness were driven out of Judaea altogether, at least temporarily. The account of 3 Maccabees (late first century BC to early first century AD) conceived of vengeance by pious Jews against those who had fallen away. Although the work is fiction, it captured the intensity of inter-Jewish violence at times:

> [Jews] petitioned the king that they might carry out the punishment deserved by those Jews who had voluntarily turned aside from the holy God and God's Law ... [The king] gave them a free hand to utterly destroy those who had violated God's Law in every place within his kingdom, and to do so with confidence and without needing royal approval or supervision ... they punished and killed any fellow Jews they came upon who had polluted themselves, making a public example of them. On that day they killed more than three hundred persons ...

King Alexander Jannaeus killed Pharisees. Samaritans were considered defective Jews, disparaged and harassed. In addition, authorities Roman, Greek and Judaean alike used violence to put down what they considered to be political threats posed by Jewish men and mobs. Persecution of adherents of early Christianity was not unusual in this violent, harassing environment.

Besides these general similarities between the early Christian movement as a Jewish group and the general traditions of the Jewish people of the time, there are more specific resemblances between the group and other existing groups. In particular, the Qumran texts and the Essene community they are embedded in show many similar and so familiar traits. The shared meal as a centrepiece of cult and a priest blessing the bread and wine; the emphasis on a new covenant; the expectation of a last judgement with victory and revenge for the righteous; the use of similar proof texts from a similar selection of scriptures and sharing a similar social justice message all point to the growth of early Christianity from the Essenes' complex of ideas.

Jesus also showed many points in common with a famous teacher from among the Pharisees, Hillel. Among commonalities is an emphasis on reaching every person, not just the already religious, with the promise of attaining righteousness through study of the Torah. The Hillel tradition stated that 'one must instruct every man, for there were many sinners in Israel and they were brought into close contact with the study of the Torah and out of them came forth righteous, true and pure men'. In addition, the formation of a group following a teacher was a common phenomenon. Outstanding Pharisees such as Hillel acquired followers, as did John the Baptist and other charismatic leaders. Even the Samaritan Simon Magus, vilified in the tradition of Christianity as an evil magician, had around him a group of followers who continued to honour him for some time after his death. The survival of a group committed to the ideas and ideals surrounding Jesus of Nazareth followed a familiar pattern.

The basic message of early Christianity found adherents among some Jewish people, but it also alienated others. Varying interpretations of how the covenant should be lived out could create very strong feelings, sometimes spilling over into violence. Such opposition could quash a differing view, or strengthen adherents' belief in their own correctness. In the face of opposition and doubt which sometimes grew into charges of blasphemy and even persecution, early Christians rallied. They steadfastly asserted that Jesus was the Messiah, the Son of God – not just another prophet. This conviction became the focal point for a feeling of group identity and mission: they knew the way to a righteousness that would end in glory as their God preserved them and destroyed their enemies at the last judgement – something virtually all Jewish people believed in. It was Jesus's claim to equality with Yahweh that alienated many Jews, not his message.

Polytheist and Christian relationships with the supernatural were similar in many ways. There were obvious and important differences that I will discuss in the next chapter. But it is important to appreciate their common ground.

In general moral attitudes, early Christians fitted in with the polytheistic world around them. They differed in some fairly noticeable respects, such as strong opposition to abortion and the disposal by exposure of unwanted newborns. But their basic morality of family, honesty and loyalty would have resonated with the norm in the polytheistic world (however often that norm might have been violated in practice). They shared basic attitudes towards the supernatural powers such as the importance of worship, dietary restrictions and sacred days. They shared language and culture. Nor did adherents have physical markers that distinguished them from their neighbours. They had no distinctive dress. They generally ate what others ate, with the exception of food dedicated to idols. They did not set themselves off in a separate geographical space. They had no architecturally distinctive meeting places. In many cases they must have been invisible. That is not to say that they could not be stirred up and act as a group, but in the everyday life of the polytheistic world, adherents could have blended in without difficulty and usually did.

The monotheism of early Christianity found some resonance in the cult of Zeus Hypsistos – a populist movement that I have mentioned before. There is no evidence of animal sacrifice in that cult. The antiidolatry theme of the Christian movement fitted with the lack of a statuary representation of the god. In addition, many polytheists were exposed to deities claiming to be the composite of all other deities, and in this way a sort of monotheistic conception existed. The high goddess Isis is a famous example.

Early Christianity shared belief in basic approaches to the supernatural such as astrology, exorcism and the role of Fate (thought of as Providence). There was some belief among polytheists of an afterlife beyond a shadowing existence. The early philosopher Pythagoras believed in reincarnation; it is hard to know how many of his followers were around in the first century AD. The idea that Jesus was Elijah redivivus, for example, might have resonated with some, at least, as would the idea of punishment and reward according to righteousness in a future world. Some mystery religions promised rewards in the afterlife as well. Those mystery religions also provided a personal, emotional connection with a deity.

Polytheists needed to be able to relate to the various supernatural forces they believed created problems or provided benefits around them. The ability of practitioners of early Christianity to affect these forces was impressive. Later, the martyrs of the movement would, as saints, accumulate the helpful abilities that the polytheists' minor supernatural powers displayed.

However deeply philosophic thought penetrated the general populace, the basic thrust of such speculation in the first century was towards developing a good way of life in tune with the cosmos. This resonated with the goal of early Christians of living a life of piety and righteousness leading to happiness and final reward.

1. Ten tribes of Israel were led into exile in 722 BC by order of the Assyrian conquerors. Their plight was the same as this family driven into exile by the Assyrians after their city, Lachish, was crushed by the Assyrian king, Sennacherib (705–681 BC).

2. The storm god Baal. Hebrews entering Canaan encountered and mixed with peoples worshipping this god in his various forms.

3. The Prophets of Baal on Mount Carmel. The contest of Yahweh and Baal is one of the most famous miracles of the Old Testament (1 Kings 18:16–45). The challenge was: Who can light an altar pyre? The winner would prove himself the true god. When the priests of Baal failed to ignite the wood, Elijah called on Yahweh who answered with an incinerating flame.

4. Herod the Great (King of Judea 37–4 BC) expanded and refurbished the Second Temple in Jerusalem. Festival sacrifices of ordinary Jewish people took place in the gigantic courtyards as shown in this reconstruction.

5. Polytheists avidly worshipped their gods. Here a group of women pay honor to the god Dionysus.

6. The lararium housed a small statue of the household god, often in a wall niche. This example from Pompeii is missing its statue; it has a household sacrifice scene painted in the background.

7. The father leads a family sacrifice before the household god.

8. Festivals often included processions. Here devotees of the goddess Cybele form up to carry her on a platform to the location of the festival celebration in Pompeii.

9. Animal sacrifice was a central feature of polytheist and Jewish cult alike. On this Attic red-figure cup, a pig is about to be sacrificed on an altar.

10. Ordinary people knew enough of elite wisdom to recognise the famous Seven Sages. The latrine of the Tavern of the Seven Sages in Pompeii has images of the wise men along with parodic 'sayings' meant to amuse those using the latrine. Here for example, Chilon of Sparta is invoked, 'Cunning Chilon taught how to fart without making noise.' Below, men defecating are painted on the wall.

11. In this Pompeian fresco, a Cynic appears in his ragged tunic and typical staff and pouch. Note the dog at his feet, a reminder that Cynics barked like dogs at passersby.

12. Wall painting from the House of Julia Felix, Pompeii, depicting scenes from the Forum market. A bustling area like this was the scene of Cynic and Christian preaching.

13. Isis was very popular with ordinary people. She presented herself as a super-goddess, subsuming all other major female deities. Her healing was especially famous. Originally from Egypt, her devotees were to be found throughout the Roman Empire.

14. A ceremony at the temple of Isis in Herculaneum.

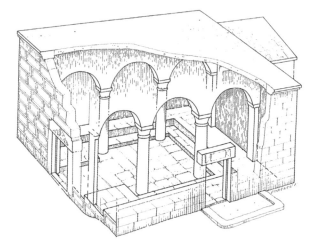

15. The synagogue at Kiryat Sefer, Israel, pictured here in
a reconstruction, dates from the 1st century BC.

16. Sica in the hand of a gladiator on a mosaic from Kourion, Cyprus, 3rd century
AD. The curved blade tore viciously when withdrawn from an enemy's body.

17. The Temple Scroll is one of the longest of the Dead Sea Scrolls. These documents revolutionized our knowledge of the Second Temple period. The Book of Isaiah, a fragment of which is shown here, was one of the most valued texts.

18. The only female Jesus had an extended conversation with was the Samaritan woman at the well.

19. Women as well as men attended Christian association events such as the agape meal and the eucharist ritual. Here women enjoy the meal.

20. Men at an early Christian agape meal and eucharist. The loaves and fishes remind of one of Jesus's miracles, the feeding of the five thousand.

21. Victorious Assyrians impaling defeated Jews
after the surrender of Lachish (701 BC).

22. This nail driven
through the bones in
the foot of a 25-year-old
man is our only human
archaeological evidence
for a crucifixion.
Found in a grave of
the Herodian period
in Givat ha-Mivtar
to the north-east of
Jerusalem (extra muros).

23. Christianity appealed to ordinary people
such as this potter, working at his wheel.

24. A late 2nd century graffito from Rome parodies Christians. It
reads, 'Alexamenos worships god.' The 'god' is a crucified, ass-
headed figure, a caricature of Jesus on the cross.

25, 26. The praying position was among the many polytheist habits Christians retained. *Left*, Chairemon raises his hands in prayful worship of the Egyptian god Anubis whose symbolic jackals sit at either side. A funeral stele from Egypt, 3rd to 4th centuries AD. *Right*, a praying Christian woman from the Coemeterium Maius, Rome, 3rd century AD.

27. An early 3rd century epitaph from the Vatican collection shows the polytheist D(is) M(anibus) applied to the Christian Licinia Amias: 'To the shades of Licinia Amias. Greatly esteemed, she lived …' Note the Greek phrase, 'fish of the living' as well as the anchor and fish, both Christian symbols.

28. Jesus raises Lazarus using a magician's wand. Christian gravestone from the Roman catacombs of the 3rd century.

29. Emperor Constantine the Great (274–337 AD) embraced the god who had miraculously aided him in victory. He in turn encouraged a Christian-friendly elite that in the course of a century created a Christian-dominated empire.

Public speaking was a well-recognised method of communicating ideas and passions among both early Christians and polytheists. Likewise, letter writing was a popular form of communication. In telling the tale of famous people, biography had existed for centuries. The Gospels lived in that tradition. So the various means of propagating the Christian messages found complete familiarity among polytheists. Finally, as far as social order was concerned, early Christians fitted in well with polytheist habits. They were encouraged to honour the authorities by whom they were governed. They held slaves, just as polytheists did. Their meetings were very similar to the association meetings of their neighbours.

In many ways, adherents of the early Christian movement were unexceptional. Adherents shared a wide range of attitudes with, on the one hand, their fellows in the larger Jewish tradition and, on the other, with polytheists. They shared basic moral values with traditional Jews as well as with polytheists. They believed in demons and in astrology. Magic and miracles played a large role in their lives. Their magicians were just like Simon Magus and innumerable other practitioners of the magic arts. Their best spokesmen were much like polytheist holy men such as Apollonius and Poimandres or Jewish charismatics. Their monotheism, with its angels and demons, was fuzzy enough to make sense to polytheists.

Their Jewish roots made them acceptable to many of the Jewish tradition. It is easy to imagine early Christianity co-existing among the options Jewish people followed during the first century. Yet this did not happen. Adherents confronted their Jewish brethren who favoured more traditional practices of their common tradition. Their shared ideas and practices did not overcome the discomfort of the deviations early Christians advocated, specifically Jesus as the Son of God.

For polytheists there should have been the same fairly easy accommodation for the movement as there generally was for accommodating Jewish traditions. From the outside, polytheists would have had a hard time distinguishing between the traditional Jew and an adherent of the early Christian movement that had developed from the traditions of the Jewish people. At the most, a polytheist might have noticed some quirkiness in what the adherents said and did, much as Pliny the Elder noted the peculiarities of the Essene group in Judaea.

But some in both the Jewish and polytheistic traditions came to detest the new movement and its members. From the start accommodation into the general world of Jews and polytheists hit speed bumps, then walls. In the next chapter I outline the differences that caused these problems.

HOSTILITY TO CHRISTIANITY

THE FOLLOWERS OF JESUS OF NAZARETH proclaimed a message that attracted Jew and polytheist alike during the course of the first century AD. By mid-century they had a name: Christians. During the first century the new movement fought for survival among the welter of possibilities in people's lives. During his lifetime, few objected to Jesus's message of repentance, reconciliation with Yahweh and preparation for the last days – all well within the Jewish religious life of his day. But he sowed seeds of hostility by claiming divine authority. Then his popularity raised the spectre of civil unrest. After his death, his followers set themselves apart from mainstream Jewish tradition by claiming his execution and resurrection had brought about a new relationship between Jews and their god. This radical break brought renewed hostility even as the movement pressed hard to fit its message into traditionally acceptable Jewish moulds. Beyond Judaea, the new movement reached out aggressively to polytheists. But these non-Jews pushed back hard against a proselytising movement that challenged a most basic element of their traditional relationship to the supernatural, the community's relationship with their gods.

As far as the Jewish tradition is concerned, the defining action of Jesus was his claim not to speak *for* Yahweh, but to be Yahweh's *son*. Prophets from the beginning of the Israelite tradition had close relationships with Yahweh, listening to him and announcing his opinions,

wishes and actions to the people of Israel. They spoke *for* him or channelled speech *from* him. No one in the tradition ever claimed to share
Yahweh's essence. Jesus did just this by claiming agency deriving from
paternity, not from a mere spiritual link. He was connected to Yahweh
as a son was connected to his father, not as an agent was connected to
his master: 'All things have been committed to me by my Father. No one
knows the Son except the Father and no one knows the Father except the
Son.' One Christian tradition even claimed outright genetic relationship
between Yahweh and Jesus through his mother Mary.

Yahweh was acknowledged as the father of the Israelites. As Isaiah
said, 'You, Lord, are our Father. We are the clay, you are the potter; we
are all the work of your hand.' But this parental metaphor did not imply
any literal connection. The terminology Jesus used stated an actual, not
metaphorical, relationship. The Messiah was not just a king or prophet
or priest acting on Yahweh's behalf. He was the anointed Son of God.
His relationship allowed Jesus to speak directly as Yahweh. He spoke
'with authority', not merely as an interpreter of the law or confronter of
demons, but as a supernatural voice.

The step Jesus took might be extreme, but the description of his
arrival in Jerusalem at the Passover shows that the people were ready to
give him the benefit of the doubt with regard to his demonstrated powerful supernatural connection, as son or no, to Yahweh. His arrest, trial
and crucifixion, whatever the details, would have dashed such expectations in the minds of most people – he would have become just another
charismatic the authorities had removed. The remarks alleged at the
cross, 'Come down from the cross if you are the Son of God,' and, 'He
saved others but he can't save himself,' would be the natural response of
people to the sight of a popular charismatic suffering a torturous death
instead of victorious triumph.

Contention subsequent to the crucifixion focused on disputes about
who Jesus had been (whether he was, indeed, the Messiah and Son of
Yahweh) and how his death fitted with the traditions of the Jewish people.
The crucifixion of Jesus caused difficulties. This form of execution had
by his time become commonplace in the entire eastern Mediterranean
and beyond. Roman legal sources routinely list it as a punishment for
capital crimes of various sorts committed by ordinary people (elites were
exempt, being beheaded or exiled instead). Hellenistic Greeks crucified

Jews and others. Alexander Jannaeus, a Hasmonean king, crucified eight hundred of his fellow Jews, even going so far as to kill the wretched men's wives and children before their dying eyes. Varus as governor of Syria crucified two thousand Judaeans; Quadratus, also a governor of Syria, crucified Judaeans and Samaritans. Governors of Judaea crucified men they considered bandits and rebels regularly. In Alexandria, Egypt, there were mass crucifixions in AD 38. During the Great Revolt the Romans crucified recalcitrant enemies. Pilate authorised the crucifixion of Jesus. As frequent as it was, the punishment was nonetheless universally viewed as a horrendous penalty. Josephus called it 'the most pitiable of deaths'. It was also popularly connected, correctly, with the execution of low sorts of people – bandits, rebels, bad slaves and so on.

Paul stated that the crucifixion was 'a stumbling block to Jews'. Deuteronomy spoke of the 'stumbling block': 'If someone guilty of a capital offence is put to death and their body is exposed on a pole, you must not leave the body hanging on the pole overnight. Be sure to bury it that same day, because anyone who is hung on a pole is under God's curse.' The 'body hanging on a pole' might have been impaled – a widely practised form of torturous execution or post-execution public display in the Near East. But it came to be widely interpreted as crucifixion. So to believe that the Jewish Messiah, an anointed of Yahweh, died on a cross seemed scripturally impossible. Paul tried to explain the paradox away, accepting the Deuteronomic curse but saying that the crucified Messiah 'redeemed us from the curse of the law by becoming a curse for us, for it is written: "Cursed is everyone who is hung on a pole."' Others could believe that crucifixion of a faithful Jew by the polytheists did not acquire a stigma. The crucifixion of a steadfastly righteous Jewish rebel such as Eleazar and his sons during the Maccabean period was viewed as praiseworthy; no Deuteronomic curse attached. Indeed, in this view the fact of crucifixion did not negate and indeed enhanced the hero rebel's reputation. Because of martyrdoms like that, crucifixion could be viewed as one of the greatest sufferings the righteous would endure in the run-up to judgement day.

How people viewed the fact that a person was crucified could to some extent depend on point of view. But Paul's attempt to explain away the problem showed that belief in a crucified Son of God was a focal point of incredulity, even hostility to the movement.

The movement claimed that Jesus's death had special significance. They pointed to Isaiah, who had prophesied that a man would meet a gruesome death as a blood sacrifice that would reconcile the faithful to Yahweh:

> But he was pierced for our transgressions, he was crushed for our iniquities; the punishment that brought us peace was on him, and by his wounds we are healed ... The Lord has laid on him the iniquity of us all ... Yet it was the Lord's will to crush him and cause him to suffer, and though the Lord makes his life an offering for sin, he will see his offspring and prolong his days, and the will of the Lord will prosper in his hand ... Therefore I will give him a portion among the great, and he will divide the spoils with the strong, because he poured out his life unto death, and was numbered with the transgressors. For he bore the sin of many, and made intercession for the transgressors.

They might also have had in mind the ideology of the Qumran community. There, the suffering of the leadership brought atonement for the whole group. The twelve members of the community's Council along with three priests were especially adept at 'truth, righteousness, justice, loving-kindness and humility'. The community's rule went on:

> They shall preserve the faith in the land with steadfastness and meekness and shall atone for sin by the practice of justice and by suffering the sorrows of affliction ... They shall atone for the land and pay to the wicked their reward ... They shall be an agreeable offering, atoning for the land and determining the judgement of wickedness and there shall be no more iniquity.

His followers interpreted Jesus's death in this prophetic vein as a sacrifice of atonement and reconciliation of the people to Yahweh: 'God presented Christ as a sacrifice of atonement, through the shedding of his blood.'

The idea that the bloody crucifixion was an atonement blood sacrifice has a precedent in Jewish tradition. Atonement was achieved by blood sacrifice. Atoning lambs were sacrificed every morning and evening in the temple and priests performed special sacrifices in the temple each year at the Day of Atonement. The blood of a dead martyr could conceivably fill the bill on an even grander scale. The suffering and death of martyrs could offer atonement for the sins of the people. In particular, the martyrdoms of Eleazar and his seven sons during the Maccabean period offered a direct example. The early Christians certainly thought that Jesus's blood provided atonement for humanity's sins since Adam.

Jesus's followers added another claim. They stated that Jesus's blood was the blood of a new, human, Pascal Lamb, delivering humans from the bondage of death. The first Passover occurred in Egypt at the time of the Exodus. Moses confronted Pharaoh, trying to force him to release the Israelite slaves he held. As Pharaoh was intransigent, at Yahweh's command Moses promised that the firstborn in the land would be killed. Israelites marked their doorposts with lambs' blood so that the death being visited upon the Egyptian firstborn would not touch their households. Jesus's sacrificial blood gave deliverance to the faithful at the last judgement, as the slaughtered lambs' blood had marked those delivered from death in Egypt.

The early Christians put forward claims such as these. To many in the Jewish tradition it all sounded like blasphemy, particularly the claim that Jesus was the Son of Yahweh.

> Then came the Festival of Dedication at Jerusalem. It was winter, and Jesus was in the temple courts walking in Solomon's Colonnade. The Jews who were there gathered around him, saying, 'How long will you keep us in suspense? If you are the Messiah, tell us plainly.' Jesus answered … 'I and the Father are one.' His Jewish opponents picked up stones to stone him, but Jesus said to them, 'I have shown you many good works from the Father. For which of these do you stone me?' 'We are not stoning you for any good work,' they replied, 'but for blasphemy, because you, a mere man, claim to be God.'

Blasphemy was a serious accusation that justified the most extreme measures. Blasphemers had suffered horrendous deaths throughout the history of the people. Violence against false prophets such as Jesus, the man who claimed to be divine, seemed fully justified.

Enemies of the new movement focused on Jesus as a blasphemer because he claimed to be at one with or like Yahweh. The major differences between what adherents of early Christianity preached and what Jewish people most readily believed were that Jesus spoke with authority, i.e. as a supernatural being, not a mere agent (prophet) of Yahweh, and that his human sacrifice superseded the traditional sacrifices of atonement and deliverance, replacing their performance in the temple with a one-time-forever act. These differences provoked openly hostile actions.

Harassment by Judaeans of other Judaeans was a commonplace in Judaea. A good comparison is with the Samaritans, people of mixed background who chose to keep worshipping Yahweh on Mount Gerizim when others demanded that he be worshipped only in the temple in Jerusalem. A dispute over the right place to worship Yahweh led to a deep suspicion and hatred that marked their relationship with Jerusalem-centred Jews, a hatred that spilled over into violence at times. Similarly, the claim of Jesus to be a second Yahweh triggered hostility. As in the case of Samaritans, violence was taken as justified against people who seemed to be apostates and blasphemers.

That said, there is no evidence that Jesus or his followers were seriously persecuted right up to the final Jerusalem events of entrance, confrontation with the priests and Romans, trial and execution. During Jesus's life, the tough questioning by Pharisees was not persecution but the usual habit of one group challenging the practice and doctrine of another, all within the Torah traditions. Opposition to Jesus during his lifetime seems to have come from other religious factions disagreeing with his claims, not from any large group from the general population. That opposition turned violent only when blasphemy and political nervousness intertwined to present what seemed to be a clear and present danger to the established religious and civil order.

When the trial and execution of Jesus did not end his influence, opposition immediately threatened the survivors of his movement. These men proclaimed the fulfilment of the Mosaic Law in Jesus's death and resurrection and his atonement for sins. Others on the contrary saw this as blasphemy. One of the early Christians, Stephen, alienated Jews in a synagogue where he presented the message. These men lodged a complaint against Stephen with the religious authorities in Jerusalem: 'We have heard Stephen speak blasphemous words against Moses and against God,' they claimed. Put on trial, Stephen defended himself with scripture, claiming that Jesus had lived out the Biblical prophesies of reconciliation to Yahweh and salvation. He even quoted Moses himself who had predicted the man Stephen claimed to be the Messiah: 'The Lord your God will raise up for you a prophet like me from among you, from your fellow Israelites. You must listen to him.' In closing, Stephen seemed to welcome the hostility arrayed before him: 'You are just like your ancestors: You always resist the Holy Spirit! Was there ever a prophet your ancestors did not persecute? They even killed those who predicted the coming of the Righteous One. And now you have betrayed and murdered him – you who have received the law that was given through angels but have not obeyed it.'

The authorities were not impressed. The penalty for blasphemy was death by stoning. Moses had spoken Yahweh's instructions to his people: 'Anyone who blasphemes the name of the Lord is to be put to death. The entire assembly must stone them. Whether foreigner or native-born, when they blaspheme the Name they are to be put to death.' Stephen was condemned and stoned.

As in the Gospel narratives of Jesus's life, much of the drama after his death took place in synagogue settings. The accepted dynamic of debate among supporters of various versions of the tradition played out. But opposition was strong in the Jewish community because some saw the proclamation of a new relationship with Yahweh as striking at the heart of traditional religious life. When Paul tried to drag a Roman official into their disputes, Gallio wisely identified the issue as intra-tribal and shied away: 'If you Jews were making a complaint about some misdemeanour or serious crime, it would be reasonable for me to listen to you. But since it involves questions about words and names and your own law – settle the matter yourselves. I will not be a judge of such things.' So he drove them off.

Paul took this internal theological dispute to the Jewish and god-fearing audience of the synagogues of the diaspora. For the Jews who listened, the response was often, perhaps even usually, hostile. Paul's experience in the town of Psidian Antioch, in Asia Minor, illustrated the hostility the new proclamation inspired among some Jews. Paul and his travelling companion, Barnabas, came to the town and attended the Sabbath meeting at the local synagogue. The leaders invited Paul to make a presentation of his views. This was normal in the context of the synagogue meeting, but Paul's message was startling. He began with a standard summary of the history and trials of the Jewish people from the time Yahweh chose Abraham, through slavery in Egypt to the Exodus, occupation of Canaan and, finally, to the reign of King David. From David's offspring, Paul said, Yahweh promised a future messiah who would offer salvation from sin: 'Therefore, my friends, I want you to know that through Jesus the forgiveness of sins is proclaimed to you. Through him everyone who believes is set free from every sin, a justification you were not able to obtain under the Law of Moses.' In his presentation, Paul touched on the essence of the Christian message. The prophet John the Baptist, Paul stated, had declared that Jesus would go beyond a call for repentance and baptism; Jesus would offer salvation itself through his atoning sacrifice. The proof of this was that Yahweh had raised Jesus from the dead:

> Fellow children of Abraham and you God-fearing Gentiles, it is to us that this message of salvation has been sent. The people of Jerusalem and their rulers did not recognise Jesus, yet in condemning him they fulfilled the words of the prophets that are read every Sabbath. Though they found no proper ground for a death sentence, they asked Pilate to have him executed. When they had carried out all that was written about him, they took him down from the cross and laid him in a tomb. But God raised him from the dead.

At first the synagogue members reacted positively and asked Paul to return the next week for more discussion of his presentation. But the leaders, whose type Paul had obliquely criticised in his description of Jesus's death, rallied in opposition. 'They stirred up persecution against Paul and Barnabas and expelled them from their region.' Paul and his companion were forced to leave.

This scene repeated itself again and again as Paul travelled from synagogue to synagogue. At Iconium, Paul and Barnabas hurriedly left as the opposition planned to mistreat and stone them. At Lystra, Paul was stoned and left for dead. In Thessalonica a mob even assaulted Paul and Silas.

These dramatic incidents were somewhat embellished by the author of Acts, but Paul himself validated the violence that he faced as he presented his message in the synagogues: 'I have worked much harder, been in prison more frequently, been flogged more severely and been exposed to death again and again. Five times I received from the Jews the forty lashes minus one. Three times I was beaten with rods, once I was pelted with stones …'

While some Jews, prepared by the contemporary currents of thought described in the last chapter, accepted the new message, the proclamation of Jesus as the fulfilment of prophecies and, indeed, of the historical destiny of the Jewish people in their relation to Yahweh continued to incite hostility among other Jews throughout the early years of the Christian movement.

On the one hand, polytheists often had a fair tolerance for a wide range of social and religious behaviour. They welcomed astrologers, dream interpreters, purveyors of strange cults, or social criticism in the form of wandering Cynic philosophers exposing the illogicalities and hypocrisies of everyday life. On the other hand, people also defended traditional ways, especially religious ways. The Roman author Cicero captured the people's attitude towards traditional religion. He wrote: 'In all probability, disappearance of piety towards the gods will entail the disappearance of loyalty and social union among men as well and of justice itself.' He further noted that 'when [piety, reverence and religion] are gone, life soon becomes a welter of disorder and confusion'. In an earlier age, one can readily think of Socrates' problems as he corrupted the youth of Athens with his attitude towards the gods, custom and normative thinking. Thus although there was curiosity and a certain acceptance towards the new, there was also ambivalence towards an explicit, visible hostility to religious (and so community) tradition.

In particular, polytheists felt uneasiness towards the, to them, abnormal habits of Jewish people such as circumcision, observing the Sabbath and not eating pork, not to mention the monolatry of the tradition that stressed opposition to the idols of the polytheists. Probably the clannishness of the Jews, setting themselves apart with their covenant even while within the society of their diaspora, added to the feeling that they were 'not like us'. But many realised that Jewish people, while strange, came to their strangeness in a respectable way – they inherited it from a long tradition. The antiquity of the Jewish ways fitted well with the honour to tradition in the polytheist culture as a whole. Therefore the customs of the Jews, although odd, fell within the bounds of acceptability, because polytheists recognised that different peoples had inherited different and often strange customs and 'to each his own'. This knowledge mitigated ill feeling, preventing it from seriously affecting relationships between Jewish people in the diaspora and polytheists. In addition, the Jewish people clearly maintained the idea that their tradition was specifically their own. Curious polytheists could learn about Jewish ways and even convert. If reluctant to undergo the initiative custom of circumcision they were still welcome as god-fearers. But there is only scattered and uncertain evidence that Jewish people actively proselytised among polytheists.

Jews were usually treated by polytheists as possessing a strange superstition, but basically harmless, like so many other strange superstitions around them in their daily lives. Jewish habits offered only an indirect and weak critique of polytheist culture and society, one that could be ignored much of the time by polytheists.

There were exceptions to this generally benign relationship between Jewish and polytheistic people. The Greco-Roman elite found little to value in the Jewish tradition, so it had scant appeal for them. Jewish traditions aroused mostly curiosity and ridicule – but also occasional overt hostility. From time to time writers universalised these oddities into Jewish opposition to polytheist culture. As purveyors of magical arts or as 'haters of the human race', as Tacitus put it, Jews were sometimes accused of being troublemakers. Four thousand were expelled from Rome in 19. There were riots involving Jews in Alexandria in the 30s and in Rome in the late 40s. They were accused of trying to burn down Rome in 64 and Antioch in 67. In Judaea, political opposition to their Greek and later Roman overlords made the Judaeans seem like a rebellious, stiff-necked people.

The normal imperial procedure was to co-opt the elite of a people to be Roman agents in managing their empire. But the religious focus of the Jewish people seemed to work against that methodology and caused trouble for the ruling powers that local elites could not or would not control. This led to attempts to suppress the traditions that seemed to breed opposition. The Jewish tradition, in turn, called upon Yahweh to defeat the polytheist oppressors. During the Maccabean revolt, a prayer went like this: 'Gather together our scattered people, free the ones enslaved among the nations, watch over those who are despised and loathed and let the nations know that you are our God. Punish the oppressors and those who commit arrogant acts of violence. Plant your people in your holy place, just as Moses said.' Roman elites, therefore, had some reason to view Jewish traditions negatively.

Life was local in the ancient world. Unless war or some other major catastrophe affected an area, the people had no knowledge of or concern for the political problems their elites faced in dealing with Jews in the diaspora and, especially, in Judaea during the first century. So it is very uncertain how widely and how far down the socio-economic scale elite feelings would penetrate. Jews experienced some unpleasantness in their daily lives around polytheists. Polytheists sometimes took the socio-religious exclusivity of Jewish people personally – the special food markets for kosher food and its preparation, the emphasis of Jewish people on their monotheism, their clannishness because their traditions were deeply, although not exclusively, tied to ethnic membership. But if Jewish people kept their idiosyncrasies to their in-group and stayed out of conflict with neighbours, those neighbours had no reason to express more than mild cultural criticism.

Problems could arise, however, if those practising Jewish traditions seemed to challenge basic elements of polytheistic life. Then the otherwise anodyne idiosyncrasies could provide vitriol. The cultural flashpoint, when there was one, was Jewish opposition, real or imagined, to the worship of the traditional gods who were intimately connected with the identity of the local community. 'If they wish to be members of the community, let them worship the community's gods,' was a polytheist's standard response.

Polytheists were aware of the groups that stood outside their general view of the gods. By the mid-second century they actively knew the categories – atheists (probably meaning Jews), Christians and Epicureans. Alexander, a polytheist charismatic of the second century, established his own celebration of mysteries for his cult and excluded just these people.

On the first day [of Alexander's celebrations] ... there was a

proclamation, worded as follows: 'If any atheist or Christian or Epi-
curean has come to spy upon the rites, let him be off, and let those
who believe in the god perform the mysteries, under the blessing of
Heaven.' Then, at the very outset, there was an 'expulsion', in which
he took the lead, saying: 'Out with the Christians,' and the whole
multitude chanted in response, 'Out with the Epicureans!'

So polytheists clearly noticed the habits of Jewish people living among
them.

Life was not only local but also public. People interacted constantly
in the markets, the street corners, the festivals and the entertainments in
towns small and large. And, of course, they talked, compared, praised
and criticised family, friends, elites, everyone. People of the Jewish traditions recognised that their habits brought attention to themselves and
sometimes hostility:

> Some people plotted to injure the Jewish nation by circulating a
> hostile report against them on the pretext that the Jews were hinder-
> ing others from practising their own customs ... [Polytheists] kept
> harping on the differences in worship and diet, and claimed that the
> Jewish people were loyal neither to the king nor to the authorities,
> but were hostile and strongly opposed to the [rulers].

That evidence is from Judaea. Relationships were a bit different there,
but tension of this sort sometimes developed between Jewish people
and their neighbours in the diaspora as well. In Alexandria relations
with native Egyptians were particularly bad. In AD 38 a serious pogrom
was launched against the Jews because of socio-political tensions within
the wider Alexandrian community:

> [Those accused as Jews] were dragged away as captives, not only in
> the marketplace, but even in the middle of the theatre, and dragged
> upon the stage on any false accusation that might be brought against
> them with the most painful and intolerable insults; ... And if they
> appeared to belong to our [Jewish] nation, then those who, instead
> of spectators, became tyrants and masters, laid cruel commands
> on them, bringing them swine's flesh, and enjoining them to eat it.

Accordingly, all who were pressured by fear of punishment to eat it were released without suffering any ill treatment; but those who were more obstinate were given up to the tormentors to suffer intolerable tortures.

Antioch in Syria was the scene of yet another outburst of hostility. There was a very large population of Jewish people in that city. In 67 they were accused of trying to raze Antioch. A Jew named Antiochus, son of a leader of the Jewish community in the city, spoke before the citizens assembled in the theatre. He accused his father and other Jews of plotting to burn down the entire city in a single night. He also accused non-resident Jews of complicity in the plot. 'When the people heard this, they could not restrain their passion, but commanded that those who were delivered up to them should have fire brought to burn them, who were accordingly all burnt in the theatre immediately.' Antiochus himself showed his apostasy by sacrificing to a polytheist god. Then 'he persuaded the rest also to compel [the Jews] to do the same, because they would by that means discover who they were that had plotted against them, since they would not do so; and when the people of Antioch tried the experiment, some few complied, but those that would not do so were slain'. These episodes show how intense hostility could be. But they were isolated. In general, Jews got along well with their polytheist neighbours and their neighbours with them.

The Christians came out of the Jewish traditions. They expected the same tolerance other Jews received. But as the movement developed, Christianity increasingly seemed to be different. They were clannish, but unlike the Jewish people, they were an artificial clan: their consanguinity was one of ideology, not blood. Their groups had no solid cultural pedigree to appeal to, no traditional ethnic foundation. Although they originally were grounded in Jewish traditions and claimed to be the fulfilment of that tradition's hope for a messiah, their deviance from the most traditional interpretations of Jewish fundamental laws left them in an ambivalent position vis-à-vis whatever tolerance there was among polytheists for those traditions. When the early Christian version of Jewish traditions actively reached out to polytheists, what was usually seen as the oddities of other Jews became an overt attack on basic polytheist life.

Given that Christianity shared many basic polytheist cultural approaches to the supernatural, what was it that made at least some polytheists angry enough to try to get the authorities to squash them? There were religious, cultural and economic factors.

One might think that the incarnation, the claim that a god had caused a divine being to be brought into the human world, would have raised eyebrows among some polytheists. But within the polytheist traditions themselves many interactions with gods and humans bore the fruit of humans who were godlike. The most famous were Hercules, the hero who particularly cared for humans, and Asclepius, who healed humans. People were quite prepared to accept supernatural appearances in the human world. Peter, James and John assumed that they had actually seen Elijah and Moses on a mountain top and that these prophets had conversed with Jesus. Polytheists accepted that gods could walk among humans. The people of Lystra, including their priest, had no hesitancy in assuming that Zeus and Hermes walked among them in the guise of Paul and Barnabas. This attitude prepared polytheists to accept Jesus as godlike. Nevertheless, a central fact of the Christian proclamation caused polytheists to recoil. Polytheists knew that only those of low status were crucified. They had a hard time believing that someone of proven low status was, in fact, a divinity's son, the saviour of the world, as adherents of early Christianity claimed. They saw that as 'foolishness', as Paul himself noted.

But religious relations with the polytheist world were more complicated than just that one issue. Adherents of the movement had to deal with another tenet that seemed within the polytheist traditions inherently unlikely to be true: a final judgement.

Reference to the final days, when the unrighteous would be judged and punished by a god, Yahweh, is laced through the Gospels and Paul's writings. The moral habits of polytheists were not far from those advocated by early Christians. Those Christians ranting about the immoral lives polytheists lived – the murder, strife, arrogance, disobedience of children and so on and so on – was at the least insulting and injudicious and at most hypocritical. Indeed, Paul, seeing this, admonished his people: 'You, therefore, have no excuse, you who pass judgement on someone else, for at whatever point you judge the other, you are condemning yourself, because you who pass judgement do the same things.'

Somewhere around 175, Celsus wrote an attack on Christianity. Origen, who flourished a half-century later, took up Celsus's challenge and wrote a refutation. We have Origen's work, but not that of Celsus. Luckily, Origen quoted long passages in his refutation. These are valuable as the earliest sustained polytheistic critique of Christianity. Celsus described the sort of preaching Paul had criticised:

> There are many who, although of no name, with the greatest facility and on the slightest occasion, whether within or without temples, assume the motions and gestures of inspired persons; while others do it in cities or among armies, for the purpose of attracting attention and exciting surprise. These are accustomed to say, each for himself, 'I am God; I am the Son of God; or, I am the Divine Spirit; I have come because the world is perishing, and you, O men, are perishing for your iniquities. But I wish to save you, and you shall see me returning again with heavenly power. Blessed is he who now does me homage. On all the rest I will send down eternal fire, both on cities and on countries. And those who know not the punishments which await them shall repent and grieve in vain; while those who are faithful to me I will preserve eternally.'

Presuming Celsus in his enthusiasm to criticise the Christians was exaggerating about preachers claiming to be God or the Son of God, his screed helps us imagine street-corner preaching, much in the mode of Cynics lambasting passersby. The image of forum life set out in the fresco from the Praedium of Julia Felix at Pompeii captures the frenetic activity of the marketplace. Holy men, astrologers, magicians, philosophers – all vied for attention in what must have been a cacophony of voices. Of course, we do not know if Paul's speaking in the markets was like Celsus's description, but public proclamation was important in early Christianity.

Early Christians could not seem to resist pillaring their polytheist neighbours in their effort to save them from themselves. So the homogeneity of moral ideals shared by polytheists and Christians was trumped by a desire to separate into a community to be rewarded by eternal life from another to be punished by eternal torment. This did not sit well with polytheists who, not surprisingly, resented the arrogance of

Christians sequestering the moral high ground, disparaging the morals of others and attacking the very cultural foundation of their lives, the gods. The use of the threat of afterlife punishment for the unrighteous upped the ante.

A hellish punishment after death for the ungodly is very difficult to discover in polytheist understandings of the supernatural. Celsus affirms that some mysteries advocate this, but identifying those has proven difficult for modern scholars. An analogous claim, that adherents lived in the flesh after death, likewise is almost impossible to find in the inscriptions and other evidence of how people thought. While elite literature is full of Tartarus, Elysian Fields and the like, most people had a much less clear concept of what happened to a person after death. Those hazy concepts did not include being in some sort of semi-live condition in an afterworld, or being revived from death at some future time. Dedications to 'gods of the underworld' and offerings at the grave were at best based on nebulous beliefs of post-mortem survival.

The either/or theology of Christians took polytheists aback. The whole concept of polytheism was that the supernatural could be accessed in many different ways, under many different names. Certainly, the idea of divine powers fighting each other on their own or on behalf of favoured humans goes back to Homer. But there was no popular idea of an apocalyptic contest between the forces of good and the forces of evil. Such an idea assumed a religious, cultural and moral duality. A supernatural 'good' and a supernatural 'evil' were battling it out on the cosmic level while that struggle was mirrored in the human sphere. Humans had to decide if they would crusade for good against cosmic forces of evil. The reward for the good was eternal bliss; for the evil, eternal punishment. Polytheists did not experience such a 'with us or against us' attitude in their relationships with the supernatural.

The being leading the fight for good was the Jewish god, Yahweh. Atheism was a common charge against Christians (and Jews). This could mean actually not believing in the gods, as some philosophers taught. It could also mean 'impious', i.e. not giving a supernatural power or powers due respect. Finally, it could also mean believing in one's own supernatural power while denying the power or even reality of another's. Christians sometimes actually denied the reality of the polytheists' gods, sometimes merely claimed to have one of superior importance and power. Either way, they denied the power of others' gods. The Christians' view of their god meant for polytheists that Christians were atheists. This was a flashpoint for hostility.

Christians directed most vehement criticism at the polytheism of the polytheists. They focused verbal attacks on idols and on eating food sacrificed to idols. Jews shared the same sentiments. The crucial difference seems to be that the Jews kept these harsh assessments of iconic paganism and its practitioners within their circle; their faith was justification of their own lives, set off from the faults and miscues of the polytheists, not an attack on them per se. The early Christians' criticism of polytheists' ways was much more offensive. Paul specifically preached against iconic worship: 'Flee from idolatry,' he taught. 'Do I mean then that a sacrifice offered to an idol is anything, or that an idol is anything? No, but the sacrifices of polytheists are offered to demons.'

Lucian, writing in the late second century, gave a synopsis of the theological stumbling blocks for polytheists:

> The poor wretches [Christians] have convinced themselves, first and foremost, that they are going to be immortal and live for all time, in consequence of which they despise death and even willingly give themselves into custody, most of them. Furthermore, their first lawgiver [Jesus] persuaded them that they are all brothers of one another after they have transgressed once for all by denying the Greek gods and by worshipping that crucified fraud himself and living under his laws.

For most people, the fundamental issue was not only theological, however. In addition to the emotional shock of having their gods impugned, the whole polytheist cultural background and explanation system seemed to come under fire. In a world understood by myth or in mythic ways, denial of the gods would cripple the ability to relate to the story world. What would replace the myths as religious stories shared by the community? As Walter Burkert pointed out, the purpose of the Greeks' relationships with the supernatural was 'not just to embellish but to shape all essential forms of community: the definition of membership [was] participation in a cult'. Romans agreed: 'Men wisest in all divine and human law used to judge that nothing was so potent in destroying a community's bonding through worship as where sacrifices were performed, not by native, but by foreign, ritual.'

Cultic and related activities provided the most common opportunity to experience a collective identity. Refusal to participate in a civic cult meant a person refused to be part of the community. Refusal to be a part of the community one lived in was an attack on the identity of everyone in that group. Denial of a community's gods was metonymy for an assault on that community's very existence. So destruction of the gods was the destruction of humanity. People who wanted to destroy the gods must hate humanity. It was all very logical.

The response to this threatening self-righteousness was suspicion and accusation. The early second-century letters attributed to Peter and to James talk about what sounds like social persecution – scoffing, resentment at not participating in polytheist things like festivals, and accusations of engaging in unauthorised sexual activities. During that century, such actions escalated. Tertullian spoke of the joy of common people in their persecution of Christians, sometimes even persuading magistrates to go along with them:

> How often, too, without regard to you [the magistrates], does the unfriendly mob on its own account assail us with stones and fire? Mad as Bacchanals, they spare not even the Christian dead ... And it is in savagery and injustice of that sort that this blind rabble exults and triumphs over us – and not they alone, but some among you, who make use of this injustice to win the favour of the rabble, boast of it.

Polytheists suspected that such atheists – for Christians denied the existence or at least the power of all their gods – must be doing evil things in their meetings: 'a people skulking and shunning the light, silent in public, but garrulous in corners'. They must be engaged in foul rites, activities such as cannibalism (reference to the easily misunderstood Eucharist of the body and blood of Christ), incest (all called each other 'brother' and 'sister') and sexual promiscuity (the kiss of peace). They were also suspected of being magicians and sharing the practices of those skilled in the occult arts. These people hated not only the gods, but indeed all mankind, for they looked with longing to its destruction in a final, pitiless judgement.

So polytheists accused Christians. Ordinary people led the charge. 'There are none more apt to shout for the death of the Christians than the common herd,' wrote Tertullian. The *Apology* of Athenagoras, a Christian work dated to 177, takes note of this hostility in his defence of the faith:

> [T]he stories told about us rest on nothing better than the common undiscriminating popular talk ... I must at the outset of my defence entreat you, illustrious emperors, to listen to me impartially: not to be carried away by the common irrational talk and prejudge the case ... Thus, while you on your part will not err through ignorance, we also, by disproving the charges arising out of the undiscerning rumour of the multitude, shall cease to be assailed ... most of those who charge us with atheism ... are doltish and utterly unacquainted with natural and divine things, and such as measure piety by the rule of sacrifices ... the multitude, who cannot distinguish between matter and God, or see how great is the interval which lies between them, pray to idols made of matter ... they (ordinary people) have further also made up stories against us of impious feasts and forbidden intercourse between the sexes.

These accusations were long-standing. And somewhat justified. Libertine actions on the part of some Christians was real. Paul noted miscreants within the Christian community at Corinth, who were committing the very incest the polytheists criticised. There was, moreover, sexual immorality, idolatrous behaviour, drunkenness and swindling going on. 'Expel the wicked person from among you,' he admonished.

A faction used the ideology of freedom from Jewish law and the promise of salvation through grace to endorse and engage in carnal as well as other sins. The second letter of (pseudo-) Peter noted, 'They promise freedom, while they themselves are slaves of depravity,' and how some engage in 'depraved conduct' that will 'bring the way of truth into disrepute ... Their idea of pleasure is to carouse in broad daylight. They [i.e. some Christians] are blots and blemishes, revelling in their pleasures while they feast with you. With eyes full of adultery, they never stop sinning; they seduce the unstable; they are experts in greed – an accursed brood!'

14. Golden votive statue (Ephesus, fifth century BC). Local artisans enraged by Paul's preaching created and sold small votives such as this made of silver.

The author went on to threaten such false Christians with 'blackest darkness'. It was not surprising that polytheists noted these antisocial habits that were so clear to the Christians themselves.

As community identities were closely allied with local cultic activities, so, too, was the identity of political power. The position of the emperor and, implicitly, the entire panoply of Roman power, were linked to the favour of the Roman gods. No living emperor was declared divine during the first or second centuries AD. However, dead ones had regularly been made divine by decree of the Senate of Rome.

So the boundary between the all-powerful living emperor (non-divine but with almost godly power) and his dead predecessors (mostly now gods) was fluid. Recognition of the position of the emperor as divinely protected came through the imperial cult and through specific prayers and sacrifices for his well-being.

Just as Christians refused to acknowledge the existence and importance of local community gods, they refused the same to the gods of the imperial community. The test of being a Christian was twofold, first to offer prayer and wine to the image of the emperor and those of Roman gods; second to curse Christ. Because refusal to sacrifice in the imperial environment was so clearly rejecting the community of the empire, asking Christians to sacrifice was a sure litmus test and one that resonated negatively much more than, for example, forcing Jewish people to eat pork.

Rejection of the gods naturally meant that those disrespected supernatural powers would wreak their vengeance. Christians were therefore suspected of causing all manner of disasters. Origen states that polytheists blamed various calamities on Christians for abandoning the gods – famine, plague, earthquake, pestilence: 'We know that in our own regions, there are earthquakes in some places and some destruction has been wrought, with the result that persons impious and outside the faith declared Christians the cause of the earthquake; and on that account the churches have suffered persecutions and have been burnt down.'

As a final accusation, polytheists said that Christians harmed the economic position of those who depended on local cults to generate their business. Paul's experiences at Ephesus as told in Acts vividly illustrate the economic damage the movement might cause. A silver-smith named Demetrius had a business making souvenirs for pilgrims to the great temple of Artemis just outside the city. Paul preached his message. Demetrius then called together fellow craftsmen and incited them, claiming that Paul had turned away worshippers from idols. He mentioned the damage to their trade, but emphasised more that Artemis, the goddess of their city, and her world famous temple would be disrespected and she would be 'robbed of her divine majesty'.

When they heard this, Demetrius's fellows were furious and began shouting: 'Great is Artemis of the Ephesians!' Soon the whole city was in an uproar. The people seized Gaius and Aristarchus, Paul's travelling companions from Macedonia, and rushed as one man into the theatre. A mob gathered. Paul wanted to speak to it, but his companions feared for his life. The mob was ready to take action. Seizing perceived malefactors, dragging them to the theatre and using that venue to authorise mob violence was standard practice in towns of the Roman Empire. (As we have seen, the attack on the Jews of Antioch follows exactly this procedure.) A spokesman for the Jewish community tried to speak, but he was shouted down by the crowd screaming, 'Great is Artemis of the Ephesians!' Luckily for Paul, the leader of Ephesus calmed the crowd by urging Demetrius and his fellow craftsmen to use proper legal channels to challenge Paul and warning the crowd that persistence in mob action would bring Roman forces down upon them to enforce order. The scene is a group of artisans and businessmen suffering economic loss because of Christian preaching against pagan modes of worship and then taking matters into their own hands by inciting a mob.

An analogous episode occurred at Thyatira. There, a slave girl offered prophesy for money. Her owners suffered financial harm when Paul 'cured' the girl and she could no longer utter prophesies. The injured owners subsumed their private complaint in a larger cultural accusation of undermining the norms of society, specifically by complaining to magistrates but elevating the charge to 'advocating customs unlawful for us Romans to accept or practice', as the owners of the slave girl put it. This time, Paul was not so lucky as at Ephesus. The local officials ordered him and his companion to be flogged and thrown into prison.

In yet another example, early in the second century, in Bithynia (north-western Asia Minor), local butchers complained that Christians were keeping people away from the temples and so their sales of sacrificed meat dried up. Pliny, the Roman special governor, took up their cause and tried and executed some Christians. Here again, the citizenry initiated the hostility against the Christian activities that put their livelihood in danger. These three episodes show that Christian proclamation endangered polytheists' economic, religious and social lives. Quite understandably, those polytheists disliked Christians.

Christians and Roman authorities

Among Christian writers, 'Christian' becomes the common name for the movement around the middle of the second century. Ignatius of Antioch (early second century) is the first Christian writer outside the New Testament to use it and also the first to refer to 'Christianity'. Tatian (mid-second century) is the last Christian writer to avoid the term. Justin uses it, as does Athenagoras ('we so-called Christians'). These last two are late second-century writers. It is the mid-250s before it is found in papyri.

By the early second century, elite polytheists also began using the name to designate people following the message of Jesus. No source mentions the term Christians before the first two decades of that century. The Roman authors Suetonius, Tacitus and Pliny are the first Latin writers to use it; some Greek writers begin to adopt it in the second half of the second century. By the time the name begins to appear in the polytheist sources it has already taken on a negative tinge. Roman authorities, generally reactive to new social and cultural issues, had been forced to take cognisance of the new movement.

Suetonius in his *Life of Claudius* noted that, in the year 49, 'since the Jews were continually making disturbances at the instigation of Chrestus, [Emperor Claudius] expelled them from Rome'. Acts reflects the same disturbance: 'After this, Paul left Athens and went to Corinth. There he met a Jew named Aquila, a native of Pontus, who had recently come from Italy with his wife Priscilla, because Claudius had ordered all the Jews to leave Rome.' Some scholars doubt that Chrestus is Jesus Christ; they suppose that an otherwise unknown Jew, Chrestus, instigated the civil unrest Suetonius mentions. 'Chrestus' means 'the good one', 'the beneficent one', in Greek, whereas 'Christus' means 'the anointed one'. We know that there was confusion between the names 'Christians' and 'Chrestians' as followers of the Jesus tradition. Chrestus appears even in Christian sources referring to Christ because 'the good one' certainly described Jesus in their eyes. Suetonius's Chrestus is, in fact, Jesus Christ. The civil disorder was a conflict between followers of Jesus and more traditional Jews, the sort of confrontation that Paul and Acts document in a number of towns of Asia Minor that contained significant diaspora Jewish communities. So Suetonius gives the first glimpse in polytheist sources of Christians – and it has them involved in trouble of the sort Paul himself got into during some of his sojourns.

The next polytheist reference is in Tacitus's *Annals*, a work also written in the first decades of the second century. Tacitus writes an account of the fire at Rome in AD 64. As the centre of Rome went up in flames, people muttered that so great a disaster must have an author – and Nero was suspected of urban clearance for a desired palace complex. Nero deflected this suspicion by finding a scapegoat. He settled on the followers of Jesus, 'a class of men, loathed for their vices, whom the crowd styled Christians'. These men followed, Tacitus recounted, a man executed in Judaea under Pontius Pilate; the movement had since spread even to Rome 'where all things horrible or shameful in the world collect and find a vogue'. Nero made a spectacle of their punishment to deflect blame for the fire from himself:

> First, then, the confessed members of the sect were arrested; next, on their disclosures, vast numbers were convicted, not so much on the count of arson as for hatred of the human race [*odio humani generis*]. And derision accompanied their end: they were covered with wild beasts' skins and torn to death by dogs; or they were fastened on crosses and, when daylight failed were burned to serve as lamps by night.

Tacitus gives a clear picture of how he viewed the early Christians. He stated that they were loathed for their vices as well as being guilty of 'hatred of the human race', a trait shared according to Tacitus with the followers of Jewish traditions: 'The Jews regard the rest of mankind with all the hatred of enemies,' he wrote elsewhere. The process against the Christians was first arrest, then confessions exacted incriminating others, then further convictions, then executions. Tacitus said they earned their punishment, although surely he or his sources have embellished the horror, especially the highly unlikely tale of their being burned on crosses like torches. But he also claimed that Nero set the fire. Therefore, he must have thought that the Christians deserved their cruel punishment for either their vices or their 'hatred of the human race'.

Suetonius also commented on the fire, although in less detail: 'In [Nero's] reign … punishment was inflicted on the Christians, a set of men adhering to a novel and mischievous superstition.' Suetonius also indicated that by his time, the early second century, it had become clear that Christians stood distinct from the normal run of Jewish people. He called the Christians' approach not only troublesome but new (*genus hominum superstitionis novae ac maleficae*). The mainline Jewish tradition had already been labelled a 'superstition' for many years. By this term the Romans mean an attitude towards supernatural powers that was incongruent with traditional Roman values and procedures. The range of superstitions was very broad. Jewish traditions and now Christian were merely examples.

Looking back from the first decades of the second century to the 60s, we can combine the accounts of Tacitus and Suetonius and see that, to these Romans, early Christians were a non-mainline and therefore intrinsically suspect religious activity (*superstitio*); a group that set itself outside and/or against the rest of humanity (*odio humani generis*); a new phenomenon (*nova*); and trouble-causing (*malefica*). Any one of these characteristics was enough to bring hostility from Roman authorities. Superstitions such as astrology, Egyptian religion in the form of Isis worship, magical practice, or animal worship all had in the past been targeted and adherents punished, ejected from Rome, or both. This may seem odd, as people, elite as well as ordinary, in Rome and the empire widely utilised magic and astrology, and turned to non-Roman cults. And even the elite Roman leaders were schizophrenic about these things, at times railing against them as harmful to the body politic and expelling practitioners from Rome, while most of the time utilising just these practices themselves in their private lives. But the public norm was to consider magicians, and astrologers especially, as anti-social superstitions.

Cultural separatism such as the Christian 'superstition' advocated, implicitly or explicitly claiming superiority to the mainstream culture, seemed to criticise the mainstream. In a culture built on honour, any such attack was bound to draw ire and accusations such as 'hatred of the human race'. On the contemporary religious scene, the Jewish people from time to time were singled out for their anti-cultural ways and among the elite polytheists, Epicureans were regularly strongly criticised for their exclusivity and withdrawal from normal social life. But Christians raised the antagonism to a new level.

In addition, 'new' was a dirty word to the Roman leadership. *Res novae*, literally, the cancellation of debts, was the phrase used for 'violent revolution'. In a society based strongly on continuity and so the continued dominance of the elite, 'new' could only be bad. Finally, the Roman elite abhorred troublemakers. Social groups such as illegal associations, outlaws, even just rowdy spectators at a gladiatorial contest, could bring down the full weight of authority to restore and maintain order. Any group of troublemakers that attacked traditional gods in a new way had a lot going against it in the eyes of the Romans.

Early in the second century AD, the Roman senator Pliny the Younger served as a special imperial representative in the province of Pontus and Bithynia, in modern north-western Asia Minor. He corresponded with the emperor, Trajan, about disruptions caused by citizens colliding with Christians. Two letters in this correspondence provide important evidence about early Christianity and polytheist culture. Full quotation provides a font of information.

Pliny to Emperor Trajan

It is my practice, my lord, to refer to you all matters concerning which I am in doubt. For who can better give guidance to my hesitation or inform my ignorance? I have never participated in trials of Christians. I therefore do not know what offences it is the practice to punish or investigate, and to what extent. And I have been not a little hesitant as to whether there should be any distinction on account of age or no difference between the very young and the more mature; whether pardon is to be granted for repentance, or, if a man has once been a Christian, it does him no good to have ceased to be one; whether the name itself, even without offences, or only the offences associated with the name are to be punished. Meanwhile, in the case of those who were denounced to me as Christians, I have observed the following procedure: I interrogated these as to whether they were Christians; those who confessed I interrogated a second and a third time, threatening them with punishment; those who persisted I ordered executed. For I had no doubt that, whatever the nature of their creed, stubbornness and inflexible obstinacy surely deserve to be punished. There were others possessed of the same folly; but because they were Roman citizens, I signed an order for them to be transferred to Rome.

Soon accusations spread, as usually happens, because of the proceedings going on, and several incidents occurred. An anonymous document was published containing the names of many persons. Those who denied that they were or had been Christians, when they invoked the gods in words dictated by me, offered prayer with incense and wine to your image, which I had ordered to be brought for this purpose together with statues of the gods, and moreover cursed Christ – none of which those who are really Christians, it is said, can be forced to do – these I thought should be discharged. Others named by the informer declared that they were Christians, but then denied it, asserting that they had been but had ceased to be, some three years before, others many years, some as much as twenty-five years.

They all worshipped your image and the statues of the gods, and cursed Christ. They asserted, however, that the sum and substance of their fault or error had been that they were accustomed to meet on a fixed day before dawn and sing responsively a hymn to Christ as to a god, and to bind themselves by oath, not to some crime, but not to commit fraud, theft, or adultery, not falsify their trust, nor to refuse to return a trust when called upon to do so. When this was over, it was their custom to depart and to assemble again to partake of food – but ordinary and innocent food. Even this, they affirmed, they had ceased to do after my edict by which, in accordance with your instructions, I had forbidden political associations.

Accordingly, I judged it all the more necessary to find out what the truth was by torturing two female slaves who were called deaconesses. But I discovered nothing else but depraved, excessive superstition. I therefore postponed the investigation and hastened to consult you. For the matter seemed to me to warrant consulting you, especially because of the number involved. For many persons of every age, every rank and also of both sexes are and will be endangered. For the contagion of this superstition has spread not only to the cities but also to the villages and farms. But it seems possible to check and cure it. It is certainly quite clear that the temples, which had been almost deserted, have begun to be frequented, that the established religious rites, long neglected, are being resumed and that from everywhere sacrificial animals are coming, for which until now very few purchasers could be found. Hence it is easy to imagine what a multitude of people can be reformed if an opportunity for repentance is afforded.

Emperor Trajan to Pliny

You observed proper procedure, my dear Pliny, in sifting the cases of those who had been denounced to you as Christians. For it is not possible to lay down any general rule to serve as a kind of fixed standard. They are not to be sought out; if they are denounced and proved guilty, they are to be punished, with this reservation, that whoever denies that he is a Christian and really proves it – that is, by worshipping our gods – even though he was under suspicion in the past, shall obtain pardon through repentance. But anonymously posted accusations ought to have no place in any prosecution. For this is both a dangerous kind of precedent and out of keeping with the spirit of our age.

Pliny responded to complaints by citizens. He did not have to explain to the emperor who the Christians were. By this date, the group was known already to the emperor and, presumably, to Pliny since he said he never before had taken part in the trial of Christians, implying that he knew of such trials. Drawing on assessments of Christians such as underlay the accounts of Tacitus and Suetonius, Pliny would have expected a tight and exclusive group that set itself against the general culture, held 'superstitious' beliefs and caused trouble. Indeed, Pliny's investigations confirmed that it was an exclusive group that had organised itself as an association (although this association had disbanded upon imperial order); it had beliefs contrary to the norm ('depraved and excessive superstitions'); and it had caused trouble by assembling illegally, convincing people not to sacrifice in the temples and not to buy sacrificial meat, thus endangering the social fabric both by subverting normal religious activity in general and by compromising butchers in particular. Pliny recognised that these facts required action, and he first identified Christians and then dealt with them severely.

What exactly was the accusation levelled against these Christians? The very name, 'Christian', subsumed whatever that accusation was. No source ever defines exactly what malefaction was implicit in the name. Guesses have filled volumes. The basic facts are: some deed or deeds were deemed worthy of swift, severe, even capital punishment; admission of identity automatically convicted one of those deeds, without need for further evidence; and denial of the identity absolved one of past and present guilt.

In general, Roman law required a specific illegal deed to be proven before punishment could be meted out. There were exceptions. Roman law punished actors merely for being actors, not for any specific deed. However, the case of astrologers is the most instructive in understanding the use of the shorthand 'Christians' to define a criminal. For astrologers, too, simple admission to being one led to punishment; no further evidence was needed. If *mathematici* (astrologers) denied their art, they would be spared, just as Trajan ordered the Christians to be treated. In AD 17 Tiberius expelled astrologers from Rome, 'but if they begged him and promised to give up their art, he allowed them to stay'. A late legal record refers to this very event. 'But the question was raised, whether the knowledge of these men was punished or was it the exercise and public acknowledgment of being an astrologer? And indeed among the ancients it was said that it was their public acknowledgment, not their knowledge that was punished.' So the way astrologers were treated provides the precedent for punishing someone who simply acknowledged that he was of a group that was criminal.

Closer to the Christian situation, identification of Jewishness had led to punishment in the case of the arson at Antioch in Syria. In that situation, eating pork was the litmus test, but once eaten an accused was let off, just as one who denied Christ was let off by Pliny. The procedure Pliny conducts, whether his own invention or following (undocumented) precedent, becomes the standard in identifying Christians. Martyr after martyr glories in refusing to deny Christ and offer sacrifice and so goes to his or her punishment. Justin Martyr wrote soon after the events in Pontus and Bithynia, 'And this is the sole accusation you bring against us, that we do not reverence the same gods as you do, nor offer to the dead libations and the savour of fat, and crowns for their statues, and sacrifices.' This jibes with Pliny's experience and procedure.

This is how these men and women that the people called Christians appeared to Roman authorities. However, Roman authorities did not, so far as we know, seek out Christians – indeed, Emperor Trajan told Pliny not to do so and certainly not to accept anonymous accusations of being a Christian; Trajan's successor, Emperor Hadrian, later confirmed this order. Trajan asserted what we would call the Christians' civil rights in the face of attempted harassment. It is the polytheist masses who initiate and pursue hostility against the early Christians, not the Roman government.

Jesus of Nazareth lived the life of a Jewish charismatic prophet. He aroused hostility when he went from being a spokesman for Yahweh to claiming a more direct relationship with the Jewish people's god. After his death, his followers affirmed that Jesus had not only spoken with the authority he and his followers claimed. They expressly claimed that he was the Son of Yahweh, Yahweh's anointed Messiah who had offered himself as an atonement sacrifice and, once risen from the dead and taken up to heaven, would return to lead the righteous in victorious strife at the last judgement. Conflicting claims made both in Judaea and in the diaspora led to arguments and even violence between Jews who accepted and those who rejected this radical claim to a fundamental change in how to think about their relations with their god.

During the first century polytheists came into contact with both normative traditions of the Jewish people and the more marginal combination practised by Jesus of Nazareth's followers. Early Christianity began and to a large extent expanded within their world. The movement had no appeal to elite polytheists. Indeed, although the highest polytheist political leaders, the emperors, showed tolerance, others were angered by the Christians who seemed to call into question the most basic element of their power, the control of community and religious identity.

Although early Christians did not share as much with the polytheists as they did with their Jewish brethren, religious fundamentals were consistent. It was the differences that stood out. And it was the differences that caused hostility. Christians challenged polytheists' social order through the rejection of traditional family bonds and community-centred values. Rejection of their traditional supernatural relations put into doubt a fundamental organising principle of their lives. The power and promise of their god drove Christians to deny the efficacy and even the very existence of the polytheists' gods. Polytheists resisted such rhetoric because their gods were fundamental to their identity and to the identity of the communities that lay at the heart of their existence.

Yet by the end of the first century the early Christians had not just survived as a group, they had become significant enough to annoy their neighbours and even come into conflict with the authorities of the Roman Empire. People were drawn to the movement – ordinary people who were normally loath to trade their traditional loyalties and devotion for a culture-challenging novelty. Why did these men and women desert traditional ways for the new?

10

CHRISTIANITY'S APPEAL: MAGICIANS, MIRACLES AND MARTYRS

PEOPLE TOOK THEIR RELATIONSHIPS with the supernatural very seriously. There was too much at stake to do otherwise. Change might be disruptive. Relationships in the community might be put at risk. Ties to gods that helped guarantee success in life might be severed, with disastrous results to family, health and fortune. Christianity demanded fundamental change in a person's supernatural allegiance. People, in turn, needed unequivocal evidence that change would be beneficial. Supernatural power could convince someone to change supernatural allegiance. A god could show his power through his agents performing deeds of magic and miracles in his name. Christianity threatened basic monotheistic beliefs of Jewish tradition as well as polytheist culture centred on worship of many powers. To convert people, deeds would need to be many and great.

Conversion was hardly a topic in polytheism. The cohabitation of many gods and powers in the cosmos made rejecting new relationships unnecessary. Relationships could easily be adjusted, with one approach or favoured supernatural power rising without the fear that existing relationships had to be severed. A person could switch from Artemis of the Ephesians to Isis of the Egyptians without a problem, for Isis considered herself the sum of all other gods, including Artemis. She did not insist that one stopped worshipping at Artemis's shrine when you began to honour her. The capaciousness of polytheism meant conversion, taking up one god while rejecting another, hardly happened. Even the most famous conversion of polytheism, Lucius's adoption of Isis as his saviour and goddess, involved only a decision to make that adoption. It did not involve an overt rejection of whatever gods he had dealt with before. Such abandonment was simply not a topic of polytheism.

Conversion is a radical reorganisation of relationships with the supernatural. This involves a reorientation not only of who we see ourselves to be (self-identity), but also of what avenues we have to meet the specific psychological and material challenges we face. Contemplation of a deep meaning of life remained a luxury reserved for elite thinkers. The issue in the broadest sense was, 'What helps me survive and thrive?' Focus was on the practical.

A person came into a contact situation that made conversion possible. The most likely situations took place through exposure within the social group. Families, friends, business contacts, even one's slaves – all entailed possible exposure to different approaches to various aspects of daily life. On the street, the noisy and intrusive nature of public life in the Mediterranean world meant that street performers, hawkers of remedies and magical cures, enthusiasts for philosophic positions, beggars associated with cultic activities, cultic processions and rites including banquets in the street, all offered opportunities to see the supernatural at work, to encounter new products, advocacies and ideas. Jews assembled in synagogues where religious and secular interchange took place. Polytheists had their secular associations with a religious element. In such associations people discussed and encountered mundane as well as possibly new elements in their lives.

Conversion took many forms. An event or an idea might strike an individual in a state of psychological disarray from some contretemps in life. The supernatural solution offered met the need to re-establish equilibrium in the person's life, to relieve the stress. The person made a quick decision to accept the way out and at the same time accepted whatever baggage came along with the solution. The conversion of Paul on the road to Damascus was of this sort.

Another opportunity for change came about through an emotional relationship with people. Association with people who had different solutions to life's conditions might bring a change. The process could be slow, involving discussion and pondering. It could have been quite rapid, if the example of associates seemed powerfully to meet an individual's needs. Gradually (or not), ties with the new group outweighed ties to the old, opening the way to change.

A body of information could cause rethinking, but conversion based on contemplation was unusual. Call it intuition, spontaneity, or what you will, most people made decisions based upon past experience, emotional predilections, stereotypes, perceived cost–benefit and other factors – not on a carefully thought-out weighing of possibilities and probabilities. More usually, reorientation of basic patterns of behaviour, including relationships to the supernatural, happened only after a person had already moved to make a change, or at least to think about making one. The Christian thinker Origen, in the early third century AD, pointed out that most people made decisions without thinking about ideas, logic and so on. He wrote, 'We must say that, considering it as a useful thing for the multitude, we admit that we teach those men to believe without reasons, who are unable to abandon all other employments, or give themselves to an examination of arguments.'

Origen also indicated that usually conversion, a determination to shift supernatural allegiance, took place first, followed by actual instruction in the content of Christianity. He cited Paul as the authority for this sequence: 'My message,' Paul wrote to Christians in Corinth, 'and my preaching were not with wise and persuasive words, but with a demonstration of the Spirit's power, so that your faith might not rest on human wisdom, but on God's power'. While it is true that there are examples of polytheists or Jews converting through persuasion alone to Christian thinking, they were far outnumbered by examples of a supernatural event impelling that fundamental reorientation. Even in cases where persuasion seemed to be the main factor, we have no way of knowing how primed to believe hearers were by magic or miraculous events. The author of 2 Peter writes, 'For we did not follow cleverly devised stories when we told you about the coming of our Lord Jesus Christ in power, but we were eyewitnesses of his majesty.' He means that eyewitness accounts of the miracles of Jesus were the active factor in Christianity's outreach message.

Polytheists had to reject their gods in order to take up Christianity. This was a very hard sell. In the last chapter I outlined the tensions between polytheists, Jews and early Christians as polytheists recognised how different from themselves those traditions were. Yet some polytheists did change from their beliefs and practices, embracing Christianity. For those who had already dabbled in Jewish traditions as god-fearers, the experience was less radical. For others, conversion came as a 'cold call'.

Some Jews took the less radical, but still serious, step of moving from more traditional ways to the marginal interpretations early Christianity presented. That move was less traumatic than the move from polytheism to Christianity, but it still involved altering very basic ideas about Yahweh and his expectations. Interest of Jewish people in early Christianity had many precursors. In the diaspora, people like Philo were studying Greek philosophical models and applying them, especially Platonic ideas, to the understanding of their tradition. Jews both in the homeland and in the diaspora had a perfect opportunity to gain exposure to new ideas because of the weekly meetings, whether in synagogues, prayer houses, or private homes.

In the Judaean-Galilean homeland people had been experimenting with different approaches to the covenant with Yahweh since the return from Exile in the fifth century. In particular, the rise of a few widely known groups such as the Essenes and the Pharisees emphasised two approaches to righteousness and Yahweh's favour, the former based in asceticism and belief in a settling of scores at the End of Days, the latter based on extremely conscientious obedience to Torah regulations. Habits had formed that paved the way to considering a variety of approaches. The widespread occurrence of disciples of various leaders emphasised that actively joining a group was central to adopting its ways. The theme of social justice and egalitarianism that the Essenes especially espoused found fertile ground in a culture whose traditions emphasised the importance of all but recognised the dominance of a selfish few as the (unfortunate) norm. Led by Isaiah's cry from under the thumb of the Babylonians, suffering and redemption went hand in hand. We have seen how the epitaphs of Eleazar along with a woman and her seven sons capture the idea of atonement through suffering (see page 151). The prophet Jeremiah had long before announced that the people needed a new covenant with Yahweh. Among all of these lively elements, people were particularly drawn to restoration and/or eschatological messages. Josephus told about leaders in the first century AD who all inspired popular support based on a hope for the vindication of righteous Israel against oppressive foreigners and home-grown elites, either in the present or at a final judgement.

These are some of the various details in the theological and social teachings of current groups that might resonate with Christian proclamation. Nevertheless, changing, converting, to Christianity was a serious matter for both polytheists and Jews.

People knew how to accomplish many things on their own. In many instances tried and true methods, tested by cause and effect, worked. But people also recognised that much was beyond their human control. Supernatural powers were active in their world. People's lives were a combination of actions they could control as humans and actions to deal with the supernatural interlaced in the world around them. They lived in a multidimensional, human–superhuman world.

Magic offered a methodology to bring supernatural power to bear on a human problem. Using the black box analogy, humans had a goal: they put acts that should make supernatural powers help achieve that goal into the black box and expected a positive result to emerge. Magic supposedly controlled what happened in the black box. A person was sick. A magician claimed that uttering an incantation over certain herbs would give the herbs curative powers. Within the black box are gathered herbs and an uttered spell. The cure emerges from the box, to be performed by the sick person. All very mysterious – but all very effective, at least sometimes.

Apuleius wrote that a magician is one 'who through shared speech with the immortal gods has ability in all things that he wishes, by means of a certain amazing power of incantations'. The Roman legal scholar Paulus called rites that 'enchant, bewitch, or bind anyone' magic. He noted that it can involve such things as human sacrifice, auspices by human blood or pollution of a shrine or temple. The power of magicians was that other people believed they could, in fact, guarantee results. They could control what happened in the black box.

We know that the relation between magical action and desired effect cannot be certainly duplicated, i.e., in modern terms, it cannot be clinically tested and proven. No matter how carefully rituals are repeated, no matter how fervently incantations and sacrifices are offered, the outcome remains unpredictable. In the ancient world, people simply did not believe this. They believed in magic. Pliny the Elder understood this: '[Magic] has held sway throughout the world for many ages'; 'Magic rose to such a height that even today it has sway over a great part of mankind'; 'All our wisest men reject belief in [words and formulated incantations], although as a body the public at all times believes in them unconsciously'; 'There is no one who is not afraid of being "caught" by malevolent curses.' Pliny reckons that almost everyone, elite or otherwise, believed in magic. The exceptions were the wisest men, evidently a very small portion of the population indeed.

Magic used a wide range of methods. From the ancient perspective, the supernatural was susceptible to the same manipulative procedures that worked in the human world. Spells and incantations could beseech, bribe, appeal to past precedent, set up a 'deal', even try to intimidate a supernatural power or (very often) an array of powers. For example, a magician might claim that a demon could not resist a particular set of sounds: 'For ... sorcerers advise those possessed with demons to recite and name over to themselves the Ephesian letters.' So uttering askion, kataskion, lix, tetrax, demnameneus, aisia – the Ephesian letters – should do the trick. Physical objects could serve as energy, storing resources for breaking through to the attention of the supernatural. So magicians used or made available to users amulets, wands and other instruments. Special sacrifices could turn a power's attention; magicians knew them. The magician's toolbox was almost infinite. This was necessary because the range of actions called for was also almost infinite.

Probably the first human forays into the supernatural were to assure success in particularly problematic enterprises such as hunting, and in healing sickness. Magicians in the Greco-Roman world frequently engaged in what we would consider medicine. Doctors were mostly beyond the reach of the general population and, anyway, their skills hardly surpassed magical intervention except in areas of physical restorations such as setting bones. Cures were home preparations and interventions by knowledgeable neighbours who might have some magical resources and also might know more elaborate preparations or have special skill in preparing them. More extreme problems called for a magician.

There could be conflict with religious solutions. In Hebrew history,

King Asa, for example, became ill and consulted physicians instead of Yahweh for a cure. He died. The prophet Job in his afflictions rejected doctors in favour of Yahweh: 'I desire to speak to the Almighty and to argue my case with God. You, however, smear me with lies; you are worthless physicians, all of you! If only you would be altogether silent! For you, that would be wisdom.' On the other hand, Jesus ben Sirach had a good experience with physicians and advised their use, for they, too, worked with the help of Yahweh: 'Honour physicians for their services, for the Lord created them ... He who sins against his Maker, will be defiant towards the physician.'

Many magical healings involved mental issues in the sick that produced fever, blindness, paralysis and so on. Firm belief in the magical powers could cure such things. Petronius in his *Satyricon* has a humorous example of a witch curing Eumolpus's erectile dysfunction, but the word picture he paints replicates what we find in magical papyri and other sources for magic in the Greco-Roman world:

> After strolling to and fro for a while, I had just sat down in the same spot as the day before, when Chrysis came in sight, bringing a little old woman with her ... The old woman drew from her pocket a hank of plaited yarns of different colours, and tied it round my neck. Then putting dust and spittle together, she dipped her middle finger in the mess, and disregarding my repugnance, marked my forehead with it. 'Never despair! Priapus I invoke, To help the parts that make his altars smoke.' The incantation ended, she bade me spit out thrice, and thrice toss pebbles into my bosom, which she had wrapped up in purple after pronouncing a charm over them. Then putting her hands to my privates, she began to try my virile condition. Quicker than thought the nerves obeyed her summons, and filled the old lady's hand with a huge erection. Then jumping for joy, 'Look, Chrysis, look,' she cried, 'how I've started the hare for other people to hunt.'

A magician's most important ability was manipulating the spirit world of demons and powers. Exorcism was a speciality. Lucian in his parodic *Lover of Lies* has a fictional description that captures this ability nicely:

Everyone knows about the Syrian from Palestine, the adept in it, how many he takes in hand who fall down in the light of the moon and roll their eyes and fill their mouths with foam; nevertheless, he restores them to health and sends them away normal in mind, delivering them from their straits for a large fee. When he stands beside them as they lie there and asks: 'Whence came you into his body?' the patient himself is silent, but the spirit answers in Greek or in the language of whatever foreign country he comes from, telling how and whence he entered into the man; whereupon, by adjuring the spirit and if he does not obey, threatening him, he drives him out. Indeed, I actually saw one coming out, black and smoky in colour.

Josephus was an eyewitness to what looked to be a successful exorcism. A fellow Jew named Eleazar had been called in to cure a soldier of demon possession. The future emperor Vespasian, his sons, military tribunes and some other soldiers were present: they wanted to see it. Eleazar

put to the nose of the possessed man a ring which had under its seal one of the roots prescribed by Solomon and then, as the man smelled it, drew out the demon through his nostrils and, when the man at once fell down, adjured the demon never to come back into him, speaking Solomon's name and reciting the incantations which he had composed. Then, wishing to convince the bystanders and prove to them that he had this power, Eleazar placed a cup or foot-basin full of water a little way off and commanded the demon, as it went out of the man, to overturn it and make known to the spectators that he had left the man.

This account reminds us again that belief in magic – exorcism in this case – extended to all segments of the population.

Jewish exorcists in Ephesus claimed skill at ejecting evil spirits. Seven sons of Sceva, a Jewish chief priest, were among the practitioners. As stories about the miracles performed by Jesus and Paul spread in the Jewish community, these magicians decided to use their names in incantations. Called in to cure a demon-possessed man, they intoned, 'In the name of the Jesus whom Paul preaches, I command you to come out.' But, as Acts told the story, 'the evil spirit answered them, "Jesus I know and Paul I know about, but *who are you?*"' The possessed man then attacked the exorcists and drove them naked and bleeding from his house.

Magic could affect other areas of the physical world. Pliny wrote how common people believed in magical powers even in the face of a clear understanding of phenomena by the educated: 'Long ago was discovered a method of predicting eclipses of the sun and moon – not the day or night merely but the very hour. Yet there still exists among a great number of the common people an established conviction that these phenomena are due to the compelling power of charms and magic herbs ...' We can readily doubt that such belief was the sole property of the masses.

The general ability to do wondrous things marked the magician's profession. Snake handling is but a minor example. Pliny reported that there were people who frighten serpents. These people were able to resist serpents' poison and even their hostility. He told the story of one Euagon, a man from Cyprus, who was part of a deputation sent to Rome. The consuls, aware of his reputation as a snake handler and curious, threw him into a large vessel filled with serpents. 'To the astonishment of all, they licked his body all over with their tongues.' Dealing with snakes also appears in Jesus's prediction of the magical acts his followers will perform: they would, he said, drive out demons, speak in tongues, heal the sick by putting their hands on them and 'trample on snakes and scorpions', since they could 'pick up snakes with their hands; and when they drink deadly poison, it will not hurt them at all'.

Magicians could also get beyond the boundary of death. Communicating with the dead was another speciality. King Saul of Israel desperately needed to consult with the prophet Samuel, but Samuel had died. So the king sought a necromancer and found the Witch of Endor:

'Consult a spirit for me,' he said, 'and bring up for me the one I name.' ... Then the woman asked, 'Whom shall I bring up for you?' 'Bring up Samuel,' he said. When the woman saw Samuel, she cried out at the top of her voice ... The king said to her, 'Don't be afraid. What do you see?' The woman said, 'I see a ghostly figure coming up out of the earth.' 'What does he look like?' he asked. 'An old man wearing a robe is coming up,' she said. Then Saul knew it was Samuel, and he bowed down and prostrated himself with his face to the ground. Samuel said to Saul, 'Why have you disturbed me by bringing me up?'

Necromancy was just one way to use magic to help a customer deal with present problems. Prophecy and divination were perhaps the most popular forms of magic after healing. Prophecy required some indication of inspiration. Direct contact with supernatural powers allowed seeing into the future. Celsus described the gullibility of people for self-declared prophets in public places:

> There are many who, although of no name, with the greatest facility and on the slightest occasion, whether within or without temples, assume the motions and gestures of inspired persons; while others do it in cities or among armies, for the purpose of attracting attention and exciting surprise. [To these motions and gestures they add] strange, fanatical, and quite unintelligible words, of which no rational person can find the meaning: for so dark are they, as to have no meaning at all; but they give occasion to every fool or impostor to apply them to suit his own purposes.

Divination involved seeing the human world from a god's perspective so that hidden things (for example buried treasure) became seen and the hidden future became knowable. There are more magical papyri concerned with seeing the future than with any other matter, including success in passion. The world of divines was complex and thickly populated. Periplectomenos in Plautus's play, *The Braggart Soldier*, painted a humorous picture of a wife wedded to people of this sort:

> The wife would stir me from my sleep and say: 'My dear husband, give me something to give to my mother on the first of the month, give me something to make preserves, give me something to give to the sorceress on the festival of Minerva, to the dream interpreter, to the clairvoyant, and to the soothsayer; it's a disgrace if nothing is sent to the woman who uses eyebrows to prophesy.'

Astrologers especially were suspected by authorities because of their ability to foretell political events, especially the success or death of important players. It did not really matter if the astrological readings proved true; the mere fact that they were circulated could cause political unrest. So astrologers as well as other magicians were expelled from Rome from time to time; just being a *mathematicus* or a *magus* was enough to be condemned and driven out. We do not know if they were expelled from other cities and towns of the empire. Aside from this repercussion of their work, astrologers were in great demand. People certainly believed that their fate was in the stars.

This sketch shows the range of magical activity that interested people and most elites, because they wanted to achieve specific ends, foretell the future or deal with the vagaries of fortune. '[Our minds are] always on the lookout for something big, something adequate to move a god, or rather to impose its will on his divinity,' as Pliny says. Magic does not pre-empt or bypass the need to seek the gods' help in life. It is just another avenue in addition to prayers in temples, votive offerings and so forth. Community-endorsed rituals, festivals and sacrifices went on as usual alongside individuals' appeals to magicians or astrologers for specific, personal reasons.

One might think that magic would clash with the omnipotent and omniscient aspect of Yahweh, who demanded total obedience to his law. Magic should be ineffective in the face of divine omnipotence, immutable providence and obstinate divine egotism. But instead of claiming that Yahweh's power made magic and sorcerers impotent the Jewish tradition stressed that Israelites should stay away from such practitioners and practices, thus admitting their efficacy. The Torah strongly prohibited magical practices. Moses addressing his people said, 'When you enter the land the Lord your God is giving you ... let no one be found among you who practises divination or sorcery, interprets omens, engages in witchcraft, or casts spells, or who is a medium or spiritist or who consults the dead. Anyone who does these things is detestable to the Lord.' The Torah never claims that magic might fail to work.

Roman tradition also tried to circumscribe magicians and their superstitions. But the repeated attempts to denigrate and marginalise magic by the central authorities only show that people continued to treat magic as functional and useful in the struggle to deal with the challenges of life.

There was no denying that someone who could work magic had a connection with the supernatural. The magician had a relationship with godly powers. Magical ability opened an audience up to the authority of the magician. This power and authority stood in competition with the rituals, prayers and sacrifices of priests so, naturally, priests were generally hostile to magic. Polytheist and Judaic traditions both made a distinction between 'magic' and 'religion'. But for the majority, this distinction was unimportant. People did not reject the authority of religion and its purveyors whether they were fathers, priests, or magistrates. Rather, they added magic and the authority of magicians to their resources for dealing with the supernatural. For them, it was a very thin line that separated 'magic' from 'religion', however much priests and elites tried to thicken that line.

In the ancient world, the difference between magic and religion was only perspective anyway. Religion was the people and traditions authorised by the community to interact with the supernatural. Magical actions worked with the supernatural outside those established avenues. Methods of religion can seem to an outsider very much like magic with its incantations and special substances. The Book of Numbers presents the Israelite test for adultery as part of religion, but it certainly looks like magic. The allegedly cuckolded husband was to bring his suspected wife to Yahweh's priest. In the following narrative, note the special substance used, the written curse that is literally mixed with it, and the incantation:

> The priest shall bring her and have her stand before the Lord. Then he shall take some holy water in a clay jar and put some dust from the tabernacle floor into the water. After the priest has had the woman stand before the Lord, he shall loosen her hair and place in her hands the reminder-offering, the grain offering for jealousy, while he himself holds the bitter water that brings a curse. Then the priest shall put the woman under oath and say to her, 'If no other man has had sexual relations with you and you have not gone astray and become impure while married to your husband, may this bitter water that brings a curse not harm you. But if you have gone astray

while married to your husband and you have made yourself impure by having sexual relations with a man other than your husband' – here the priest is to put the woman under this curse – 'may the Lord cause you to become a curse among your people when he makes your womb miscarry and your abdomen swell. May this water that brings a curse enter your body so that your abdomen swells or your womb miscarries.' Then the woman is to say, 'Amen. So be it.' The priest is to write these curses on a scroll and then wash them off into the bitter water. He shall make the woman drink the bitter water that brings a curse, and this water that brings a curse and causes bitter suffering will enter her. The priest is to take from her hands the grain offering for jealousy, wave it before the Lord and bring it to the altar. The priest is then to take a handful of the grain offering as a memorial offering and burn it on the altar; after that, he is to have the woman drink the water.

If the woman were guilty, her belly would swell and she would miscarry. This was proof of adultery and she would be cursed. If nothing happened, she was proven innocent.

Note that Yahweh was brought directly into the process even though the process had all the marks of magic. Likewise Naaman the Syrian's experience seeking a cure for his leprosy. He went to the prophet Elisha and asked for a cure. He expected Elisha to come before him 'and stand and call on the name of the Lord his God, wave his hand over the spot and cure me of my leprosy'. Naaman expected a magical cure for his leprosy. Elisha responded with instructions for just such a cure – bathing seven times in the Jordan. After protest, Naaman came around, followed Elisha's instructions and was cured.

Both these magical processes were embedded in the authorised actions of Jewish traditions and so were 'religious', not 'sorcery'. Magic was viewed as deviance from community-sponsored religion, not as a separate, identifiable spectrum of actions. Especially considering the fluidity of ancient polytheism, the categories were confused, mixed up and unclear to most. No matter. Magical acts were entangled in medicine, religion, divination – magic involved them all. People would try what seemed to work, without careful thought about what category an act fell into.

There was a deep belief in the Jewish tradition that evil came from disobedience and that Yahweh would protect and aid a devout, purified person. Yet magic came to the fore from almost the earliest days. Josephus noted King Solomon as the source for magical lore and incantations. Outside the Jewish people, their reputation as sorcerers was strong. Pliny the Elder in his encyclopaedia said, 'There is yet another branch of magic, derived from Moses, Jannes, Lotapes and the Jews ...' The Roman satirist Juvenal made fun of that magical skill when he wrote:

> No sooner has [a priest] gone than a palsied Jewish woman will abandon her hay-lined chest and start begging into her private ear. She's the expounder of the laws of Jerusalem, high priestess of the tree, reliable intermediary of highest heaven. She too gets her hand filled, though with less, because Jews will sell you whatever dreams you like for the tiniest copper coin.

Lucian in his essay, *Gout*, noted: 'Others are mocked by chants impostors sell and other fools fall for the spells of Jews ...' Apuleius called the people 'Iudaei superstitiosi' ('Judaeans, the most magically endowed of all'). Polytheist magical papyri regularly invoked Yahweh and his other names in their incantations, indicating the magical tradition attached to the Jewish traditions. In fact, those names outnumber the names of other powers invoked in the papyri formulations by about three to one. Celsus made clear the fit between Jewish magic and polytheistic culture when he wrote:

> If, then, we shall be able to establish the nature of powerful names ... and shall be able to make out that the so-called magic is not an altogether uncertain thing, but is, as those skilled in it prove, a consistent system, then we say that the name Sabaoth, and Adonai, and the other names treated with so much reverence among the Hebrews, are not applicable to any ordinary created things, but belong to a secret theology which refers to the Framer of all things. These names, accordingly, when pronounced with that attendant train of circumstances which is appropriate to their nature, are possessed of great power.

Recourse to religious activities in time of need could be thrust aside by a more immediate reality, the need for prompt and direct results, especially when the actual will of Yahweh was impenetrable and one would be compelled just to 'wait and see'. So magic continued to exist among Jewish people and to be successful. Magic was reconciled with basic monotheistic habits by assigning it to the domain of lesser supernatural powers. Yahweh was reckoned to allow these to operate so long as their actions did not actually compel (or try to compel) him to do something.

However it was understood, magic remained a lively part of the lives of Jewish people before, throughout and beyond the first century AD. While the priesthood and law experts strove to push the official line because it established and maintained their position in society, ordinary people (and at times the priests and law experts themselves) wanted to have the 'other option' available and to use it regularly. The result was an officially uneasy relationship between the two access points to supernatural aid, but an unofficial acceptance of magic. The evidence of the biblical characters and from magical formulae, amulets and actions in later times proves that exactly the same recourse was had to magic as in the polytheistic environments. The proof was in the pudding, and magic was a shortcut to dessert.

Famous magicians

In the polytheist tradition, Pythagoras was one of the most well known in a long list of magicians. This sixth-century Greek philosopher's life story was shrouded in mystery and bedevilled by later accretions. His school influenced Plato especially and survived all the way through antiquity. His followers clearly believed that he had magical powers and had performed miracles. People claimed to be Pythagorean sages and wandered about teaching his ways and ideas.

In the Jewish people's lives, Solomon was the magician par excellence, although his magic was said to have the authority of Yahweh. Josephus noted that 'God granted him knowledge of the art used against demons for the benefit and healing of men. He also composed incantations by which illnesses are relieved and left behind forms of exorcisms with which those possessed by demons drive them out, never to return.' In historical times, Simon Magus ('The Magician') stood out. He lived in the first century. From Samaria, he practised his skills alongside the Christian apostles Peter and Philip and other contemporary adepts. He was baptised by Philip and attempted to purchase the power of Jesus's name from Peter in order to enhance his repertoire. He appeared in Christian apocryphal writings such as the *Acts of Peter*, where he was given the ability to fly, and contested in magic with Peter himself. He had disciples called Simonians who founded a sect at his death. Justin elaborated on his origins and following:

> There was a Samaritan, Simon, a native of the village called Gitto, who in the reign of Claudius Caesar, and in your royal city of Rome, did mighty acts of magic, by virtue of the art of the devils operating in him. He was considered a god … and almost all the Samaritans, and a few even of other nations, worship him, and acknowledge him as the first god; and a woman, Helena, who went about with him at that time, and had formerly been a prostitute, they say is the first idea generated by him. And a man, Meander, also a Samaritan, of the town Capparetaea, a disciple of Simon, and inspired by devils, we know to have deceived many while he was in Antioch by his magical art. He persuaded those who adhered to him that they should never die, and even now there are some living who hold this opinion of his.

Simon's sect survived at least into the third century.

Among polytheists, a false prophet who was immensely popular arose in the middle of the second century. Alexander of Abonoteichus (a small town on the Black Sea) got the brilliant idea that he could use a trained serpent to convince people that he had supernatural powers. He and Glycon, his serpent, set up shop in Ionopolis, claimed to foretell the future and healed the sick. Lucian, in his essay *Alexander the False Prophet*, describes the situation:

> Alexander seated himself on a couch in a certain chamber, clothed in apparel well suited to a god, and took into his bosom his [giant serpent], who, as I have said, was of uncommon size and beauty. Coiling him about his neck, and letting the tail, which was long, stream over his lap and drag part of its length on the floor, he

15. A sorceress offers a client a potion. The pointed cap is doffed
in imitation of the garb of Etruscan priests and priestesses.

concealed only the head by holding it under his arm – the creature
would submit to anything – and showed the linen head at one side
of his own beard, as if it certainly belonged to the creature that was
in view ... Alexander announced to all comers that the god would
make prophecies.

He issued oracles supposedly from the serpent himself. The cult of
Glycon actually existed – there is a coin of Ionopolis showing the crea-
ture and a statue of the snake survives. Fame spread far and wide. Even
Emperor Marcus Aurelius is said to have consulted the oracle.

Jewish and polytheist sources agreed that women were most active
in the magical arts. The fictional example from Petronius cited above
is a vivid illustration. The whole plot in Apuleius's *Metamorphoses* is
activated by the magical abilities of a witch. Rabbis believed that most
women practised witchcraft and that most witchcraft was practised
by women. Pliny agreed that 'charms and magic herbs' were 'one outstanding province of women'. Mythical women such as Circe, however,

were much more famous than any actual sorceresses. But this epitaph of a little girl shows a witch at work:

> I was almost four when I was seized and laid in the ground. So sweet I could have been to my mother and father! A witch's hand – surpassing cruel! – snatched me away. While she remains on earth she harms by her art your lovely little ones. Oh parents guard them, lest grief be fixed deep in your breast.

Powerful magicians are sometimes shown in competition with each other. Whether we want to call the episode of Elijah and the prophets of Baal magic or religion, it was a contest to see who could call down supernatural power effectively. The confrontation of Paul and the Jewish magician, Elymas, before the governor of Crete showed Paul's superior power, as did the triumph of his power over the rival sons of Sceva. Simon Magus did not actually compete with Peter in the account in Acts cited just above, but in the *Acts of Peter* there is an extended contest. In all of these cases, the demonstration of greater magical power brought authority to the magician.

The ancient authorities considered magic and magicians as threatening to social and political order. The competition magic presented to community rites and practices caused understandable tensions, but the hostility of Jewish and polytheist elites goes beyond mere rivalry for people's attention in their dealings with the supernatural. Josephus treats 'magician' as interchangeable with 'imposter', and also uses the most common Greek word, *goetes* (sorcerer), instead of 'brigands' for troublemakers if they perform miracles or pretend to. For the Romans, too, magicians and their ilk had great potential for disruption. Felix (governor in Judaea c.52–60) executed not only bandits but also magicians in an attempt to control his province. In Rome, we have seen the examples of expulsions from the city. Dio, writing in the third century, has Maecenas urge the emperor Augustus to keep divination but get rid of the sorcerers (*goetes*) because they incite revolution. Roman legal texts repeated this fear that magicians are antisocial at best, politically dangerous at worst. While the main target of these fears were astrologers and fortune tellers, these were a sub-set of magicians in general.

Magic came to be thought of as a central aspect of what the Romans called *superstitio*. Practising a deviant avenue to the supernatural undermined the general welfare and could thus become 'hatred of the human race'. Tacitus labelled the Jewish tradition a *superstitio*; he, Pliny and Suetonius did the same for early Christianity. In this picture, magic and magicians played a crucial role. Embedded in Justinian's code from the time of the early Christian emperors came the statements: 'Magicians in every portion of the world should be considered the enemies of the human race,' and 'Those who, by means of magic arts, plot against the health or lives of men.' The similarity to Tacitus's language is striking, as is the sweeping implication of the danger to society presented by magicians and their kind.

Many of the things Jesus was said to have done during his lifetime a Greco-Roman observer would categorically have labelled as magic: he raised Lazarus from the dead, walked on water, withered fig trees, drove out demons, healed the sick and predicted his own death and resurrection. He used magical formulae and magical substances such as sputum. When we first encounter in art images of Jesus working a miracle, he holds the wand of a sorcerer! Unsurprisingly, therefore, polytheist sources thought of Jesus as a magician-cum-miracle worker. As Tertullian saw, 'from his lowly guise polytheists took him to be merely a man; so it followed that, confronted by his power, they counted him a magician'. Jesus declared his deeds were based on his own power. His name was invoked in magical papyri, indicating that magicians accepted him as a power to be reckoned with. In accounts of confrontations between early non-Christian and Christian writers, the accusation of Jesus being a magician repeatedly comes up.

After Jesus's death, his followers continued in magical ways. Peter raised the dead by reviving Tabitha and healed a cripple: 'Then Peter said, "Silver or gold I do not have, but what I do have I give you. In the name of Jesus Christ of Nazareth, walk."' Paul on a regular basis demonstrated magical abilities to heal. At Corinth, for example, 'God did extraordinary miracles through Paul, so that even handkerchiefs and aprons that had touched him were taken to the sick and their illnesses were cured and the evil spirits left them.' Paul also invoked the name of Jesus as a magical formula when a slave girl, inspired by an evil spirit, harassed him: 'She kept this up for many days. Finally Paul became so annoyed that he turned around and said to the spirit: "In the name of Jesus Christ I command you to come out of her!" And at that moment the spirit was said to have left her.' 'In the name of the Lord' and other such phrases were similar to standard incantational usage of divine name. Magic was used to harm as well as to heal. God struck down Ananias and Sapphira following Peter's denunciation. All such actions were recognised as magic.

Jesus and his followers did not use the full panoply of magic as it was then known. Although a number of women are mentioned in the followers of Jesus, both before and after his death, none is portrayed as a sorceress. Some standard tools of magic did not appear, for example curse tablets. Really strange substances like lizard's feet or human body parts were not used in magical acts. The Gospels present a rather benign sort of magician, but a magician nonetheless. And magical power meant supernatural connection. Jesus's magical abilities undergirded his message and the proclamations of his followers and gave it authority in people's eyes.

People believed in miracles, large or small, as they did in magic. Both were part of the way the supernatural acted in the natural world. Aelius Aristides stated that miracles were the manifestation of the power of a god. Better, 'manifestation of supernatural power', because there is little difference between miracle and magic. Both achieved the same result but, like 'magic' and 'religion', it was a matter of personal opinion. My 'miracle' was your 'magic', and vice-versa, because miracle had a more positive connotation. Both were, as the Buddhists put it, any event that does not follow from a sequence of causes that are identifiable in the natural world. There were two distinctions between miracles and magic: miracles tended to be more spectacular than magic; miracles focused primarily on alterations in the realm of healing. Miracles that altered the physical world were least common, for attempts to bring rain or part waters or move mountains were not likely to succeed. These did occur, as when Moses parted the Red Sea, Joshua brought down the walls of Jericho, or Elijah summoned up fire and rain at the sacrifice contest with the priest of Baal. But such miracles usually occurred in distant history or legend.

There are many miracles in polytheistic lore. Eunus, the leader of the great slave revolt in Sicily in the late second century BC, won and kept his leadership role through producing fake miracles that nonetheless had a profound effect on his followers. At Stymphalus in Arcadia (Greece) a festival of the huntress Artemis celebrated a hunting miracle, quite appropriately. A mid-second-century inscription said to have come from the temple of Asclepius on the island in the River Tiber in Rome testified to a miracle of the god:

> The god commanded a certain Gaius, a blind man, to go to the holy altar and worship, then go from the right towards the left, and place five fingers on the altar, then lift his hand and lay it on his eyes. Thereupon he saw perfectly well, and the people stood about and rejoiced with him because divine power was still alive in the time of our Emperor Antoninus.

Theagenes of Thasos, a man of prodigious strength and athletic prowess, set up a statue of himself in the fifth century BC which people believed cured disease. Apollonius of Tyana, a philosopher and wonder-worker of the first to second century AD, was said to have performed miracles such as this one:

> There was a girl who appeared to have died just at the time of her wedding. The betrothed followed the bier, with all the lamentations of an unconsummated marriage, and Rome mourned with him, since the girl belonged to a consular family. Meeting with this scene of sorrow, Apollonius said, 'Put the bier down, for I will end your crying over the girl.' At the same time he asked her name, which made most people think he was going to declaim a speech of the kind delivered at funerals to raise lamentation. But Apollonius, after merely touching her and saying something secretly, woke the bride from her apparent death. The girl spoke, and went back to her father's house like Alcestis revived by Heracles.

Apollonius's biography claims others.

Josephus, as we have seen, was eyewitness to a healing miracle by a Jewish magician. Along the same lines, men sought a miracle from the newly minted emperor, Vespasian. Suetonius describes how two people, one blind and the other lame, asked him for healing. Vespasian at first demurred, for he did not believe he could cure anything. But his friends insisted. He was said to have spat on the eyes of the blind man, who then saw, and to have touched with his heel the leg of the lame man, who then walked. If Vespasian was uncertain of his ability to heal, the blind man and the cripple had no such doubts.

Celsus in his diatribe against the Christians described popular enthusiasm for works of

> sorcerers who profess to do wonderful miracles, and for the accomplishments of those who are taught by the Egyptians, who for a small fee, make known their sacred lore in the middle of the marketplace and drive daemons out of men and blow away diseases and invoke the souls of hero and exhibit expensive banquets, and tables, and dishes, and dainties having no real existence, and who will put in motion, as if alive, what are not really living animals, but which have only the appearance of life.

Surely some of these demonstrations were straight deception on the part of charlatans – but in other cases, cures were real.

Miracles also had a long history in the Jewish tradition. Moses, Joshua, Isaiah, Elijah and Elisha all perform miracles through the power of Yahweh. The Nile turned to blood. Walls came tumbling down. The sun moved backwards. The dead were raised. Elisha, like Jesus after him, made bread last for a mob:

> A man came from Baal Shalishah, bringing the man of God twenty loaves of barley bread baked from the first ripe grain, along with some heads of new grain. 'Give it to the people to eat,' Elisha said. 'How can I set this before a hundred men?' his servant asked. But Elisha answered, 'Give it to the people to eat. For this is what the Lord says: "They will eat and have some left over."' Then he set it before them, and they ate and had some left over, according to the word of the Lord.

He also performed a miraculous multiplication of wine.

In contrast to magic, there was little social objection to miracles because, by definition, they were seen as positive. Although authorities from time to time tried to suppress magicians as they did astrologers and other diviners, miracle workers were never attacked. Miracles were often used as proof of a god's power. Marcus Aurelius wrote, 'If any ask, "Where have you seen the gods or how have you satisfied thyself of their existence that you are so devout a worshipper?" I answer ... from the continual proofs of their power I am assured that gods also exist and I reverence them.'

The ability to do magic or miracles proves effective connection with the supernatural. A magician or a miracle worker had to have a powerful relationship with the cosmos. If the adept wished to persuade an audience to a certain path, be it so mundane as a request for money or so emotional as a change of heart, the demonstration of power validated the message he sought to convey. For a religious practitioner, the challenge was not to persuade an audience that magic or a miracle had taken place – people were more than ready to believe. The task was, first, to identify for the audience which god performed the miracle and then, second, to translate the belief in the miracle into support for that god. The process took place across the experience of many religions. For example, in the Buddhist tradition miracles played an important role in demonstrating to the Buddha's enemies and possible converts alike his supernatural power. People had every reason to continue with their relationships with the supernatural in the same manner as their ancestors. Until a better, proven option came along.

As a charismatic, Elijah-like figure, Jesus claimed to speak not as a prophet, but as more than a prophet, as the Son of Yahweh. This intrigued some of his fellow Jews and alienated others. To have people believe such a radical claim, Jesus needed to prove ability to direct and control supernatural power. The magic and miracles Jesus performed supplied a powerful proof of his connection to the supernatural (Yahweh). Such clear demonstration of superior power could persuade people to change their orientation to the supernatural.

Jesus spent much of his time performing miracles. The historicity of the miracles is unimportant. People believed that Jesus performed those miracles. That belief turned them to listen to what Jesus had to say. For example, Jesus miraculously described her life to the Samaritan woman at the well. Her witness brought Jesus many adherents. 'Many of the Samaritans from that town believed in him because of the woman's testimony, "He told me everything I ever did." So when the Samaritans came to him, they urged him to stay with them and he stayed two days. And because of his words many more became believers.' The list of miracles in the Gospels is long, perhaps numbering 200. Mark is particularly rich, but many occur in Matthew and Luke, and even in the more spiritual John. Miracles not only healed people but also were signs of the truth of Yahweh's final victory, and of reward for the righteous – in sum, the proof that Jesus was the Son of Yahweh, as Tertullian emphasised:

> For with a word he drove devils out of men, he gave light again to the blind, he cleansed the lepers, he braced up the paralytic and to crown all he restored the dead to life by his word; he made the very elements his servants, he controlled the storm, he walked on the sea, – showing that he is the Logos of God, that is the Word, original and first-begotten, attended by Power and Reason, upheld by Spirit, the same Being who by his word still made as he had made all things.

Paul had his personal miraculous vision of the risen Jesus. It was what converted him to a follower and advocate of the new sect. He also testified that many had seen the risen Christ in the flesh, as many as five hundred at one time, and they bore witness to that miracle and so helped validate the Christian message. In fact, it would be hard to find in the Gospels or in the other New Testament literature a conversion that was not the result, directly or indirectly, of the occurrence of a miracle or a magical event.

Quadratus, writing about AD 125, affirmed how important witnesses of Christ's miracles were as the movement spread. They supplied evidence for the supernatural powers of Jesus and so a reason for a movement after his death. Eusebius, the church's historian, wrote in the early fourth century AD:

> Our Saviour's works, moreover, were always present: for they were real, consisting of those who had been healed of their diseases, those who had been raised from the dead; who were not only seen while they were being healed and raised up, but were afterwards

constantly present. Nor did they remain only during the sojourn of the Saviour on earth, but also a considerable time after His departure; and, indeed, some of them have survived even down to our own times.

Justin, writing much earlier, had also emphasised the role of miracles in conversions when he wrote, 'Moreover, by the works and by the attendant miracles, it is possible for all to understand that He is the new law, and the new covenant, and the expectation of those who out of every people wait for the good things of God.'

Miracles form the heart of the apocryphal acts of various early Christian leaders. For example, in the fictional *Acts of Peter* a fish swam and people converted. In the story, Peter took down a sardine hanging up for sale and said to a crowd, 'Will you believe if I make the fish live?' When the crowd agreed that such a miracle would convince them, he tossed the fish into a pond and uttered an incantation, 'In your name, O Jesus Christ, in the sight of all these, live and swim.' The fish revived. Peter kept it swimming for a long time; people came and fed it to see if it was real. Seeing the miracle, 'many followed Peter and believed in the Lord'.

The polytheist opponent of early Christianity, Celsus, along with his contemporary, the doctor-philosopher Galen, also affirmed that it was the miracles that created Jesus as a god. Celsus wrote that Jesus, 'having been brought up as an illegitimate child, and having served for hire in Egypt, and then coming to the knowledge of certain miraculous powers, returned from thence to his own country, and by means of those powers proclaimed himself a god'. Origen, Celsus's Christian critic, agreed:

> And I shall refer not only to his miracles, but, as is proper, to those also of the apostles of Jesus. For they could not without the help of miracles and wonders have prevailed on those who heard their new doctrines and new teachings to abandon their national usages, and to accept their instructions at the danger to themselves even of death.

The answer, then, to the question, 'Why change my traditional ways?' was simple: a greater power had come on the scene; the power was incontrovertibly proven by miracles and magic; the message was worth, if not believing, at least listening to – and then perhaps believing.

Martyrdoms were also seen as miracles. As Ramsay MacMullen puts it, 'Surrender of one's life for one's faith was bound to work most powerfully on witnesses. It was quite beyond nature, a wonder.' This wonder was often inspirational. Voluntarily giving up one's life is seldom easy. To see someone doing it with an avowed purpose might induce horror if you thought it foolish or be persuasive if you admired it, even inspiring you to copy it, especially if you were already committed to the purpose.

The suffering, exemplary, inspirational martyr appeared in the Jewish tradition in the post-exilic, Second Temple Period. Although none of the authors who contributed to the book of Isaiah seems to have actually been a martyr, the post-exilic message of the prophet(s) was clear: a martyred leader would prove a salvation for Israel: 'Yet it was the Lord's will to crush [the righteous servant] and cause him to suffer, and though the Lord makes his life an offering for sin, he will see his offspring and prolong his days, and the will of the Lord will prosper in his hand.' This prophecy was directed originally at Zerubbabel or some other actual leader of the post-exile period. Later readers changed it into a prophecy of a future leader.

The model of suffering in the service of Yahweh inspired others. A tradition grew up that during the second century BC, Eleazar and his sons were such sufferers. Being tortured by his enemies and about to die, Eleazar cried out, 'God, you know that I could have saved myself; instead, I am being burned and tortured to death for the sake of your Law. Have mercy on your people. Make our punishment sufficient for their sake. Purify them with my blood and take my life in exchange for theirs.' He, his wife and their seven sons all were martyrs to their faith. The result was Isaiah-like: 'The tyrant was punished and our nation was cleansed through them. They exchanged their lives for the nation's sin. Divine providence delivered Israel from its former abuse through the blood of those godly people.' As the psalmist sang, 'Precious in the sight of the Lord is the death of his faithful servants.' These martyrs were the first attested at great length in the Jewish tradition.

At the point of death of the youngest of Eleazar's sons, his mother said to him, 'Do not be afraid of this executioner, but be worthy of your brothers and accept death, so that in the time of mercy I may receive you again with your brothers.' By this she meant that she would be reunited with her righteous son at the resurrection and final judgement.

The promise of resurrection and reward at the End of Days added significance to a martyr's death. Such martyrs set a pattern for dying in righteousness that was followed by many other Jews through the time of the Great Revolt and beyond.

The atonement imagery that accompanied these first martyrs was not repeated in every martyrdom. Death rather than betrayal of Yahweh's law was usually simply praised as innocents suffering for their faith. This seems to be the case with those crucified in Alexandria during the unrest of AD 38. During the Great Revolt thirty years later there were many steadfast martyrs, such as one who died with a smile on his face. Josephus reported that a Jewish rebel, captured during a siege, 'held out under every variety of torture and, without betraying to the enemy a word about the state of the town, even under the ordeal of fire, was finally crucified, meeting death with a smile'. As in the case of the mother of the seven martyred sons, confidence in a resurrection at the final judgement inspired such martyrs. During the Great Revolt Essenes were tortured by Roman soldiers in the most terrible way to get them to blaspheme or eat forbidden food. They resisted unto death. Josephus recorded that 'they cheerfully resigned their souls, confident that they would receive them back again'.

Martyrdom was much rarer in polytheistic traditions. In Greece, the death of Socrates was widely viewed as an example of dying to make a point; his is by far the most famous and exemplary martyrdom in the tradition. In Roman history the practice of *devotio* – self-consecration as a sacrifice to the gods in return for favourable action of the gods – is seldom attested, but does seem to have happened. The cases of the consul Decius Mus in 340 BC and, less historically secure, of his son and grandson, are the most famous examples of Roman martyrs, even being cited by Augustine as an example of polytheist martyrdom.

The habit does not, however, seem to have continued among polytheists. Death of the sort suffered by martyrs in the Jewish tradition did not happen in Roman or Greek culture. The practice of self-immolation, spectacularly demonstrated to Greeks and Romans by Indian gymnosophists, was not martyrdom in the sense of dying for a faith or cause. Lucian tells the story of Peregrinus, a second-century pseudo-martyr, who, after many adventures, including a stint as a Christian, committed suicide in a spectacularly public manner. According to Lucian, Peregrinus said he was acting for the sake of his fellow men, to teach them to despise death and endure agony. His self-sacrifice imitates Jewish and Christian deeds but does not represent any Greco-Roman habit. In Spain, the barbarian Cantabrians seemed to celebrate their martyr-like death as they sang songs of victory while executed on the cross by the Romans, but we have no details. A philosopher might die for his convictions. Socrates was the paradigm but he was rarely imitated, although Seneca made a show of his suicide to protest Nero's tyranny. Tertullian, seeking polytheist comparisons to Christian martyrs, could not name more than half a dozen in Greco-Roman history – but not even any of these replicated the habit and tenor of Jewish and Christian martyrdoms. In short, there was no widespread tradition in polytheist life that duplicated what came to be accepted in the Jewish tradition as evidence for loyalty to a god, combined with hope for reward by that god in a later life.

Martyrdom was central to early Christian experience and theology. Followers of Jesus interpreted his crucifixion as martyrdom in the mould of Eleazar's, i.e. a sacrifice having a redeeming power that looked forward to a final judgement and vindication. The claim that Jesus was not just a resistance hero or prophet, but the Son of Yahweh, made the martyr sacrifice all the more significant. Christians believed it to be a super-atonement that would cleanse whoever accepted its value. It set the stage for participation in Yahweh's eschatological kingdom. The wondrous aspect of Jesus's martyrdom – that he was willing to die a very cruel death for what he believed – was enhanced by the claimed miracles of his resurrection, his appearance in the flesh to followers and subsequent assumption to Yahweh's side, there to preside over final judgement and revenge.

Among followers of Jesus, his martyrdom thus combined with the pre-existing tradition of martyrdom in the Jewish tradition to encourage both a sense of persecution and a willingness to replicate Jesus's deed with their own deaths. According to Christian tradition, Jesus had warned that his followers would be persecuted, and that they should welcome it. The first martyr, Stephen, was stoned, as was appropriate for blasphemers, but the next known martyrdom occurred fully twenty years after Stephen's death, when Herod Antipas had James, Jesus's brother, killed in the 50s. Christians were martyred at Rome in 64. In Pliny's dealings with the Christians in Pontus Bithynia, some were executed for refusing to curse Christ and so became martyrs.

Somewhat oddly, Christians recalled martyr names from among neither the Roman nor Bithynian early martyrs. But by the mid-second century, martyrdom was well established as a fundamental Christian act; individual martyrs were remembered and honoured. Justin, himself destined to be a martyr, wrote, 'it is plain that, though beheaded, and crucified, and thrown to wild beasts, and chains, and fire, and all other kinds of torture, we do not give up our confession [of Christ]; but the more such things happen, the more do others and in larger numbers become faithful, and worshippers of God through the name of Jesus'. Tertullian famously stated that the blood of the martyrs was the seed of the church. The consistent theme was how each stubborn martyr acted in a miraculous way either to strengthen the faithful or convert the unbeliever, or both. 'That very obstinacy,' wrote Tertullian, 'with which you taunt us, is your teacher. For who that beholds it is not stirred to inquire, what lies indeed within it? Who, on inquiry, does not join us?' Justin became a Christian in just this way.

This theme flows through the nine historical acts of martyrdom – the earliest of which is that of Polycarp about 155 – before the widespread persecutions of the mid-third century. Some, such as the *Acts of Perpetua*, were clearly meant to be read to and by the faithful in order to inspire admiration and emulation.

Some polytheists saw martyrdoms as puzzlingly peculiar. Others who witnessed them felt that degenerates were getting the death they deserved. Although Christian literature consistently claimed conversions resulting from witnessing martyrdoms, it is striking that no unconverted polytheist comments on any positive, inspirational content of a Christian martyrdom. But Christian evidence shows that at least some polytheists witnessing martyrdom felt that something supernatural was happening. The power that could provoke such self-sacrifice seemed more than human. The simple determination to die for the faith rather than deny Christ was a proof, like other miracles, that here was a supernatural power worth changing for.

Only a very strong motivation could change customary relations with the supernatural. But traditional means to access the supernatural were not guaranteed. Often failures occurred. Doubts could arise. If a previously unknown or untried power came on the scene, there was a temptation to have at least a quick look. After all, there could always be supplementary ways to work with the supernatural. Friends are healed. Rival magicians are vanquished. It was said that a man, now a god, had not only done those things, but also passed on the ability to his follow-ers. A power that could demonstrate such abilities – that was worth paying attention to. A follower who could direct that power was very impressive. How would someone tap into the benefits of that power? The follower says you need to do such and such and believe such and such and the power will be at your disposal – and more than that, the power will guarantee your enemies will get their comeuppance in a final judgement while you will be rewarded with eternal bliss. This was worth trying out.

WHEN PROPHECY FAILS

TWO EVENTS CHANGED THE DIRECTION of early Christianity. The first was the destruction of the temple in Jerusalem by the Romans in the year 70. Putting down the Great Revolt in blood and destruction shook the lives of Jewish people, particularly in Judaea, but also in the diaspora. The Romans despoiled, then destroyed the centre of their cultic existence. The Sadducees disappeared from the scene, for there was no temple for a priesthood to serve. The Romans had already eradicated the Essenes, both their actively rebellious adherents and the entire community at Qumran. The Zealots' and Sicarii's last stand at Masada was in vain. That left the Pharisees. These regrouped first at Jamnia (Yavne) in Judaea and later in Galilee. They became known simply as teachers, rabbis. Over the next two hundred years these rabbis gradually established a long-lasting tradition based on their interpretation of the Torah. Christians, too, evolved in a new direction. The temple's destruction broke a crucial bond. Yahweh had missed a perfect opportunity to show his power; Jerusalem would have been the perfect stage for a scenario all expected – the return of Jesus and the ensuing end of the world. But Jesus had not returned. This non-event exacerbated existing psychological unrest at the failure over the previous forty years of his promised reappearance in power. Followers expected his Second Coming within their own lifetimes. Twenty years or more before the temple's doom, Paul had already had to settle rustlings of uneasiness about Jesus's non-appearance. He had to make constant assurances that the end was near. And yet it had not happened, even as more and more people died who had known Jesus or been personally inspired by his message.

Christian leaders sought a response. The group's emphasis flipped. From awaiting the End of Days and living a life that would ensure being on the winning side in the near future, thinking shifted to living a right-eous life over the long term with the final reward, the End of Days, receding ever more, ceasing to be the prime focus of the group's life.

By the end of the first century, some Christians feared that Jesus was not going to return, as had been promised to the early adherents. Other writers kept up the hope that the Second Coming would soon occur. But the standard explanation of the failed prophecy became that 'soon' was in God's time, not human time, so the delay in human time was unim-portant. The author of Peter's second letter encapsulates the view when he writes: 'With the Lord a day is like a thousand years, and a thousand years are like a day. The Lord is not slow in keeping his promise, as some understand slowness. Instead he is patient with you, not wanting anyone to perish, but everyone to come to repentance.' In the meantime, the righteous dead would be preserved until that glorious day, so the delay did not matter. The failure of the prophecy of a Second Coming caused this radical shift from the original, straightforward, motivating message.

Christians dealt with the disappointment and disaster by distanc-ing themselves from their Jewish roots and adopting more and more to polytheist ways. Before AD 70, the movement involved mostly pros-elytising Jews and god-fearers in Judaea and in the diaspora. After, the movement became essentially non-Jewish. From 70 onward, Christians increasingly directed their proclamation at polytheists. As a result, Chris-tianity became gradually more enmeshed in polytheist culture. Radical sloughing of polytheist habits lost its immediacy. Instead, people kept to their old ways as much as they could while also claiming to have taken up a new Christian way of life. Jewish Christians remained: there is evidence for their activity right into the fourth century. But the centre of gravity for the movement irrevocably shifted to the non-Jewish, poly-theist world.

There was no guarantee that Christianity would survive the twin shocks of Jerusalem's destruction and the failure of Jesus's End Times prophecy. They might have crippled the movement. Early Christianity might have petered out and disappeared, as did the movements inspired by so many other miracle workers. The followings of John the Baptist, Simon Magus and Alexander's divining serpent were only a few examples. The Jesus movement had survived the shock of Jesus's arrest, trial and execution. Now once again it faced disappointments that might lead to extinction.

There was, however, no overt recognition of the need for action, nor was there a carefully thought-out plan, nor was there any way to implement a consistent plan for all believers. There was no centralised organisational structure. Christian communities' models within the Jewish tradition had no such structure. None had seemed necessary since the end of world had been at hand. Now, new approaches developed organically. Two adjustments were especially significant. One was intellectual: the movement downplayed its Jewish origins and explained itself more and more in the philosophical terms of the polytheist world. The other was structural: the movement established a clear distinction between leaders and followers. It also revised its basic rituals and began to build permanent structures for worship and community organisation.

Early on, there was little attempt to formulate the Christian story. The end was near. Paul, for example, did not dwell on Jesus's life, but on his final days, crucifixion and resurrection. But as the End faded further and further into the future, the story itself became more and more important. It was formulated in a culturally recognisable context – the Gospels – which in turn allowed, even encouraged, discussion in the terms of the culture understood, i.e. philosophy. As far as impressions went, the story also allowed cultural interpretation: Jesus as a 'deceiver' (sophist) and/or magician. Thus the faith was increasingly put into categories familiar to polytheists – philosophy and magic.

Tacitus, Pliny and Suetonius were unable to understand the new movement. They thought in terms of a deviant mystery cult whose problem was in the actions of its participants, not in an intellectual formulation. In their elite environment, however, the explanation and justification of Christian ideas increasingly donned the habit of polytheistic philosophy. Tertullian criticised his educated polytheist enemies but he and Justin Martyr and many others employed exactly their moves, bringing philosophic categories and ideas into play while defending Christian ideology. They treated Christianity as a philosophic school. A mythology even developed that saw early philosopher-Christians prominent enough to address material to Roman emperors: 'Aristides, a most eloquent Athenian philosopher, and a disciple of Christ while yet retaining his philosopher's garb, presented a work to [the emperor] Hadrian. The work contained a systematic statement of our doctrine.'

Tertullian went so far as to say that in his day not wonders and miracles, but only persuasion, caused converts. He claimed that 'all who once hated Christianity because they were ignorant of the nature of what they hated, so soon as they cease to be ignorant of it, leave off hating it. From their number come the Christians; it is on the basis of knowledge, nothing else.' Of course he spoke only of educated men such as himself, and of those rather optimistically. Origen properly noted that miracles were far more persuasive than message.

Not that close argumentation over points of action and belief had ever been absent. Virtually from the beginning of the Christian movement there were arguments over the meaning of a wide range of issues. The writings of Paul illustrate numerous disagreements on dogma and action within the community. For example, some thought that food sacrificed to idols could be eaten safely while others did not. The Gospels themselves embodied differing interpretations of Jesus and his message. Some thought that message was for Jews only while others held that it extended to polytheists as well. This was all in the Jewish tradition of examination and dispute. Once the philosophically inclined began to gain ascendance, the full habit of polytheist philosophical disputation, with its nit-picking, often acrimonious argumentation, strongly asserted itself. As a papyrus from Egypt put it, 'philosophers agree about nothing – one of them even says that silver is black. You can hear more uproar from a household of philosophers than from a household of madmen.' Sometimes disputes led to violent altercations. Artemidorus tells us in passing of Alexander the philosopher who was living the life of an ascetic and was not interested in marriage, business partnerships, wealth or anything else. He got involved in an argument with a Cynic and was hit over the head with a wooden club. Philosophy added a polytheist dimension to the existing disputatious habits taken over with other Jewish traditions.

The intellectual approach to Christianity gained adherents, as the quotation from Tertullian just mentioned indicates. Christian authorities increasingly argued along the lines of a philosophical approach to understanding the world. Christianity was unique because its fundamental truth came by divine intervention, but the techniques of logical arguments that went forth from that truth were philosophical. By the end of the second century we find a much-philosophised Christianity. For example, the epistle to Diognetus is very Platonic, with Christians being the soul in the body of the world. In Diognetus's work there was no mention of the crucifixion or of the resurrection, nor of the ritual of the Eucharist. He wrote as though instruction was what would propagate the faith, as it would for philosophy.

The way of life emphasis of philosophy particularly suited the moral and even theological orientation of early Christianity. When we begin to get apologies (explanations) for Christianity around the middle of the second century, they are often framed as a discussion of competing philosophies, i.e. ways of life.

Hegesippus, writing in the early second century, stated that, while blood relatives and witnesses of Jesus's life survived, Christianity remained 'like a virgin pure and uncorrupted'. But once 'the sacred band of the apostles and the generation of those to whom it had been vouchsafed to hear with their own ears the divine wisdom had reached the several ends of their lives', false doctrines began to proliferate. Polytheist philosophical concepts and categories insinuated themselves into Christian thinking.

In particular, the tendency to assimilate the movement's ideas to known philosophical schools such as Stoicism and Platonism proved irresistible. Stoicism seemed particularly fertile ground. Seneca expressed the sort of sentiment that even led later Christians to forge a correspondence between him and Paul. For example, in correspondence with a friend, Seneca wrote:

We do not need to uplift our hands towards heaven, or to beg the keeper of a temple to let us approach his idol's ear, as if in this way our prayers were more likely to be heard. God is near you, he is with you, he is within you. This is what I mean, Lucilius: a holy spirit indwells within us, one who marks our good and bad deeds, and is our guardian. As we treat this spirit, so are we treated by it. Indeed, no man can be good without the help of god. Can one rise superior to fortune unless god helps him to rise? He it is that gives noble and upright counsel.

The gods, Seneca writes elsewhere, 'neither give nor have evil; but they do chasten and restrain certain persons and impose penalties and sometimes punish by bestowing that which seems good outwardly. Would you win over the gods? Then be a good man. Whoever imitates them, is worshipping them sufficiently.'

Platonism offered a high divinity who fashioned the earth and controlled all in it. This philosophy evolved over the centuries after Plato's death in the fourth century BC. It was extremely influential. It drew in a wide range of thinkers, including some of the Jewish intellectuals. Philo, in particular, had drunk deeply from this well. Many of his writings show an effort to reconcile Jewish traditions about Yahweh, his covenant and the cosmos with Platonic concepts. Platonism taught that every person had a spark or 'daemon' that was potentially connected to the divine essence. It is small wonder that this mode of exploring the relationship of human and divine in the universe appealed to early Christian thinkers as well.

Various philosophical schools had long insisted on the existence of one ultimate deity. Christianity's high god concerned with humanity and its morality fitted well with a philosophical way of life with an emphasis on such a high divinity, beyond human comprehension, singular, but also concerned with humanity and its morality. Note, for example, the Stoic take on reverence according to Epictetus:

Be assured that the essential property of piety towards the gods lies in this, to form right opinions concerning them, as existing, and as governing the universe justly and well. And fix yourself in this resolution, to obey them, and yield to them, and willingly follow them amidst all events, as being ruled by the most perfect wisdom. For thus you will never find fault with the gods, nor accuse them of neglecting you.

This Stoic perspective fits well with the Platonic view as expressed by Apuleius:

It is the goal of wisdom that the wise man should advance to the merit of a god, and that his task will be to approach the conduct of the gods by imitating them in his life; moreover, this will come about for him if he shows himself a perfectly just, pious, and thoughtful man.

Stoic thought also held that a divine spirit was inside every human. Celsus pointed out how the Stoics called their god a spirit, 'diffused through all things, and containing all things within himself'. This, Celsus claimed, was just how Christians saw their god. He also pointed out many similarities to famous philosophers. Indeed, he claimed that Christians had put their words into Jesus's mouth. He wrote,

we are told that Jesus judged the rich with the saying 'It is easier for a camel to go through the eye of a needle than for a rich man to enter the kingdom of god.' Yet we know that Plato expressed this very idea in a purer form when he said, 'It is impossible for an exceptionally good man to be exceptionally rich.'

He also claimed a Platonic source for Jesus's saying, 'Don't resist a man who insults you; even if he strikes you, offer your other cheek as well.' This, supposedly, was taken from Plato, with Socrates stating that 'it is never right to do wrong and never right to take revenge; nor is it right to give evil for evil, or in the case of one who has suffered some injury, to attempt to get even'. Jesus, Celsus claimed, simply took this over when he said, 'Don't resist a man who insults you; even if he strikes you, offer your other cheek as well.'

Tatian in the late second century was, like Justin fifty years earlier, a good example of someone trained in philosophy who converted to Christianity. He began by seeking truth through traditional polytheist approaches to the supernatural, experiencing mystery religions and traditional polytheist worship of such gods as Jupiter and Diana. Finding these wanting, he took up philosophic inquiry, again in search of truth. He chanced upon (so he wrote) the Jewish scriptures. There he found what he was looking for, proof of prophetic power, high-minded social and personal precepts and 'the declaration of the government of the universe as centred on one Being'. In comparing his philosophical investigations with the Hebrew scriptures, he realised that both led to the same place, only that the scriptures took the better route.

> I discerned that the philosophical writings lead to condemnation, but that the Hebrew writings put an end to the slavery that is in the world and rescued us from a multiplicity of rulers and ten thousand tyrants, while they gave us, not indeed what we had not before received, but what we had received through philosophy but were prevented by error from retaining.

Tertullian, also late second to early third century, writes that he had in his hands works that polytheist converts had written tying their pre-conversion polytheistic culture into their new beliefs. They had gathered testimonies of polytheist philosophers, poets and other intellectuals from all of ancient literature. They then showed that Christianity embraced nothing new or monstrous – nothing that could not be supported by existing polytheist writings. This intellectual exercise meant that they could embrace the new approach without abandoning all they had previously learned through cultural heritage and philosophical inquiry. Celsus confirmed that Christian intellectuals 'weave together erroneous opinions drawn from ancient sources, and trumpet them aloud, and sound them before men, as the priests of Cybele clash their cymbals in the ears of those who are being initiated in their mysteries'.

Tatian, Tertullian and Justin were exceptional. Polytheist philosophers generally rejected fundamental claims of Christianity, alienated by the anti-intellectual appeal. Celsus wrote, 'No wise man believes the Gospel, being driven away by the multitudes who adhere to it.' Also, some claims were simply too outlandish to believe. As a philosopher, Celsus, using Platonic concepts, pointed out the absurdity of a god becoming incarnate in human form:

> And I make no new statement, but say what has been long settled. God is good, and beautiful, and blessed, and that in the best and most beautiful degree. But if he come down among men, he must undergo a change, and a change from good to evil, from virtue to vice, from happiness to misery, and from best to worst. Who, then, would make choice of such a change? It is the nature of a mortal,

indeed, to undergo change and remoulding, but of an immortal to remain the same and unaltered. God, then, could not admit of such a change.

For educated persons such as these, the supernatural claims and the authoritative nature of Christianity were hard to accept. As Celsus wrote, 'One ought first to follow reason and a rational guide in accepting doctrines because anyone who believes people without so doing is certain to be deceived.' Philosophy in principle worked by logic and argumentation. Christianity proclaimed divine truths without giving ground to what polytheists considered logical. Not surprisingly, many educated people preferred their traditional approach to life.

The tendency to meld philosophy and the theology of early Christianity removed that faith further and further from what everybody could understand. Tertullian made the soul a witness to things that should persuade a polytheist that Christianity was better. His stated audience was people 'of the road, the street, the work-shop'. Supposedly this was directed at the common people's views – views which were beyond the reach of philosophical argument. However, despite this claim to be directed at the citizenry and their thought processes, his whole treatise was actually yet another intellectual confrontation of polytheist philosophy with Christian views and actions. Fundamentally, philosophy struggled with reconciling theoretically ideal lives with people's everyday experiences in a very real, very challenging world. While some concepts overlapped, such as friendship, courage and justice, the approaches of the intellectual and the ordinary were in fact quite different. An educated leadership was trying to fit Christian thought into moulds that were increasingly distant from the lives of ordinary people.

The movement continued to attract relatively unsophisticated people such as artisans and the poorer members of society. A two-track Christianity began to emerge. One track carried the educated Christian leaders increasingly intent on fitting into the educated polytheist world; the other, everyone else, trying as usual to relate effectively to the supernatural.

Celsus, dismissing Christian attempts to philosophise their religion, claimed that Christians only wanted to convert 'foolish and low individuals, and persons devoid of perception, and slaves, and women, and children'. He claimed that they purposefully rejected the wisdom of educated people. The Christian watchword was, he wrote, 'Let no one come to us who has been instructed, or who is wise or prudent (for such qualifications are deemed evil by us); but if there be any ignorant, or unintelligent, or uninstructed, or foolish persons, let them come with confidence.' Galen, a contemporary of Celsus, agreed: 'Most people are unable to follow any demonstrative argument consecutively; hence they need parables, and benefit from them ... just as now we see the people called Christians drawing their faith from parables and miracles.'

The appeal was to 'only the silly, and the mean, and the stupid, with women and children' and to 'workers in wool and leather, and fullers, and persons of the most uninstructed and rustic character'. Philosophy offered help in forming a successful way of life; why, Celsus asked, should it be rejected? Origen in his turn tried to defend philosophy as legitimate: 'For why is it an evil to have been educated and to have studied the best opinions and to have both the reality and appearance of wisdom? What hindrance does this offer to the knowledge of God? Why should it not rather be an assistance and a means by which one might be better able to arrive at the truth?'

But Christianity, Celsus insisted, rather used disreputable, popular methods to convert. Tricks and deceptions were their stock in trade:

> Christians are sorcerers who flee away with headlong speed from the more polished class of persons, because they are not suitable subjects for our impositions, while they seek to decoy those who are more rustic ... but wherever they see young men, and a mob of slaves, and a gathering of unintelligent persons, thither they thrust themselves in, and show themselves off.

These accusations emphasise that Christianity attracted ordinary people. Preachers tried to proclaim to them in ways they could understand.

Along with an intellectual shift toward philosophical categories came a cultural one. During the first century, adherents had met in small, ad hoc communities awaiting the Second Coming. That event had not happened; the prophecy had failed. Those who did not fall away in disappointment now awaited a delayed final judgement. That meant living in this world indefinitely. They gradually shifted to a long-term organisational structure that could better help members successfully navigate the difficult waters of the polytheistic culture around them. Besides importing the methodology and vision of polytheist philosophies, they also imported the hierarchical leadership structure of the polytheist cultural package.

During the first century, the movement had no set organisation. A charismatic person, Jesus of Nazareth, had proclaimed a future Kingdom of Heaven. Yahweh would reward those who lived in a new covenant according to his ways. At a last judgement he and his son, Jesus, would reward these righteous as well as those who had gone before, punish all others and establish his rule for ever. The resurrection of Jesus proved the truth of the proclamation of the imminent End of Days. In Jerusalem, Jesus's disciples and others who had directly experienced Jesus's life and the miracle of his resurrection lived in anticipation. These 'brothers', as they called themselves, selected leaders based upon an individual's closeness to Jesus. Peter, John and Philip of the original twelve emerged as leaders among those with a personal relationship with Jesus. James and Jude, two of Jesus's brothers, emerged because of their blood relationship to him. The group accepted new leaders when they received clear proof that Yahweh approved. In the case of choosing a substitute disciple to replace the traitorous Judas Iscariot, they relied on casting lots – letting Yahweh decide through those lots. In the case of Paul and others, proof of a miraculous connection between Jesus and a new devotee was sufficient.

Indeed, Paul's example set the tone for leadership since neither new disciples who had travelled with Jesus, nor new blood relatives could possibly appear. Charismatic connection with Jesus became the touchstone for leadership. This meant that anyone who could claim that connection could and often did, claim authority to lead in the new movement. So Paul at Corinth came into competition with Apollos, a person who asserted, exactly as Paul did, authority to interpret what Jesus meant in the lives of followers.

The loosely organised movement of the first century gave way to a structured leadership by the elite. This was not the high elite of the empire – senators and equestrians and local town bigwigs – but the educated class of the movement. Paul had shown the way with his emphasis on a sub-group who had special knowledge and so, presumably, leadership potential. We cannot trace in detail how that sub-group slowly solidified leadership. It was a messy process because Christianity, as was also the habit of Jewish sects and polytheist philosophical schools, fragmented into groups, with different interpretations of who Jesus had been and how his movement should unfold. When the end of the world failed to materialise, this fragmentation continued with renewed energy, as warnings about proliferating heresies recorded in 2 Peter, James and the *Didache* amply attest. Different groups had different structures. Nevertheless, we can see a durable structure of orthodox ('right-thinking') Christianity forming.

The basic organisational outline became clear by the turn of the third century. A tripartite division separated adherents into bishops (high-level leaders), priests and deacons (low-level leaders) and laity (everyone else). During the first century, community meetings focused on three central elements, instructional and inspirational activity, a common meal and the celebration of the Eucharist. Group faith affirmation might include scripture reading and interpretation, baptism and admission of new members, presentation and discussion of contemporary material such as letters from fellow communities, or ecstatic experiences such as speaking in tongues and spontaneous prophecy by members. The meal exemplified the family spirit of the community. The Eucharist ritual affirmed the centrality of Jesus of Nazareth as Lord and Saviour. At first, all participated equally in these activities, sharing both property and resources. Only a loose structure facilitated individual preparation for the end of the world.

Almost immediately the strong cultural pull of both Jewish and polytheistic life worked to undermine and change this situation. From the first, the Christians who gathered together in the diaspora did not establish the truly egalitarian community that existed, Essene-like, among the first expectant followers of Jesus in Jerusalem. Paul's letters paint a picture of a movement struggling against the strong, indeed irrepressible, cultural tendency towards social differentiation and hierarchy. At the community meal, the wealthier, put off by the common fare, had to be admonished not to bring their own, unshared, food. Those same people tried to claim preferential seating at services. By the early second century, the cultural pull towards prestige and status plagued the Christian communities. An author writing under the pseudonym James, the brother of Jesus, admonished:

> My brothers and sisters, believers in our glorious Lord Jesus Christ must not show favouritism. Suppose a man comes into your meeting wearing a gold ring and fine clothes, and a poor man in filthy old clothes also comes in. If you show special attention to the man wearing fine clothes and say, 'Here's a good seat for you,' but say to the poor man, 'You stand there,' or, 'Sit on the floor by my feet,' have you not discriminated among yourselves and become judges with evil thoughts?

The letter of James also preached against 'envy and selfish ambition' that some members were demonstrating. The letter attributed to Jude, another of Jesus's brothers, lashed out against those who 'boast about themselves and flatter others for their own advantage'.

Paul himself fell prey to the hierarchising tendencies of the cultures. He sought to suppress the spontaneity of self-expression at meetings, claiming that excesses like speaking in tongues put off potential converts. He also stressed submission to authority. He used the human body as a metaphor for the community – saying how its various components played important roles in the overall functioning. However, that very image made it clear that some(one) had to be the 'head', while others took non-leadership positions. He also affirmed that some had a deeper understanding of the truths that Jesus represented. For example, he said that those with a deeper knowledge could eat food sacrificed to idols without harm, while less thoughtful followers falsely believed that just eating that food endangered their immortal souls.

In other ways Paul put a premium on special knowledge that only a select few possessed. His argumentation in the letters sometimes wandered into virtually impenetrable verbal thickets reminiscent of philosophical parsing. He was, after all, educated in at least the basics of polytheist culture. This is clear from his allusions to cultural activities such as athletic contests, as well as references to polytheistic literary and philosophical motifs he learned in his basic polytheistic educational exercises. His training as a Pharisee inculcated a belief that some had a greater knowledge of scriptural interpretation than others. He was, as

Eusebius pointed out, 'the most powerful of all in the preparation of argument and the strongest thinker'. Special knowledge meant special leadership privilege. In sum, Paul had a theoretical dedication to a communitarian, egalitarian movement, but his whole life-experience as we know it left him deeply influenced by the hierarchical cultural imaginations of his day, both polytheistic and Jewish.

The group of early Christians who remained focused on Jerusalem and the Judaea-Galilee area had their own organisational trajectory. Peter, James and a few others emerged as leaders. None of these, as far as the tradition tells us, was formally educated, as Paul had been. They had a knowledge of the Jewish scriptures, as had Jesus himself, but there was no indication of instruction within the Jewish environment, much less of extensive exposure to polytheist cultural habits in general. Rather, these men relied upon personal charisma and magic, as Eusebius observed when he wrote:

> Christ's Apostles were but simple men in speech. Though they were indeed bold in the divine and wonder-working power given them by the Saviour, they had neither the knowledge nor the desire to represent the teachings of the Master in persuasive or artistic language, but they used only the proof of the Spirit of God which worked with them, and the wonder-working power of Christ which was consummated through them.

This group huddled together in Jerusalem after the crucifixion and resurrection, awaiting the Second Coming. Subjected to persecution for blasphemy by more traditional Jewish elements, they doubled down on their Jewishness, keeping Jewish feasts, attending temple worship and even trying to force Peter to abjure the relatively benign habit of eating with non-Jews. As in the case of Paul and diaspora Christian groups, the Jerusalem group soon began a gradual shift to a traditional leadership model. The selection of James, Jesus's brother, is an example of bowing to cultural pressure. James was not one of Jesus's disciples – indeed, one tradition states that Jesus's family did not understand or respond to his message. Yet James, along with Mary his mother and Judas his brother, popped up immediately in the aftermath of the crucifixion – he and other family members were part of the small group that the Holy Spirit visited on Pentecost. Passing leadership through family ties was fundamental to Jewish traditions. Kingship was supposed to pass through the line of King David. The Maccabee brothers took turns leading the community during the mid-second century BC and their descendants, the Hasmoneans, clung to the kingship for a century thereafter. During the first century AD, charismatic leaders such as Judas the Galilean passed on the torch of banditry and resistance to Rome through family descent. The high priesthood of the temple was held within a close clan. It was only natural, therefore, for Jesus's male relatives to assume a leadership position alongside those leaders chosen by Jesus himself during his lifetime.

Still, the structure was rather loose. Individuals claiming inspiration from the Holy Spirit proclaimed and prophesied at will. For example, the four daughters of the disciple Philip were all prophets of this sort. Agabus roamed as far as Antioch issuing prophecies, including a prediction of widespread famine, presumably as antecedent to the last days. Secular as well as religious authorities found the community troubling. Prophets such as Agabus were disruptive. King Herod Agrippa of Galilee had James, the brother of John, both disciples of Jesus, beheaded around AD 40. Herod also threatened Peter, but did not punish him.

The Jerusalem community began as a communitarian endeavour. It included Jesus's original group – minus those who had deserted in the aftermath of the crucifixion – as well as people who had witnessed Jesus either in the flesh or resurrected, or had been convinced by miracles or persuasion that Jesus was the Messiah. Movement members described themselves in terms such as 'apostles', 'disciples', 'brethren' and 'the faithful'. After the initial description of this community, we have virtually no knowledge of how the organisation grew and changed in the course of the next forty-odd years. Paul's negotiations with Peter and James during the 40s show that their leadership continued. However, after the destruction of the temple in 70 and the failure of Jesus to return, initiating the last days, the organisational structures of the movement began to change. Christians had fled from Jerusalem across the River Jordan to the town of Pella just before the Romans took and destroyed the city. There, the surviving apostles and disciples (i.e. those people who had direct connection to Jesus) gathered along with Jesus's surviving family members. Acting like a synagogue congregation, they met and selected a new leader. The group unanimously chose Simeon, the son of Clopas – apparently a cousin of Jesus, accepting the tradition that Clopas was Joseph's brother. But this 'cousin' Simeon might actually have been Jesus's brother of the same name. Eusebius deduced that he must have been an eyewitness of Jesus's life, but a close blood relationship to Jesus would have provided his most important credential. With Peter's death, perhaps in the early 60s, the rule of the disciples had died out but the family of Jesus remained influential in the local group – the last physical descendant, a grandson of Jesus's brother, Judas, seems to have lived into the early second century.

The ideal of a Jewish messiah sent to the Jews alone dominated the ideology of the Jerusalem element. They somewhat grudgingly acceded to non-Jewish adherents. They focused on the Jewish population of Judaea-Galilee and on the semi-Jewish Samaritans, although they did range into nearby areas such as Phoenicia, Cyprus and Syria, where they directed their message to Jews living there. Even as late as the early second century, Justus, chosen leader after Simeon, was a Jewish convert to Christianity.

Among the diaspora and non-Jews of the empire, at first the authority of surviving apostles and disciples held sway. John lived in Ephesus, in Asia Minor. He was influential in determining the leadership of Christian groups in the towns of that area. He and other eyewitnesses survived into the second century. Quadratus, a Christian writing in Athens around 120, noted that people who had personally experienced Jesus's miracles 'were real, consisting of those who had been healed of their diseases, those who had been raised from the dead'. These people were a constant presence in the communities; some lived into the second century. Prestige and authority adhered to those who could claim even tangential connection as or to an eyewitness. Ireneaus, for example, a leader of the late second century, sought validation by claiming to have been connected with Polycarp, a martyr of the mid-second century, who had in turn been converted by the apostle and disciple John, and had been 'appointed to the bishopric of the church in Smyrna by the eyewitnesses and ministers of the Lord'.

These diaspora groups included men and women of various talents. Acts recognised prophets and teachers. Paul listed in addition, apostles, miracle workers, healers, interpreters of doctrine and speakers in tongues. The author of the letter to the Ephesians added preachers and shepherds (presumably metaphorical shepherds) to the list. The Mediterranean cultural values of honour and prestige infiltrated the idealistic world of the early communities. Apostles, prophets and so on vied for importance – hence Paul's strong admonishment that they should stop such pettiness. Nonetheless, he prioritised apostles (such as himself), prophets and then teachers.

But authority fragmented as the influential apostles (eyewitnesses) died off. Eusebius idealised the situation, claiming that all was concord, sweetness and light while the apostles lived – but believing and living the truth became much more difficult thereafter as false teachers intruded with their false knowledge. There is some truth to this description. In the welter of claims and counterclaims regarding Jesus and his message, eyewitnesses provided some anchor for deciding among options and for distributing authority in Christian groups. Even in the third generation after Jesus, a man like Papias, Apostolic Father and Bishop of Hierapolis, continued to try to discern a true tradition by relying on eyewitnesses:

> And I shall not hesitate to append to the interpretations all that I ever learnt well from the elders and remember well, for of their truth I am confident. For unlike most I did not rejoice in them who say much, but in them who teach the truth, nor in them who recount the commandments of others, but in them who repeated those given to the faith by the Lord and derived from truth itself; but if ever anyone came who had followed the elders, I inquired into the words of the elders, what Andrew or Peter or Philip or Thomas or James or John or Matthew, or any other of the Lord's disciples, had said, and what Aristion and the elder John, the Lord's disciples, were saying. For I did not suppose that information from books would help me so much as the word of a living and surviving voice.

But for the less conscientious, with the eyewitnesses and their immediate successors gone from the scene, the floodgates of inspiration and deception opened wide. Anyone claiming a vision or other spiritual connection to Jesus and his father could proclaim even the most outrageous message. The movement faced centrifugal destruction.

Contrary to the later rosy view, already in the age of the apostles Paul had had to fend off what he considered false doctrine. The Jerusalem church endeavoured to wield central authority over some matters, for example over the question of whether a non-Jewish convert to Christianity had to be physically circumcised, but independent agents went their own way. Once the first generation passed from the scene, doctrinal discipline became ever more difficult to maintain. Early in the second century someone writing under the pseudonym 'Paul' admonished:

> These are the things you are to teach and insist on. If anyone teaches otherwise [than what I write] and does not agree to the sound instruction of our Lord Jesus Christ and to godly teaching, they are conceited and understand nothing. They have an unhealthy interest in controversies and quarrels about words that result in envy, strife, malicious talk, evil suspicions and constant friction between people of corrupt mind, who have been robbed of the truth and who think that godliness is a means to financial gain.

A subsequent letter harps on the same thing:

> Preach the word; be prepared in season and out of season; correct, rebuke and encourage – with great patience and careful instruction. For the time will come when people will not put up with sound doctrine. Instead, to suit their own desires, they will gather around them a great number of teachers to say what their itching ears want to hear. They will turn their ears away from the truth and turn aside to myths.

Writing pseudonymously as 'Peter', an early Christian loosed a bitter, abusive screed against false prophets and false teachers: 'They are like unreasoning animals, creatures of instinct, born only to be caught and destroyed, and like animals they too will perish.' The *Didache* emphasised again and again the need to vet carefully people coming to the community with claims to apostolic or prophetic talents – these latter seem to have taken up the scam of posing as prophets in order to be taken in, fed and housed by Christian communities.

In this environment the only way for a group to survive was to endorse an authority that could separate wheat from chaff and cast the waste into the fire. Of course, one person's wheat was another person's chaff, but agreement within a particular group made possible the expulsion of the unorthodox and the strengthening of the orthodox, whatever 'orthodox' might mean. Apostles and prophets, at least, were beyond the control of any local group because they claimed authority directly from the Holy Spirit. The synagogue (from the Jewish tradition) and the association (from the polytheist tradition) provided a more controllable authority scheme. In both cases the group chose its leader or leaders, controlled its membership, agreed upon procedural rules and so on. So the president of an association, or a synagogue head, became a teacher and general overseer (bishop) in a Christian context; a board of senior members became elders (presbyters); while assistants in organising activities and taking care of daily business were servants (deacons). The general membership became the people (laity). Since at first there was no central authority to control how individual groups organised themselves, different communities had different permutations of this organisation. For example, in some groups the bishop was simply the chief elder. The general scheme does, however, replace the agency of apostles, prophets and teachers of earlier days.

Ignatius, leader of the Antioch community of Christians at the turn of the first to second centuries AD, advocated the strongly hierarchical bishop-deacon-laity authority model that would become standard in Christian groups empire-wide. Paul had stated that Jesus was the 'head' of any Christian group. Ignatius said that the bishop, to whom God delegated power, now took that place. This delegated divine authority gave him (and it was always a man) complete control over the central rites of the Christian community: initiation (baptism), the communal feast (agape) and the central cultic act (the Eucharist). 'Let no one do anything pertaining to the church without the bishop's consent.'

About the same time, Clement of Rome in a letter to the Christians in Corinth set out the principle that a bishop was not only chosen by a congregation but also explicitly authorised by other bishops who had, in turn, been authorised by previous bishops going back to the eyewitness disciples and apostles. This line of authority reaching back in theory to Jesus himself was intended to guarantee the legitimacy and force of a bishop's actions and words. The second and third centuries saw a battle

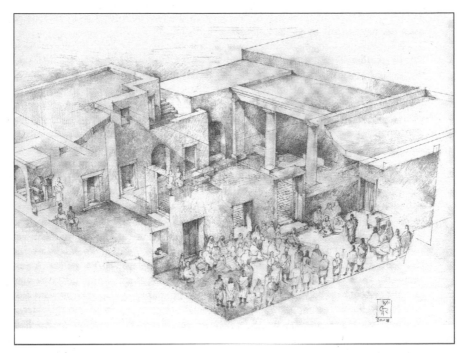

16. An imaged Christian assembly in the building discovered in Dura-Europos.

waged by bishops against the competing authority of 'prophets' and other charismatics who claimed independent authority to define and carry out Christian doctrine.

The emergence of bishops and elders and deacons as leaders marked the beginning of systematic differentiation within the movement. It only gained momentum. The agape meal as a community-participant common event disappeared towards the end of the second century. At the same time, the Eucharist performed and controlled by the leadership replaced the Eucharist as a community event embedded in the agape meal. Now, the rest of the people assembled looked on as the leaders performed the Eucharistic ritual. The formalisation of the Eucharist was modelled on the procedures and space of the Roman law court. There, spectators standing before a raised dais for the magistrate set the tone. The magistrate presided over a formal procedure. The priest claimed this function in the earliest church buildings, remodelled private homes with the congregation seated or standing in front of him. But by the end of the third century Christians had begun to adopt a very useful public building plan, the basilica. Here a long central nave allowed spectators to assemble while a presiding magistrate seated himself on a dais in front of a curved background that provided good acoustics for his pronouncements. In a way, the Church was taking over the whole hierarchical governmental structure of the Greco-Roman town: the bishop was chief magistrate; the elders were the wealthy members of the town council; the laity were the plebs. In the fine churches that began to be built in the later third century, bishops addressed an audience of wealthy adherents who represented perhaps the upper 5 per cent of all Christians – we know because their sermon references clearly mark out just such an audience. The seizure of the central Christian sacraments by the community's educated leadership and the focus of that leadership on people like themselves was symptomatic of a movement shifting away from the centrality of the general population.

But the people did not give up so easily. In fact, they did not succumb to the new organisational and leadership model. The tailors and weavers and women and children – those so disparaged by the likes of Celsus – did not supinely submit to the hierarchisation of Christianity by means of the institution of a hierarchical leadership, dedicated buildings, carefully defined sacraments, specified rituals and scriptural priorities. Ramsay MacMullen has shown how archaeology and scattered texts can reveal this two-track Christianity. About 5 per cent of Christians found satisfaction in a Christianity that replicated the familiarities of polytheist religion in a new guise – leadership of an elite, hierarchical distribution of rights and privileges, financial support and control by the better off. The elite found satisfaction because it continued these social and economic habits they held in common with the polytheists. They also continued their traditional derision of the lesser beings in their field of vision. Admonished to care for the poor and socially disadvantaged in sermon after sermon, they in fact cared little for any truly egalitarian, much less social revolutionary, advocacy within a Christian tradition that would have allowed it, had they cared.

The second track saw the rest of the population in their own way taking the same path. That is, they adhered to a Christianity that continued their old polytheistic ways as much as possible. As to the worship

17. Dancing at a festival of Isis. Aricia, Italy.

venues of the better off, the very small size of church structures proves that large numbers of worshippers never gathered within them. When the leaders worshipped in their purpose-built structures led by a recognised clergy, those allowed into the relatively constrained spaces could shuffle in, stand at the sides or in the back of the worship space and participate by meekly listening to a priest or bishop admonishing their betters – if they could understand the Greek of the service at all. Where was the raucousness, the food, the sociability that so often went with polytheistic sacrificial ceremonies followed by free food and drink – a real feast? It had existed in the beginning for Christians. The agape meal from the very first, as we know from Paul's admonitions, provided the opportunity for excessive eating, drinking and raucous argument. As the more sedate elite gained control, the agape meal disappeared from the repertoire of Christian activity by the later second century. No food, no drink, no outlandish behaviour: Churches did not appeal to most people. In fact, churches were not meant for ordinary people and ordinary people's Christianity did not centre on the churches. They

18. An imaged family burial celebration in Tipasa, North Africa.

gathered elsewhere. The 'elsewhere' were the cemeteries outside the walls of every town.

Even without worked-out ideas of life after death, people felt a close connection with those who had gone before. People maintained the link between generations by gathering at the gravesite of a forebear. Remembrance at the grave followed ritual burial. They regularly returned to the burial place. There the living shared a meal and poured a libation for the dead. For the poor, it might be a modest picnic. For others, there might be a permanent structure where the family regularly gathered. On days commonly recognised to remember the dead, crowds gathered in the cemeteries, each participant to commemorate his or her own links to the past. Such gatherings often turned into wholesale celebrations of family. Visiting and remembering went on year after year. Libations were poured, presuming some actual presence of the deceased. Prayers were offered. Raucous meals followed with much drinking, singing and dancing, often through the night.

Christians retained this habit. Burial customs remained much the

19. A Christian funerary offering plate from Sardinia, fourth century AD. Note the polytheist formula D.M. (*Dis Manibus* = 'to the spirits of the dead') at the top flanked by Christian chi-rho symbols and also the chi-rho Christian symbol at the bottom.

same before and after a population became Christian, although the explanations understood for those customs changed. People threw away the old, polytheistic relationships to the supernatural in favour of a new god and his son, resurrected from the dead and presiding over an antici-pated End Time when the living and the dead would be reunited in a victorious, glorious heavenly kingdom. But their actions in burying and remembering the dead continued as before. Recognition of the spirits of the dead (*Di Manes*) appeared via the initials 'DM' on thousands of polytheist gravestones over the centuries. There are hundreds of Chris-tian gravestones with the same 'DM' – somewhat astonishing, until you realise that Christians continued polytheistic habits of commemoration of the dead. For example:

Here lies a dear and pious wife, Yugia, fully committed to her husband. Because of her funeral, we grieve wholeheartedly. I,

Cominienus Amantius, prepared this eternal home for the two of us. May your holy *manes*, we ask, be present so that always and freely we can sing psalms to you. Aurelia Yugia lived 38 years, 4 months, 2 days. She was a firm companion for her husband 24 years, 4 months, 2 days. She was buried the day before the first of May, in the fourth year of rule of the emperors Valentinian and Valens [368].

In another example, a chi-rho, the first two Greek letters of *Christ* and so a Christian symbol, is etched below this epitaph: 'To the immortal powers (*Di Manes*). Valeria Rode saw to it that this be built for Valeria Rode, her very dear and well deserving mother.' And this late fourth century epitaph mixed polytheist symbols with a Christian message:

To the Underworld Spirits (*Di Manes*). I, his wife, set this up from my own resources to the resting spirit of Karissimus, a stalwart supporter of all his friends, a servant of the poor's needs. By the mercy of Christ he lived a good life in all ways. He lived 65 years, 3 months, and 12 days. Rest in peace.

The martyrs of the faith attracted the sort of remembrance and celebration appropriate for important members of the larger Christian family. These particular dead had shown exemplary strength and courage. In fact, they had supernatural power derived from their heroically faithful fate, their sacrifice in Christ's service. With that power, they became intermediates between the human and the superhuman. So celebrations at martyrs' graves were also the time to ask a favour or to seek a miracle from these powerful dead. Clergy in vain attempted to control these festive outpourings of devotion. A priest named Vigilantius, writing in the fourth century, complained that Christians mimicked polytheistic habits as they worshipped relics of the martyrs:

Why do you pay such honour, not to say adoration, to the relic, whatever it may be, which you carry about in a little vessel and worship? Why do you kiss and adore a bit of powder wrapped up in a cloth? Under the cloak of religion we see what is all but a polytheist ceremony introduced into the churches: while the sun is still shining,

20. An imaged martyr's memorial service.

heaps of tapers are lighted, and everywhere a paltry bit of powder, wrapped up in a costly cloth, is kissed and worshipped. Great honour do men of this sort pay to the blessed martyrs.

Elite patrons increasingly poured money into formal structures enhancing a martyr's gravesite, seeking to seize and control this aspect of worship as well. But people went on with their celebrations and devotions at the graves.

The examples of Christian habits of worship and relationship to supernatural powers that mimicked polytheistic habits could be greatly multiplied. Augustine, like many other elites, railed against Christians who continued with polytheistic habits, people who proclaimed, 'I certainly go to idols, I consult demoniacs and soothsayers – but nevertheless I do not deny the Church of God; I am a Catholic.' The basic point is clear. In the eyes of the elite, whether polytheist or Christian, the people were poorly educated, given to raucous behaviour, dressed badly and generally were dolts and boors. In their own eyes, these people were following well-trodden paths in their desire to bring to bear supernatural power on their contingent lives. The tension between the elite track and the popular track in Christianity continued well past the time of Constantine and the coming of a religion of empire, even to the present day.

Christianity en avant

In the world of ideas, Christianity consciously, by the fourth century AD, had wedded philosophy ('wisdom') and cult. To paraphrase Lactantius, a Christian philosopher: in our worship we ought to be wise like philosophers, i.e. we ought to discover the proper object and mode of worship and in our worship we ought to carry out that knowledge by deed and action. The educated could understand this and relate to it. But as from the very first days, the movement continued to have popular appeal. Disregarding the increasing separation of the leadership and thought from the people's lives, they went about their daily affairs attuned, as always, to approaches and beliefs that proved effective. As the educated moved towards polytheist intellectual approaches and attitudes, and as they adapted to the culture of elite leadership, ordinary people, in the words of Ramsay MacMullen, 'made the least possible tear in the fabric of already held beliefs'. This meant that many polytheistic practices were covered by Christianised understandings. Their needs for the supernatural were now met by a Christianity going forward into the brave new world of acceptability, then dominance in the West for the next millennia.

Such changes were not instantaneous. Christianity did not assume the wardrobe of the polytheists immediately or entirely. The habits of the elite as leaders in education, birth and wealth did nestle into the new faith, but not quickly or universally, by any means. The conversions by 'signs, miracles, prophecies', as Tertullian says, continued but fell far short of convincing more than a small minority in the towns, and practically no one in the countryside. The movement's crucial moment came when Constantine saw a cross in the sky, defeated his enemy Maxentius under its miraculous power and decided that he had found a very powerful god indeed. Embraced by a powerful patron, Christianity quickly gained the adherence of an important component of the polytheist elite of the empire. From there in less than a hundred years the movement begun among commoners on the shores of the Sea of Galilee moved to complete imperial ascendency. Along the way, from its Jewish roots grew a lush greenery that fitted well into the polytheist landscape. Adjusting to the needs of ordinary people as well as elites, 'the Christian culture that would emerge in late antiquity carried more of the genes of its "pagan" ancestry than of the peculiarly Christian mutations'.

Throughout the Jewish, polytheist and early Christian traditions, people desired results from their relationships with their gods. In the Jewish tradition, a desire for social justice as well as for immediate solutions to immediate problems combined to make some open to a new, powerful interpretation, one based on the divine sonship of one of their own, a sonship proven by supernatural deeds. For polytheists, the appearance of a charismatic leader with supernatural powers was sufficient to turn some to a message that rejected core elements of their traditional approaches to the gods. For early Christians, the conviction that their time had come, that following their divine, martyred leader's message and prophecies would gain them eternal life and vengeance against their earthly enemies, proved overwhelmingly persuasive – persuasive enough to reject both core Jewish and polytheistic beliefs and live in a sometimes hostile cultural environment, awaiting final vindication. The failure of Jesus's main prophecy affected potential recruits among Jews and polytheists, as well as already convicted believers in the early Christian communities. There had been no miraculous reappearance, as promised. Rather than die right then and there, the movement was able gradually over the second century AD to transform itself into a shape that was recognisable and sometimes acceptable to elite and ordinary polytheists alike. It could then hang on until the miracle of the cross in the sky saved it for another day.

VALEDICTORY

PEOPLE IN THE ANCIENT WORLD maintained a deep connection with the supernatural. Powers could help or destroy. Success in life depended on a fruitful relationship. Cultural tradition determined what personal behaviour, prayer, ritual, sacrifice, or magic might persuade the supernatural to be benign. Danger lurked for those who left the well-trodden path. In the Jewish tradition, deviation invited Yahweh's wrath. Polytheists had a wider range of possibilities, but denial of the gods themselves brought disintegration of family and community life. Yet in the first century AD some Jews and polytheists broke with their traditions. Jesus of Nazareth in his lifetime demonstrated to his followers by magic and miracle that he spoke as a god. He promised them reward in this life and a happy immortality in the next. After his death his disciples and apostles were also reported to have performed miracles and magic. They proclaimed their message to Jews and polytheists. Magic, miracles and message convinced still more to change from traditional ways.

Jewish and polytheist traditionalists strongly opposed the new movement. Disaster in Judaea shook it free from Jewish roots; failed prophecy seemed to doom it. Reorientation saved it. Christianity was flexible enough to meet the most basic needs of polytheist people. It melded human and superhuman powers into tools to deal with life. It showed itself a supernatural force powerful enough to bring people out of their traditional ways. Miracles and magic continued to prove their worth among people. The educated worked Christianity's message into an acceptable, philosophical way of life. People incorporated it into their daily religious habits.

By the end of the third century Christianity had become a movement with an organisational structure, theology and popular appeal. Perhaps as many as 10 per cent of urban dwellers and 3 per cent of rural inhabitants believed in one way or another. In all likelihood the movement would have continued as one option among many in the polytheist world, no better, no worse than others, appealing to a few but hardly to all. Constantine's cross in the sky cancelled that trajectory. Instead, Christianity became an imperial religion. Its appeal and spread no longer depended on meeting the people's needs through demonstrations of power. Top down replaced bottom up. Hand in hand with empire, it began its march through history, Christ's triumphant return and the end of time always receding before it. Supernatural power remained at the centre, but now in the service of a much grander movement than Jesus of Nazareth could ever have imagined as magic and miracles proved his authority to proclaim salvation for the righteous in the dust and heat of far-off Judaea.

WHO'S WHO AND WHAT'S WHAT

Abraham	Hebrew patriarch traditionally dated to around 2000 BC. Isaac was his son, Jacob his grandson.
Adiabene	A small kingdom located in the upper reaches of the Tigris valley.
Aelius Aristides	A Greek orator and writer (AD 117–81). Besides being a great orator, he is known as the most famous hypochondriac of antiquity. He spent long periods seeking cures from the healing god Asclepius.
Albinus	Lucceius Albinus, Procurator of Judaea AD 62–4.
Alexander	Tiberius Julius Alexander, Procurator of Judaea about AD 46–8.
Alexander of Abonoteichus	A charismatic magician, oracle and fraud from northern Asia Minor. In the second century AD he used the prop of a tame snake to issue oracles in the name of Asclepius. He established a cult and gained followers.
Ananias, Jesus ben	A charismatic Jewish prophet who predicted the destruction of Jerusalem in the mid-60s AD.
Antioch	The major city of Syria, the third largest city in the Roman Empire in the first century AD.

apocalypse	*Apokalypsis* means a 'disclosure', a 'revealing'. It comes to have the more specific meaning, derived from the most famous apocalyptic work, the Book of Revelation, of a prediction of disaster, particularly one leading to the end of the world.
Apocrypha	*Apokruphos* means 'hidden' or 'obscure'. In post-antiquity usage, 'obscure' came to mean 'of dubious authenticity'. The Apocrypha are religious books such as Judith and first and second Maccabees that some believers hold to be 'of doubtful authenticity' compared to the canonical books of the Bible. It is now used of the many early Christian works claiming to be inspired but not included in the canon – works such as the Acts of Peter or the Gospel of Thomas.
Apuleius	A rhetorician and novelist of the second century AD. He was a Platonist and a devotee of several mystery cults. His work, *Metamorphoses* (*The Golden Ass*), focuses on the evils of magic and the saving powers of the goddess Isis. It contains the best description of conversion in polytheist literature.
Artemidorus	Greek author of the second century AD. He wrote a book about the interpretation of dreams.
Athenagoras	A philosopher and convert to Christianity who lived in the later second century AD. He wrote an *Apology* defending Christianity in philosophic terms.
Baal	A Semitic word meaning 'Lord'. It became applied to gods, especially Hadad, the high god of the Canaanites.
Bannus	A charismatic desert teacher who had Josephus as one of his students. Probably he was an Essene.
Ben Sirach	See Sirach.
Celsus	A Roman philosopher who wrote a scathing and knowledgeable attack on Christianity in the late second century AD called *The True Word*. It survives only in fragments as quoted by Origen in his refutation.

charisma
: Charisma is a personal essence deriving from a special relationship with the supernatural. This essence brings a charismatic person out of the ordinary and allows him or her to access supernatural power.

Clement of Rome
: A bishop of Rome in the late first and early second centuries AD. He wrote a letter that survives in which he admonished Christians in Corinth about obedience in church governance.

Cumanus
: Ventidius Cumanus, Procurator of Judaea AD 48–52.

Cynicism
: A philosophical movement begun by Antisthenes, a follower of Socrates, and best exemplified by Diogenes of Sinope (fourth century BC). The main tenet was that people should live according to Nature, which was interpreted to mean contrary to conventional social life. Cynic philosophers therefore criticised conventions such as wealth and sexual pleasure and advocated a simple life of begging and preaching, often in a confrontational manner.

Daniel
: The Book of Daniel is a piece of historical fiction dating to the second century BC. The titular author is a Jew living in Babylon during the Exile following a supposed defeat of a Jewish king in 606 BC. There are six discrete tales in the work. His loyal adherence to the law during his exile becomes his hallmark. He receives divine visions of a final apocalypse.

David
: The first king of a united Kingdom of Israel (in the north) and Judah (in the south). His rule is given traditionally as 1010–970 BC. He made Jerusalem his capital city.

Day of Atonement
: Yom Kippur, the Day of Atonement, is an autumn Jewish festival of repentance and atonement, looking forward to the coming year which begins ten days before, at Rosh Hashanah.

Deuteronomy
: The fifth book of the Torah.

Didache	'Teaching of the Twelve Apostles'. This non-canonical work dates from the end of the first or beginning of the second century AD. It is a Jewish-Christian guide for the community of the faithful. It deals with ethics, rituals and organisation.
Dio Chrysostom	A Greek philosopher, orator and historian of the later first and early second centuries AD. His eclectic philosophical bent is representative of the 'way of life' direction philosophy took in the second century AD.
Diognetus	Recipient of a letter from one Mathetes ('Disciple'). The composition is an apologistic defence of Christianity written in the later second century AD.
Ecclesiasticus	See Sirach.
Egyptian, The	A charismatic Jewish leader in the 50s AD.
Eleazar	A Jewish martyr during the Maccabean period. He chose to die rather than to betray his duty to Yahweh by eating pork.
Elijah	A Hebrew prophet in the Kingdom of Israel during the ninth century BC. He performed miracles. Rather than death, he experienced assumption to heaven in a chariot of fire uplifted by a whirlwind. He will return to earth. The much later prophet Malachi has Yahweh promise, 'See, I will send the prophet Elijah to you before that great and dreadful Day of the Lord comes.'
Enoch	According to Hebrew tradition, the great-grandfather of Noah. He did not die, but was taken up into Heaven. As an angel, he became Yahweh's right-hand man and a potent access point for cosmic knowledge. His prestigious name was taken by the authors of three non-canonical Books of Enoch. 1 Enoch dates from the third–first centuries BC; 2 Enoch to the first century AD; 3 Enoch to the fifth century AD. Probably none is a single composition. 1 Enoch, for example, may have as many as nine discrete sections, including matters such as cosmic astronomy, human morality and the End of Days.

Epicureans
: A philosophical movement begun by the Greek, Epicurus (341–270 BC). Self-sufficiency was the way to happiness; being at peace with oneself, free from fear and pain, was the goal. Gods are not an important part of human life; they do not reward good and punish evil; death is the dissolution of atoms.

eschatology
: *Eschatos* means 'last'. Eschatology deals with events of the 'Last Days', the end of the world as we know it and the initiation, whether violent or peaceful, of another, supernatural, existence.

Essenes
: A Jewish movement of the second century BC to the first century AD. Individually and in communities, Essenes emphasised withdrawal from normal social interaction and concentration on ritual cleanliness as the avenue to righteousness and ultimate favour from Yahweh at the End of Days.

Eusebius
: The earliest (about AD 260–340) historian of the Christian church whose work, the *Ecclesiastical History*, is extant in full. He wrote in the early fourth century AD under Emperor Constantine. His work contains important quotations from earlier, now lost, sources on the early years of the movement.

Exile
: Twice the Jewish nation was vanquished and part of the population destroyed or exiled. The Assyrians deported most of the northern peoples after 722 BC. The Babylonians deported the elite after 586 BC. The term 'post-exilic' refers to the period after the 586 event.

Exodus
: The second book of the Torah.

Ezekiel
: A prophet of the seventh to sixth centuries BC. He predicted the fall of Jerusalem, as did Jeremiah. Then he was one of the men deported to Babylon after the city was captured in 587 BC.

Fadus
: Cuspius Fadus, Procurator of Judaea AD 44–6.

Felix
: Antonius Felix, Procurator of Judaea AD 52–8.

Festus
: Porcius Festus, Procurator of Judaea AD 60–62.

Florus
: Gessius Florus, Procurator of Judaea AD 64–6.

Galen	A Greek physician and intellectual of the later second century AD.
Galilee	A geographical area in the northern portion of Palestine.
Gallio	Lucius Junius Gallio Annaeanus was Governor of Achaea (which included the city of Corinth) in AD 51–2. He heard Jewish complaints against Paul. He was the famous Seneca's brother.
god-fearers	Polytheists attracted to the Jewish traditions but not actually converted to Judaism.
Great Revolt	In AD 66 a combination of religious fervour and elite in-fighting impelled some of the Jews in Judaea to revolt from Rome. This movement gained momentum and despite many setbacks the rebels held out until the destruction of their last stronghold, Masada, in 73. Jerusalem itself was taken and destroyed after a siege by the Romans in 70. Josephus gives us a detailed although prejudiced account in his *History of the Jewish War*.
Hasidim	'Pious ones'. A personal characteristic becomes a label, just as those especially zealous for Yahweh became known as Zealots in the first century AD. Hasidim felt that righteousness came from close adherence to the Torah's strictures.
Hasmoneans	The name of the family that included the Maccabees. Asamoneus was supposedly the great-grandfather of Mattathias, father of Judas Maccabeus and his brothers. The Hasmonean dynasty supplied kings to Judaea from about 167 until the Romans installed Herod the Great as king in 37 BC.
Hebrews	Descendants of Abraham are conventionally called 'Hebrews' until the destruction of the temple in Jerusalem by Babylonians in 587 BC. Thereafter by convention the term 'Jew' is used. See also Israelites, Jews.
Hegesippus	A second-century Christian who wrote against heresies. The work survives in only eight quotations in Eusebius's history of the early Christian church.

Hemerobaptists	'Daily baptisers'. One of the sects within first century AD Judaic traditions. Their name comes from the fact that they used a purificatory bath every day.
Herod Antipas	Son of Herod the Great. Appointed by the Romans to govern Galilee and neighbouring Perea, AD 6–39.
Herod the Great	King of Judaea 37–4 BC. With the aid of the Romans he displaced the Hasmonean dynasty and ruled with lavishness and oppression. His remodelling of the temple in Jerusalem made it one of the wonders of the ancient world.
Hippolytus	A Christian writer of the third century AD. His *Refutation of all Heresies* described early Christian aberrations.
Ignatius	A Christian leader and early martyr from Antioch in Syria. He lived during the later first and early second centuries AD. He wrote letters in which he discussed church organisation and sacraments.
Irenaeus	A second-century Christian apologist and theologian.
Isaac	Hebrew patriarch traditionally dated to around 1900 BC. Abraham was his father, Jacob his son.
Isaiah	Writings by a group of Hebrew prophets whose works were united in a single prophetic Book of Isaiah in the fifth or fourth century BC. It is possible that some material (chapters 1–39) goes back to an actual man named Isaiah in the eighth century BC. Other material dates from the mid-seventh century BC while the final portion was written in the context of the Babylonian destruction of the temple in 587 BC.
Isis	A major divinity in Egyptian religion. During the Hellenistic and Roman periods she assimilated other goddesses (Demeter, Aphrodite, etc.) to herself and assumed a position as supreme (mother) goddess. Her cult was widespread and very popular.
Israelites	The descendants of Jacob, grandson of the first patriarch, Abraham. Jacob was called 'Israel' and so his descendants became 'Israelites'. See also Hebrews, Jews.
Jacob (Israel)	Hebrew patriarch traditionally dated to around 1700 BC. Abraham was his grandfather, Isaac his father.

Jeremiah	A prophet of the late seventh and early sixth centuries BC.
Jews	In the tenth century BC, Judah was the southern Hebrew kingdom, Israel being the northern. It much later became the Roman province of Judaea. Its inhabitants were therefore 'Jews'. See also Hebrews, Israelites. The usage becomes muddled after 587 BC when descendants of Jacob in the diaspora were called 'Jews', even though they did not live in Judaea. In that sense it does not reflect a place name, but a cultural designation.
Job	The Book of Job is a work of fiction designed to probe the fundamental issue of theodicy, why bad things happen to good people if Yahweh is omnipotent, omniscient and benevolent.
John the Baptist	A charismatic Jewish leader active about AD 30.
Josephus of Jerusalem	Josephus (AD 37–c.100) was a Jewish leader and historian. After going over to the Romans during the Great Revolt (AD 66–73), he went to Rome where he composed works on Jewish traditions and culture as well as his narration of that Revolt and its causes.
judge	In early Hebrew history, a leader chosen by consensus to provide leadership and conflict resolution to fellow Israelites.
Justin Martyr	An early Christian apologist of the second century AD. His writings defended the Christian movement against its Jewish critics and justified its morality to polytheists.
Leviticus	The third book of the Torah.
Middle Platonism	A version of Platonism that melded philosophical ideas of its day, the first century BC to the third century AD. Ideas from the Peripatetics (followers of Aristotle's notions) and from the Stoics combined with basic ideas of Platonism. Matter and the body were evil, while the soul was immortal and could unite with the soul of the universe (God). Freedom of will meant that humans could choose (or not) to follow their soul-ness rather than the evils of the material world.

Mishnah	A collection of material attributed to Jewish teachers (rabbis). The collection aims to offer interpretations of the Jewish oral traditions. It was assembled early in the second century AD.
Mithras	A god arisen, probably, from the area of Persia. His cult was adapted and adopted within the Roman Empire as a mystery religion, especially by soldiers and merchants. Its theology is poorly understood.
mystery religions	Religious activities that contained a special knowledge as part of their teaching and practice. Those with the knowledge participated as initiates (*mystai*) in the cultic events. The Eleusinian Mysteries in Attica were the most famous, but numerous cults of this sort existed throughout the Greco-Roman world. Keeping the special knowledge secret from the uninitiated was a crucial element in these cults.
Numbers	The fourth book of the Torah.
Origen	A Christian philosopher of the late second and third centuries. He wrote a refutation of the polytheist Celsus who had, in turn, written a skilful attack on Christianity in the 170s.
Palestine	In the ancient world, this was the area east-west between the Mediterranean Sea and a strip of land east of the River Jordan and north-south from just beyond the Sea of Galilee to the south of Jerusalem. The name comes from the Philistines, inhabitants of part of this territory from the twelfth century BC. The Greeks called it Palaistina, while the Romans in the second century AD ceased calling the area Judaea, renaming it Syria Palaestina.
Passover Feast	Hebrew Pesach. The spring Jewish festival celebrating the liberation of the Hebrews from slavery in Egypt.
Pentateuch	See Torah.
Pentecost	See Weeks Feast.
Pharisees	A school of Jewish thought and action. They focused on the interpretation of the Torah and living out its instructions as fully as possible. Later, rabbinic tradition emerged from Pharisaic thought and action.

Philo of Alexandria	Philo lived from about 25 BC to AD 50 in the Jewish diaspora. He was an intellectual and a leader in the Jewish community in Alexandria, Egypt. Highly educated, he melded material from the Hebraic tradition with that of the Hellenistic world around him.
Platonism	A philosophical movement founded by Plato in the fourth century BC.
Pliny the Elder	A Roman polymath of the first century AD. His encyclopaedia offers wide-ranging information and insights regarding the Greco-Roman world of this time. He died near Pompeii while investigating the eruption of Mount Vesuvius in AD 79.
Pliny the Younger	A Roman senator, governor and epistalographer (AD 61–c.113). His correspondence with Emperor Trajan provides us with the earliest certain reference to Christians by a Roman author. A contemporary of Tacitus and Suetonius.
Plutarch	A Greek prose writer (c.AD 46–120). He composed history, biography and philosophy.
polytheism	Polytheism has almost infinite variety; there is no unified theology beyond the belief in many gods.
Porphyry	A neoplatonic philosopher of the third century. He attacked Christians and philosophical Christianity in a lost work, *Against the Christians,* that survives only in quotations from Christian authors refuting his arguments.
Pythagoras	A Greek philosopher, mathematician, mystic and magician of the sixth century BC. He believed in the transmigration of souls.
Quadratus (1)	A Christian apologist of the late first and early second centuries AD. His work survives only in quotations by later authors.
Quadratus (2)	Gaius Ummidius Durmius Quadratus, governor of Syria in 52 BC when he marched into Samaria and put down unrest.
Quintilius	Publius Sulpicius Quintilius, Roman governor of Syria with authority over Judaea, AD 6–12. He conducted a census in Judaea that caused an uprising.

Sadducees	The hereditary priestly cast in Judaea.
Samaritan, The	A charismatic Jewish leader in AD 36.
Samaritans	Inhabitants of the land between Judaea to the south and Galilee to the north. The population is a combination of Israelites and immigrants who arrived after the destruction of the Kingdom of Israel in 722 BC. They practised a version of Judaism that focused on Yahweh's presence on Mount Gerizim, in Samaria.
Scribes	A group within the Jewish community whose original task of copying the Torah and other religious documents led to their being experts in the interpretation of the Mosaic Law.
Second Temple Period	The Babylonians destroyed the first temple of Yahweh in Jerusalem in 587 BC. A replacement temple was rebuilt with the permission of the Persian overlords in the later sixth century. Destroyed again by the Romans in AD 70, the time between the construction and destruction of the second temple is called the Second Temple Period.
Seneca	A Roman philosopher and political figure of the first century AD.
Shavuot	See Weeks Feast.
Simon Magus	A Samaritan wonder-worker who lived in the first century AD.
Sirach	Ben Sirach's book of ethical teachings dates to the second century BC. It is also called the Book of Ecclesiasticus – not to be confused with the Book of Ecclesiastes.
Solomon	Kind David's son and the second king of Israel (traditionally 970–931 BC). He built the first temple of Yahweh in Jerusalem.
Stoicism	A philosophical movement founded in the third century BC. Stoics believed that living a virtuous life – one in accordance with Nature – led to happiness. Stoics valued highly self-control and strength in adversity. Imperviousness to the blandishments of wealth and success as well as to the evils of pain and suffering led to a happy life.

Suetonius	A Roman biographer (about AD 69 to sometime after 122). Little remains of his prolific works, but his multi-biographical *Twelve Caesars* is a fundamental source for the period of early Christianity. A contemporary of Tacitus and Pliny the Younger.
Sukkot	See Tabernacles, Feast of.
Syrus	Publilius Syrus, a first-century BC former slave; author and compiler of Roman moral sayings.
Tabernacles, Feast of	Hebrew Sukkot. The autumn Jewish festival celebrating the harvest of fruit.
Tacitus	A Roman senator and historian (about AD 56 to sometime after 117). His works deal with the first century AD, including parts of the Jewish wars. His account of the fire at Rome and the punishment of Christians in 64 is a classic document of early Christianity. A contemporary of Pliny the Younger and Suetonius.
Talmud	A compendium of material in the Mishnah and the commentaries on the Mishnah called the Gemara. It dates from around AD 400.
Tanakh	The Hebrew name for the holy scriptures of the Jews. New material ceased to be added at about the end of the fifth century BC. It includes three genres: the five Books of Moses; the Prophets; and the Writings (all other material).
Teacher of Righteousness	An unknown charismatic Jewish leader of the second (or perhaps the first) century BC. He is an important figure in some of the Dead Sea Scrolls. Probably the founder or most famous leader of the Essene movement.
Tertullian	A second to third century Christian theologian and apologist. The first great Church Father who wrote in Latin, not in Greek.
Therapeutae	A Jewish group in Egypt living in community and dedicated to a pure and righteous life.
Theudas	A charismatic Jewish leader in the mid-40s AD.
Torah	The first five books of the Old Testament and the fundamental texts of the Hebrew tradition. Also called the five Books of Moses or the Pentateuch.

Varus   Sextus Quinctilius Varus, governor of Syria 7/6–4 BC.

Weeks Feast   Hebrew Shavuot, Pentecost. The summer Jewish festival
                     seven weeks after Passover celebrating the wheat harvest.

Wisdom of   A second- or first-century BC work that combines Jewish
Solomon   and Hellenistic philosophical and religious teachings. It
                     presents justification, guidelines and praise for a godly
                     way of life.

Yahweh   The name of the Hebrew god was never to be spoken,
                     but the usual transcription of the consonants YHWH is
                     Yahweh. His original home was Mount Sinai, his original
                     people nomads of that area.

Yom Kippur   See Day of Atonement.

Zadok   King David's High Priest.

SOURCES

Ordinary people lie hidden in the nooks and crannies of ancient history. The elites had a virtually complete monopoly on telling the story. Their vision from the pinnacle of society sometimes included notice of the masses, sometimes not. Even when seen, the prejudices of the elite meant that ordinary people were viewed through elite-tinted glasses. So something like 1–2 per cent of the population has left us a picture of culture, society and religion congruent with their vision of the world. It is possible that their vision could include observations that revealed conditions and thinking among the general population. They, of course, participated in many of the same activities, rubbing shoulders with – or with shoulders at least in proximity to – the army and so on, during festivals, public events and entertainments. But common activities did not necessarily mean common understandings, common problems, or common outlooks. Indeed, it is very unlikely that an elite had a clear concept of life on an everyday level unless he (and it would have been a he) went out of his way to observe and think about it, as an author like Pliny the Elder or Apuleius or Petronius must have done.

Nevertheless, elites crossed paths with the public in various ways and so were not completely ignorant about their lives. Since especially literary material often involved ordinary people in the telling of an event or in the course of a poem, it is possible to extract evidence of real lives even from the work of the high elite. Some elites came from fairly unremarkable backgrounds, so a person of the artisan class such as Lucian knew the world he lampooned in some of his writings. Among Christians too, many elites, at least early on, came from the ranks of the ordinary and so had some sense of their attitudes, hopes and dreams. Compiling such extracts, combining the result with more direct evidence and using comparative material from other times and places intelligently can produce a reasonable, if incomplete, picture of everyday religious activity.

Jewish material includes not only the writings in what Christians call the Old Testament and Apocrypha but also a wide variety of literary works from the period after about 500 BC and extending right through the first two centuries AD. The discovery of the Dead Sea Scrolls in the middle of the twentieth century opened a floodgate of new information and speculation about a wide variety of topics, including ordinary people's religious lives. As is the case with all sources, an essential question is, to what extent do Jewish sources reflect actual practice? Do they present a picture of real life, or an idealised one? How skewed are they by one perspective or another? A further difficulty comes in separating material relevant to the actual period described, for example the time of the Assyrian conquest of Jerusalem in the eighth century BC and how much it has been adjusted to reflect the concerns of the time of composition or editing, often hundreds of years after the fact. The material in the Old Testament and Tanakh was not edited into its present form until sometime in the fifth to fourth centuries BC. It is a challenge to disentangle the 'facts' of tenth- or eighth- or sixth-century religious and political history after traditions and data have been massaged into production hundreds of years later. Finally, there are Jewish sources from after our period, i.e. from the second century AD onward. After the destruction of the temple in Jerusalem in 70, followed by the failed diaspora and Judaean revolts of 117–18 and 130–33, rabbis in Judaea and Babylon compiled material and gradually gained control over Jewish activities and historical memory. Their writings provide some information about our period, particularly the first century, that is unclear at best. Reading back conditions, attitudes and actions from Mishnah and Talmud material (200–400 and later) is almost irresistible, but too often leads to false conclusions about first-century conditions and events, a time radically different from the later Jewish experience. Great care is necessary.

Finally, Jewish material from the diaspora. One of the casualties of the rabbinic takeover of Jewish culture was material written in Greek. The Septuagint is a Greek translation of the Tanakh made in the late fourth century BC in Egypt; it was the standard for centuries. Philo was a prominent Jewish intellectual in Alexandria during the early first century. His writings give great insight into the more philosophical direction of some Jewish thinking of the time. The historian Josephus's wide range of writing during the later first century provides us with rich material about many Jewish historical and cultural topics. All three of these sources were preserved not in the Jewish tradition, but in the Christian. The Septuagint provided their Bible and both Philo and Josephus seemed to provide validation for later Christian constructions of their history and faith.

As to sources about early Christians, the New Testament material is, of course, crucial, and contested almost beyond belief. At one extreme lie the 'hand of God' advocates who see the material as dictated directly by the Christian god, word for word, revealed to the faithful and so complete, true and transparent, without any need for historical or other dissection. At the other extreme lie scholars who seek to interpret in a radical fashion almost all historical elements of the material in the Gospels. Recent trends have seen the rise of anthropological and sociological interpretations that seek understanding in theory and comparative cultures.

Within the New Testament, the earliest material comes from the genuine epistles of Paul – 'genuine' because over half the Pauline corpus was composed by persons other than Paul who falsely claimed Paul's authorship as a way to valorise their own instructions to the faithful. The true Pauline letters date from the mid-40s until the late 50s, earlier than any of the canonical Gospels. They provide a picture of the contemporary urban Greek world as the scene of the spread of early Christianity. It was in this environment that Jewish communities argued over the merits of the new message and that polytheists first came to learn of it.

The Synoptic Gospels, so called because they offer a vision of the life of Jesus that shares many elements, portray the world of the Jewish artisan-peasant in Galilee-Judaea. Mark, Matthew and Luke were probably all written at least a generation after the death of Jesus, either in the run-up to or, more probably, in the aftermath of the destruction of the temple in Jerusalem in 70. They present a story that melds Jewish and non-Jewish ('gentile') elements into a whole that can appeal to believers in both groups and at the same time work in the task of proselytising outsiders. The Gospel of John, written later than the other three, brings a different mix of fact and culture. Finally, the non-canonical *Gospel of Thomas*, a work that may date from the first century but more likely from the second, provides a different perspective altogether, one that emphasises the message of Jesus in his sayings rather than the message in the miracles, especially in the resurrection, so emphasised by Paul and in the other Gospels. The Acts of the Apostles, written by the gospeller Luke, continues the story after the resurrection of Jesus. In many ways, Acts is a history in the contemporary Greco-Roman mode. That certainly does not mean that it is factually accurate in all details – far from it – but it does attempt to outline the expansion of early Christianity.

Material written by Christians during and after the period when the New

Testament contributions were composed (c.45–110) adds distinctively to the mix. The *Didache*, a somewhat peculiar work on religious discipline, the first letter of Clement and, perhaps, the *Gospel of Thomas*, along with other works, fall into this category.

None of this material was written by highly educated elites. Obviously, the writers were literate. That literacy came from a basic education that inculcated the standard fare of Hellenistic Greek (everything is written in that language) and Jewish culture. But there is no indication in either style or content that the authors were from the elite as represented by the ruling class, or the leaders in communities. They represent what I am calling ordinary people – perhaps not from the lower echelons of minor artisans or peasants, but non-elite nevertheless. Their views and materials are crucial to understanding how such people, both polytheist and Jewish, thought and acted during the first century.

Later, in the second century, works by Justin Martyr and Tertullian, among many others, provide still more material, although it is crucial to realise that second-century Christianity had already become a very different animal from that of the first century, for by that time the segue from the first-century communal organisation to a hierarchical, philosophising approach was well underway. Eusebius, writing in the time of Constantine the Great, quotes other valuable material from the second century. The Nag Hammadi texts, discovered hidden away in the Egyptian desert much as the Dead Sea Scrolls had been hidden in Judaean caves, offer new material bearing on early Christianity, especially a complete *Gospel of Thomas*. As with everything else in this field, disagreements about almost all facets make their use for historical investigation a challenge.

Other sources for the views of ordinary Roman and Greek adherents of Christianity hardly exist. There is a bit of information in Roman law codes. Inscriptions for Christians appear by the third century. They mention labourers, bankers, stonecutters, weavers, traders, tailors, mule keepers and the like – the sort of people we expect from written sources. During the first two centuries, papyri add little of use to the other sources I have mentioned.

Translations and Editions

Material from the main sources is given from others' excellent translations. Specific translators are given in brackets. Other translations are my own.

The following authors are from the Loeb Classical Library editions: Apuleius, *Florida* (Butler); Apuleius, *Metamorphoses* (Hanson); Augustine, *City of God* (Green); Babrius, *Fables* (Perry); Cicero, *De Natura Deorum* (Rackham); Cicero,

Tusculan Disputations (King); Dio, *Discourses* (Cohoon and Crosby); Eusebius, *Ecclesiastical History* (Kirsopp-Lake); Homer, *Iliad* (Murray); Josephus, *Jewish Antiquities* (Thackeray, Marcus and Feldman); Josephus, *Jewish War* (Thackeray); Josephus, *Life of Josephus* (Thackeray); Juvenal, *Satires* (Braund); Livy, (Sage); Lucian, *Gout* (MacLeod); Lucian, *Icaromenippus* (Harmon); Lucian, *Peregrinus* (Harmon); Marcus Aurelius, *Meditations* (Haines); Martial, *Epigrams* (Shackleton Bailey); Petronius, *Satyricon* (Heseltine, Rouse and Warmington); Philo, *Embassy to Gaius* (Colson); Plautus *Braggart Soldier* (de Melo); Pliny the Elder, *Natural History* (Rackam & Jones); Pliny the Younger, *Letters* (Radice); Plutarch, *Moralia: Table Talk* (Clement & Hoffleit); Plutarch, *Moralia: Obsolescence of Oracles* (Babbitt); Plutarch, *A Pleasant Life Impossible* (Einarson & De Lacy); Publilius Syrus (Duff & Duff); Seneca, *Letters* (Gummere); Strabo, *Geography* (Jones); Suetonius, *Life of Vespasian* (Rolfe); Tertullian, *Apology* (Glover & Rendall); Xenophon, *Hellenica* (Brownson).

Other classical sources: Artemidorus, *Interpretation of Dreams* (Robert J. White, *Artemidorus Daldianus, The Interpretation of Dreams = Oneirocritica* (Park Ridge, NJ: Noyes Press, 1975)) and Xenophon of Ephesus (Graham Anderson in Bryan P. Reardon, *Collected Ancient Greek Novels* (Berkeley: University of California Press, 1989)).

Scriptures

Old and New Testaments: *The Bible: New International Version* (Colorado Springs: International Bible Society, 1984); Sirach: *Good News Bible: Good News Translation* (New York: American Bible Society, 2000); *Acts of Peter*: M. R. James, *The Apocryphal New Testament* (Oxford: Clarendon Press, 1924); Maccabees 1–4: *The Common English Bible* (Nashville: Common English Bible, 2011).

The following works are from Alexander Roberts and James Donaldson, eds, *The Ante-Nicene Fathers: Translations of the Writings of the Fathers Down to AD 325* (Buffalo: The Christian Literature Publishing Company, 1885–96): Athenagoras, *Apology* (Pratten); Irenaeus, *Against the Heresies*; Justin Martyr, *Dialog with Trypho*; Lactantius, *Divine Institutes* (Fletcher); Minucius Felix, *Octavius*; Origen, *Against Celsus*; Tatian, *Address to the Greeks*; Tertullian, *On the Soul's Testimony* (S. Thelwall); Tertullian, *Prescription against Heretics*.

Other apocryphal and early Christian texts: Dead Sea Scrolls: Michael Owen Wise, Martin G. Abegg and Edward M. Cook, *The Dead Sea Scrolls: A New*

Translation (San Francisco: HarperSanFrancisco, 1996); *Didascalia Apostolorum*: R. Hugh Connolly, *Didascalia Apostolorum* (Oxford, Clarendon Press, 1929); Enoch: R. H. Charles, *The Apocrypha and Pseudepigrapha of the Old Testament* (Oxford: The Clarendon Press, 1913); *Epistle of Mathetes to Diognetus*: J. B. Lightfoot, *The Apostolic Fathers* (London & New York: Macmillan, 1885–90); Eusebius, *Preparation for the Gospel*: Edwin Hamilton Gifford, *Eusebius, Preparation for the Gospel* (Oxford: Clarendon Press, 1903); Jerome: *Against Vigilantius*: W. H. Fremantle in Philip Schaff and Henry Wace, eds, *From Nicene and Post-Nicene Fathers* (Buffalo: Christian Literature Publishing Co., 1892).

FURTHER READING

Sources for the study of religious practices among the general population provide a rich if, as always, incomplete picture. The scholarship on all these sources is simply immense – almost defying comprehension. Each year scores, even hundreds of articles or books are written just on someone like Jesus or Paul. Interpretations of people, events and literary works appear with, what must seem to an outsider, unfathomable frequency. Scholarly combat ensues on hundreds of topics, large and small. Sorting out a general treatment that offers something new, even in a small way, proves daunting. The suggestions below list the scholarly material I found most helpful.

Chapter 1: The Journey

John Bright, *A History of Israel* (Louisville: Westminster John Knox Press, 2000), tells the story down to the Maccabean revolt in the mid-second century BC; thereafter, Shaye J. D. Cohen, *From the Maccabees to the Mishnah* (Louisville: Westminster John Knox Press, 2006), and Seth Schwartz, *Imperialism and Jewish Society, 200 BCE to 640 CE* (Princeton: Princeton University Press, 2001). For archaeology and society see the essays in Thomas E. Levy, ed., *The Archaeology of Society in the Holy Land* (New York: Facts on File, 1995). Robert Knapp, *Invisible Romans* (London: Profile, 2011), provides a look at how ordinary people in the Greco-Roman world lived. Gildas Hamel, *Poverty and Charity in Roman Palestine, First Three Centuries CE* (Berkeley: University of California Press, 1990), treats the Jewish material.

Chapter 2: Polytheists, Jews and the Supernatural

The anthropology of religion documents how intertwined the natural and the supernatural world are in cultures worldwide. Annemarie de Waal Malefijt, *Religion and Culture: An Introduction to Anthropology of Religion* (New York: Macmillan, 1968), and Fiona Bowie, *The Anthropology of Religion* (Oxford: Blackwell, 2000), offer good basic information and approaches. James B. Rives, *Religion in the Roman Empire* (Oxford: Blackwell, 2007), provides an excellent introduction to religious habits in the Roman world; Teresa Morgan, *Popular Morality in the Early Roman Empire* (Cambridge: Cambridge University Press, 2007), addresses how ordinary people thought and acted. For the earlier Greek period Walter Burkert, *Greek Religion: Archaic and Classical* (Oxford: Blackwell, 1985), remains fundamental. Dale B. Martin, 'Hellenistic Superstition', pp. 110–27 in P. Bilde, et al., eds., *Conventional Values of the Hellenistic Greeks* (Aarhus: Aarhus University Press, 1997), emphasises popular attitudes. E. P. Sanders, *Judaism Practice and Belief 63 BCE–66 CE* (London: SCM Press, 1992), offers interesting analysis of developments in Jewish culture and religion. For an excellent assessment of polytheism as it worked in the Roman world, Ramsay MacMullen, *Paganism in the Roman Empire* (New Haven: Yale University Press, 1981), is still the best; Giulia Sfameni Gaspero, 'Daimôn and Tuchê', pp. 67–109 in P. Bilde, et al., eds., *Conventional Values of the Hellenistic Greeks* (Aarhus: Aarhus University Press, 1997), is useful in understanding Fate and Fortune in polytheist approaches.

Chapter 3: Ordinary Jewish People

For general background on the political scene, see Seth Schwartz, *Imperialism and Jewish Society, 200 BCE to 640 CE* (Princeton: Princeton University Press, 2001). For a solid treatment of ordinary people c.1200–587 BC, see Oded Borowski, *Daily Life in Biblical Times* (Atlanta: Society of Biblical Literature, 2003). Jody Magness, *Stone and Dung, Oil and Spit: Jewish Daily Life in the Time of Jesus* (Grand Rapids: Eerdmans, 2011), presents many down-to-earth aspects of life. For full and up-to-date material on a wide variety of daily-life subjects, Catherine Hezser, ed., *The Oxford Handbook of Jewish Daily Life in Roman Palestine* (Oxford: Oxford University Press, 2010), provides rich resources. Jodi Magness's *Archaeology of the Holy Land: From the Destruction of Solomon's Temple to the Muslim Conquest* (New Haven: Yale University Press, 2012), offers a readable, reliable and well-illustrated introduction to the archaeology. For more detailed treatments, see Eric M. Meyers and Mark A. Chancey, *Alexander to Constantine: Archaeology of the Land of the Bible*, vol. III (The Anchor Yale Bible Reference Library) (New Haven: Yale University Press, 2012). On the Jewishness of Galilee, see S. Freyne,

'Jesus and the Galilean Am ha-Aretz: A Reconsideration of an Old Problem', pp. 37–54 in Lee I. Levine and Zeev Weiss, *'Follow the Wise': Studies in Jewish History and Culture in Honor of Lee I. Levine* (Winona Lake, IN: Eisenbrauns, 2010), and Jonathan L. Reed, 'Archaeological Contributions to the Study of Jesus and the Gospels', pp. 40–54 in Amy-Jill Levine, Dale C. Allison Jr and John Dominic Crossan, eds., *The Historical Jesus in Context* (Princeton: Princeton University Press, 2006). Martin Goodman's *The Ruling Class of Judaea* (Cambridge: Cambridge University Press, 1987), remains the best treatment of the upper classes and their traumatic internecine struggles under Rome. For common people see A. Oppenheimer, *The 'Am Ha-Aretz: A Study in the Social History of the Jewish People in the Hellenistic-Roman Period* (Leiden: Brill, 1977). For those of Jewish traditions living outside Judaea, Erich Gruen's magisterial *Diaspora Jews Amidst Greeks and Romans* (Cambridge MA: Harvard University Press, 2002), gathers much information and puts it into understandable form. For women in our period see Tal Ilan, *Integrating Women into Second Temple History* (Peabody MA: Hendrickson, 1999); Eileen M. Schuller, 'Women in the Dead Sea Scrolls', *Annals of the New York Academy of Sciences* 722 (1994): 115–31; and Bernadette J. Brooten, *Women Leaders in the Ancient Synagogues: Inscriptional Evidence and Background Issues* (Chicago: Scholars Press, 1982); Ross Kraemer, 'Jewish Women and Christian Origins', pp. 35–49 in Ross S. Kraemer and Mary Rose D'Angelo, eds., *Women and Christian Origins* (Oxford: Oxford University Press, 1999). For an aggressive view of unrest in Judaea-Galilee, see Richard A. Horsley and John S. Hanson, *Bandits, Prophets, and Messiahs: Popular Movements at the Time of Jesus* (Minneapolis: Winston, 1985).

Chapter 4: The Justice of Yahweh

Victor Matthews, *Hebrew Prophets and Their Social World* (Grand Rapids: Baker Academic, 2012), discusses each prophet and his social message. Alex P. Jassen treats the Dead Sea Scroll evidence in 'The Presentation of the Ancient Prophets as Lawgivers at Qumran', *Journal of Biblical Literature* 127 (2008): 307–37. John S. Kloppenberg, 'Symbolic Eschatology and the Apocalypticism of Q', *Harvard Theological Review* 80 (1987): 287–306, treats the origins and development of the End of Days theology. John J. Collins collects and explains the material in *The Apocalyptic Imagination: An Introduction to the Jewish Apocalyptic Literature*, 2nd edn (Grand Rapids: Eerdmans, 1988).

Chapter 5: Polytheists in Their World

On mystery cults see Walter Burkert, *Ancient Mystery Cults* (Cambridge MA: Harvard University Press, 1987). Teresa Morgan deals with how ordinary people thought in her *Popular Morality in the Early Roman Empire* (Cambridge: Cambridge University Press, 2007). Polytheism gets magisterial treatment in Ramsay MacMullen's *Paganism in the Roman Empire* (New Haven: Yale University Press, 1981). On current philosophical movements see A. A. Long, *Hellenistic Philosophy: Stoics, Epicureans, Sceptics*, 2nd edn (Berkeley: University of California Press, 1986); Pierre Hadot, *What is Ancient Philosophy?* (Cambridge MA: Harvard University Press, 2002), has a good treatment of ancient philosophy as a way of life. For Cynics, see R. Bracht Branham and Marie-Odile Goulet-Cazé, eds., *The Cynics: The Cynic Movement in Antiquity and Its Legacy* (Berkeley: University of California Press, 1996). Hans Dieter Betz, 'Jesus and the Cynics: Survey and Analysis of a Hypothesis', *Journal of Religion* 74 (1994): 453–47, dispatches the once popular idea that Jesus himself was some sort of Cynic. Stephen Mitchell and Peter van Nuffelen write about Zeus Hypsistos in *One God: Pagan Monotheism in the Roman Empire* (Cambridge: Cambridge University Press, 2010). On conversion, A. D. Noch's classic, *Conversion: The Old and the New in Religion from Alexander the Great to Augustine of Hippo* (Oxford: Oxford University Press, 1933), still stands tall. Also see Martin Goodman, *Mission and Conversion: Proselytising in the Religious History of the Roman Empire* (Oxford: Clarendon Press, 1994).

Chapter 6: Paths to Change

On Pharisees and Sadducees, see Emil Schürer, *The History of the Jewish People in the Age of Jesus Christ (175 BC–AD 135)*, revised and edited by Geza Vermes and Fergus Millar (London: Bloomsbury, 1973), vol. II, pp. 381–414; Essenes, pp. 555–84; Therapeutae, pp. 591–7. On Zealots and Sicarii see also Morton Smith, 'Zealots and Sicarii, Their Origins and Relation', *Harvard Theological Review* 64 (1971): 1–19. On the Dead Sea Scrolls, see the fine essays in Timothy H. Lim and John J. Collins, *The Oxford Handbook of the Dead Sea Scrolls* (Oxford: Oxford University Press, 2010), and James VanderKam and Peter Flint, *The Meaning of the Dead Sea Scrolls* (San Francisco: HarperCollins, 2002). For polytheism, Ramsay MacMullen's *Paganism in the Roman Empire* (New Haven: Yale University Press, 1981), remains fundamental.

Chapter 7: Charismatics and Messiahs

For Jewish messianic beliefs see Emil Schürer, *The History of the Jewish People in the Age of Jesus Christ (175 BC–AD 135)*, revised and edited by Geza Vermes and Fergus Millar (London: Bloomsbury, 1973), vol. II, pp. 488–554. John J. Collins, '"He Shall Not Judge by What His Eyes See": Messianic Authority in the Dead Sea Scrolls', *Dead Sea Discoveries* 2 (1995): 145–64, and Matthew V. Novenson, 'The Jewish Messiahs, the Pauline Christ and the Gentile Question', *Journal of Biblical Literature* 128 (2009): 357–73 defend the argument that messiahs were not a prominent part of the Judaic experience. On messianism and the Dead Sea Scrolls, see John J. Collins, *The Scepter and the Star: Messianism in the Light of the Dead Sea Scrolls* (New York: Doubleday, 1995). On the lack of a suffering messiah in the Dead Sea Scrolls see James VanderKam and Peter Flint, *The Meaning of the Deud Sea Scrolls* (San Francisco: HarperCollins, 2002). John P. Meier, 'The Present State of the "Third Quest" for the Historical Jesus: Loss and Gain', *Biblica* 80 (1999): 459–87, offers a good summary of who historians might think Jesus was. William Horbury, *Jewish Messianism and the Cult of Christ* (London: SCM Press, 1998), is a good guide to popular feelings about messiahs in our period. The idea of Jesus as a revolutionary has been strongly argued. Reza Aslan's *Zealot: The Life and Times of Jesus of Nazareth* (New York: Random House, 2013), is overstated historical fiction while Douglas E. Oakman, *The Political Aims of Jesus* (Minneapolis: Fortress Press, 2012), offers a carefully documented discussion of an 'historical' Jesus separated from what some claim is simply later mythology. For charismatics in the polytheist world as well as the Judeo-Christian, Graham Anderson, *Sage, Saint, and Sophist: Holy Men and Their Associates in the Early Roman Empire* (London: Routledge, 1994), is fundamental.

Chapter 8: Christianity in the Jewish and Polytheistic World

Philip A. Harland's work on associations in antiquity ties together Jewish, Christian and polytheist social worlds: *Associations, Synagogues, and Congregations: Claiming a Place in Ancient Mediterranean Society* (Minneapolis: Fortress Press, 2003), and *Dynamics of Identity in the World of Early Christians* (New York: T&T Clark, 2009). On synagogues, see D. Binder, Anders Runesson and Birger Olsson, *The Ancient Synagogue from Its Origins to 200 CE: A Source Book* (Leiden: Brill, 2010). Wayne Meeks, *The First Urban Christians: The Social World of the Apostle Paul* (New Haven: Yale University Press, 1983), relates the social worlds of the polytheists and early Christians, as does his 'Social and Ecclesial Life of the Earliest Christians', pp. 145–73 in M. M. Mitchell and F. M. Young, eds., *The Cambridge History of Christianity: Origins to Constantine* (Cambridge:

Cambridge University Press, 2006). For Christian/Jewish and polytheist morality, see Wayne Meeks, *The Origins of Christian Morality: The First Two Centuries* (New Haven: Yale University Press, 1993), and Teresa Morgan, *Popular Morality in the Early Roman Empire* (Cambridge: Cambridge University Press, 2007). Ramsay MacMullen, 'Two Types of Conversion to Early Christianity', *Vigiliae Christianae* 37 (1983): 174–92, discusses how polytheists saw the early Christian phenomenon; M. David Litwa, *Iesus Deus: The Early Christian Depiction of Jesus as a Mediterranean God* (Minneapolis: Fortress Press, 2014), outlines the commonalities (not borrowings) in the polytheist world's ideas about human gods and deification and how early Christianity participated (not borrowed) those ideas in formulating what Christ was or looked like as a deity.

Chapter 9: Hostility to Christianity

Stephen Benko, *Pagan Rome and the Early Christians* (London: Batsford, 1974), looks at Christianity from the perspective of the polytheists. Ramsay MacMullen's *Christianizing the Roman Empire AD 100–400* (New Haven: Yale University Press, 1984), along with Ramsay MacMullen and Eugene N. Lane, eds., *Paganism and Christianity 100–425 CE: A Sourcebook* (Minneapolis: Fortress Press, 1992), give an excellent account of the spread of Christianity and the challenges it faced. For polytheist views, see Robert L. Wilken, *The Christians as the Romans Saw Them* (New Haven: Yale University Press, 1984), the short treatment by Gillian Clark, *Christianity and Roman Society* (Cambridge: Cambridge University Press, 2004), and a detailed treatment focusing on the ancient sources, John Granger Cook, *Roman Attitudes Towards the Christians: From Claudius to Hadrian* (Tübingen: Mohr Siebeck, 2010). For persecution see W. H. C. Frend, *Martyrdom and Persecution in the Early Church* (Oxford: Blackwell, 1965), and his 'Persecutions: Genesis and Legacy', pp. 503–23 in M. M. Mitchell, F. M. Young, eds., *The Cambridge History of Christianity: Origins to Constantine* (Cambridge: Cambridge University Press, 2006). Brent Shaw, 'The Myth of the Neronian Persecution', *Journal of Roman Studies* 105 (2015): 73–101, attempts to negate the evidence of Tacitus and Suetonius for Christians in the first century AD. On the reasons for persecuting Christians, see the classic positions in A. N. Sherwin-White, 'Why Were the Early Christians Persecuted? – An Amendment', and G. E. M. de Ste Croix, 'Why Were the Early Christians Persecuted? – A Rejoinder', both in *Past and Present* 27 (1964): 23–7 and 28–33. Heidi Wendt, 'Ea Superstitione: Christian Martyrdom and the Religion of Freelance Experts', *Journal of Roman Studies* 105 (2015): 183–202, hits upon the true reason, or, at least, the same reason I came to in my own research.

Chapter 10: Christianity's Appeal: Magicians, Miracles and Martyrs

For magic in general, see Matthew W. Dickie, *Magic and Magicians in the Greco-Roman World* (London: Routledge, 2001), and for texts Daniel Ogden, *Magic, Witchcraft, and Ghosts in the Greek and Roman Worlds: A Sourcebook* (Oxford: Oxford University Press, 2002). For Jewish magic, Gideon Bohak, *Ancient Jewish Magic: A History* (Cambridge: Cambridge University Press, 2008), is indispensable. Morton Smith wrote the classic on Jesus and magic in his *Jesus the Magician* (New York: Harper & Row, 1978). There is a good series of articles on miracles in the Jewish and Greco-Roman world in Graham H. Twelftree, ed., *The Cambridge Companion to Miracles* (Cambridge: Cambridge University Press, 2011), pp. 15–148. A still useful theoretical treatment is Howard Clark Kee, *Miracles in the Early Christian World: A Study in Sociohistorical Method* (New Haven: Yale University Press, 1983). On martyrs, see Glenn W. Bowersock, *Martyrdom and Rome* (Cambridge: Cambridge University Press, 1995), and Daniel Boyarin, *Dying for God: Martyrdom and the Making of Christianity and Judaism* (Stanford: Stanford University Press, 1999).

Chapter 11: When Prophecy Fails

Simon Dein in 'What Really Happens When Prophecy Fails: The Case of Lubavitch', *Sociology of Religion* 62 (2001): 383–401, critiques the sociology of failed prophecy in the wake of Leon Festinger, Henry W. Riecken and Stanley Schacter's path-breaking and now much disputed *When Prophecy Fails: A Social and Psychological Study of a Modern Group that Predicted the Destruction of the World* (New York: Harper & Row, 1956); Dein also presents a different way to view failed prophecy based on the experience of the Lubavitchers at the death of Rebbe Menachem Mendel Schneerson. Jean Daniélou offers a good analysis of second-century Christians coming to terms with polytheist philosophy in 'The Wisdom of the Gentiles', pp. 39–73 in his *Gospel Message and Hellenistic Culture* (Philadelphia: Westminster Press, 1973); also Frances M. Young, 'Towards a Christian Paidea', pp. 485–502 in M. M. Mitchell and F. M. Young, eds., *The Cambridge History of Christianity: Origins to Constantine* (Cambridge: Cambridge University Press, 2006). For a treatment of the theological struggles with Christianity in the second century AD see Walter H. Wagner, *After the Apostles: Christianity in the Second Century* (Minneapolis: Fortress Press, 1994). Richard Bauckham, *Jesus and the Eyewitnesses: The Gospels as Eyewitness Testimony* (Grand Rapids: Eeerdmans, 2006), rightly emphasises the importance of the witnesses to the earliest days of Christianity. Ramsay MacMullen, *The Second Church: Popular Christianity AD 200–400* (Atlanta: Society of Biblical Literature, 2009), offers fundamental insights that are directly reflected in my own analysis.

ACKNOWLEDGEMENTS

The genesis of this book, long in the thinking and long in the writing, requires more than the usual recognition of the help of others. In writing, I have noted in the Further Reading section above where my deepest debts lie. The format chosen for this book precludes the usual scholarly respect paid in footnotes; indeed, sufficient footnotes would have filled scores of pages. My colleagues in ancient history will readily recognise the breadth and depth of my reliance on their work, and I hope they will pardon with understanding my failure to give specific credit where credit is due, satisfied that the foundations they have laid allowed the present work to be erected.

I do wish to acknowledge especially four scholars who particularly facilitated the thinking and research that went into the project. Charles F. Pfeiffer, who introduced me to the ancient world; Ramsay MacMullen, who opened up the world of ordinary people; Wayne A. Meeks, who showed how the history of early Christianity could elude the grasp of the elite tradition; and Erich S. Gruen, whose approach to ancient sources is at once impeccable and inspiring. Of course none of these distinguished historians is responsible for how I have used their inspiration in this book.

As my research unfolded, patience and support came in measures above and beyond from my wife, Carolyn, who has been a steadfast enthusiast for the project even when it took me away from other things. John Davey's sensible reading, firm admonitions and friendly encouragements have seen the book to its happy conclusion.

LIST OF FIGURES

1. Conversion of the Emperor Constantine, 312. The vision at the Battle of Milvian Bridge. Illustration for History of the World by Evert A. Duyckinck (Johnson, Wilson, c 1870.). Photo: Alamy
2. Marble head of Pompey the Great (106–48 BC), Conqueror of Jerusalem. Roman, 1st BC. Ny Carlsberg Glyptotek, Copenhagen, Denmark. Photo: akg-images
3. Marble sculpture depicting Glycon serpent found at Constanza, Romania (ancient Tomis) in 1962 along with other fragments of sacred sculpture. Muzeul de Istorie Nationala si Arheologie Constantza. Photo: DEA/G. DAGLI ORTI
4. The coin, also depicting Glycon, is from Tomi.
5. The house is alleged to be the home of Peter, one of Jesus' disciples. Image after James F. Strange and Hershel Shanks, 'Has the house where Jesus stayed in Capernaum been found?' *Biblical Archaeological Review*, November/December 1982 p. 31
6. Bronze pyxis with nine shekels of Tyre minted between 13 BCE and 65 CE, used for temple taxes, fines, etc., and three Hebrew shekels, Israel Museum (IDAM), Jerusalem, Israel. Photo: akg-images/Erich Lessing
7. Tetradrachm of Antiochus IV Epiphanes (175–163 BCE). Israel Museum (IDAM), Jerusalem, Israel. Photo: akg-images/Erich Lessing
8. Lararium, fresco in House of Vettii, interior, Pompeii (Unesco World Heritage List, 1997), Campania, Italy, Roman civilization, 1st century. Photo: Martin Shields/Alamy

9. Gravestone with aperture for offerings to the deceased. Science Museum, Science & Society Picture Library, London.

10. The Fates, Puteal de Moncloa. Museo Nacional de Arqueología, Madrid. Drawing by P. Ponzano in Villa-Amil y Castro, J. (1875): 'El Puteal de la Moncloa', Museo Español de Antigüedades V, p. 235

11. Stele from Panormus (northwestern Asia Minor). Image after M. Perdrizet, 'Reliefs mysiens', *Bulletin de correspondance hellénique* 23 (1899) fig. 4

12. The 'Stele of Cyrus the Great'. Achaemenid period. Location: Palace of Cyrus the Great, Pasargadae, Iran. Photo: De Agostini/W. Buss /.Getty

13. Wall graffito, CIL IV 00202, from Pompeii. Image after J. Ward-Perkins & Amanda Claridge, *Pompeii A.D. 79* (New York: Alfred A. Knopf, 1978) p. 41.

14. Solid gold statuette of a goddess from Artemision (Temple of Artemis), located in Ephesus Archeological Museum Selcuk Izmir Turkey. Photo: Glyn Genin/Alamy

15. The wayfarer and the sibyl, fresco from Pompeii, 1st century AD, Musée Archéologique Naples. Photo: DEA/G. NIMATALLAH/Getty

16. An imaged Christian assembly in the building discovered in Dura-Europos. Drawing by Wladek Prosol in Ramsay MacMullen, *The Second Church* (Atlanta: Society of Biblical Literature, 2009 fig 1.4 p. 5

17. A relief found at Ariccia, south of Rome, which illustrates the celebration of religious rites in Egypt, identified by the ibises. The cult was probably connected with Isis. Museo Nazionale Romano, Rome, Italy. Photo: Heritage Image Partnership Ltd/Alamy

18. Family burial. Drawing by Wladek Prosol in Ramsay MacMullen, *The Second Church* (Atlanta: Society of Biblical Literature, 2009 fig 3.5 p. 61

19. A Christian funerary offering plate from Sardinia, 4th century AD. Department of History, Cultural Heritage and Territory of the University of Cagliari. Photo by O. Savio.

20. An imaged martyr's memorial service. Drawing by Wladek Prosol in Ramsay MacMullen, *The Second Church* (Atlanta: Society of Biblical Literature, 2009 fig 2.7 p. 43

LIST OF PLATE ILLUSTRATIONS

1. Assyrian relief from Palace of Sennacherib at Nineveh 650 BC Exodus of people from conquered city of Lachish, held in the British Museum, London. Photo: DEA/G. DAGLI ORTI
2. The storm-god Baal with a thunderbolt, from Ugarit (Ras Shamra) c.1350–1250 BC (sandstone), Assyrian School/Louvre, Paris, France/Alamy
3. The Prophets of Baal on Mount Carmel (tempera on plaster). Dura-Europos Synagogue, National Museum of Damascus, Syria/Photo © Zev Radovan/Alamy
4. Model of Herod's Temple in Jerusalem. Photo: Hemis/Alamy
5. Wall painting from Pompeii portraying the Dionysus cult. Photo: Eric Lessing/Alamy
6. Fresco depicting a Lararium from Pompeii (UNESCO World Heritage List, 1997), Campania, Italy. Roman civilization. Photo: De Agostini/Archivio J. Lange
7. Wall painting from a house in Pompeii. Image after Thomas Fröhlich, *Lararien-und Fassadenbilder in den Vesuvstädten* (Mainz: Philipp von Zabern, 1991) tab.28.2
8. Religious procession. Fresco on the wall of the Shop of Procession to Cybele, Pompeii. Soprintendenza Archeologica di Pompei. Archivio Fotografico degli Scavi
9. Epidromos Vase painter. Sacrifice of a pig with inscription: "Epidromos is beautiful". Attic red-figured cup (510–500 BCE). Louvre, (Museum), Paris, France. DEA/G. DAGLI ORTI/Getty

10. Wall painting, Tavern of the Seven Sages, Pompeii. Photo: Michael Larvey, translation by John Clarke

11. Wall painting of a market scene from the atrium of the House of Julia Felix, Pompeii. Museo Archeologico Nazionale, Naples. Image after A. Maiuri, *Roman Painting* (Milan: Skira Publishing, 1953) p. 140

12. Fresco of a market scene from the atrium of the House of Julia Felix, Pompeii. Museo Archeologico Nazionale, Naples. Image after A. Maiuri, *Roman Painting* (Milan: Skira Publishing, 1953) p. 143

13. Goddess Isis. Statue of bigio morato marble. 2nd century AD. Italy. National Archaeological Museum, Naples. Italy. Photo: PRISMA ARCHIVO/Alamy

14. Wall painting. Temple of Isis in Herculaneum. Photo: World History Archive/Alamy

15. The Kiryat Sefer synagogue, reconstruction drawing. Image JSP3 Khirbet Badd ISA p. 201 fig. 32, courtesy of the Staff Officer of Archaeology in Judea and Samaria

16. Mosaic from the 'House of the Gladiators'. The gladiator 'Lytras' is separated from his opponent by Darios the referee. Kourion, Limassol, Cyprus (mosaic), Roman, 3rd century AD. Photo: Heritage Image Partnership Ltd/Alamy

17. Portion of the Temple Scroll, Dead Sea Scrolls, Qumran (parchment)/Israel Museum, Jerusalem. Photo: Bert de Ruiter/Alamy

18. Samaritan at well, fresco, Via Latina Catacomb, Rome, Italy, 4th century. Photo: DEA Picture Library/Getty

19. Breaking of the Bread. Early Christian fresco. Catacomb of Priscilla, Rome, Italy

20. Agape meal, Cubicula of the Sacraments (fresco), 2nd–3rd centuries AD. The catacomb takes its name from the deacon Saint Callixtus. Rome, Italy. Photo: DEA/G. DAGLI ORTI/Getty

21. Assyrian warriors empaling Jewish prisoners after conquering Jewish fortress of Lachish in 701 BCE. Part of a relief from the palace of Sennacherib, Niniveh, Mesopotamia (Iraq). Assyrian, 8th BCE. British Museum, London. Photo: Alamy

22. Nail driven through the bones in the foot of a 25-year-old man. Found in a grave of the Herodian period in Givat ha-Mivtar to the north-east of Jerusalem (extra muros). Israel Museum (IDAM), Jerusalem, Israel. Akg-images/Erich Lessing

23. Wall painting from Pompeii. Potter at work on wheel. Pompeii Antiquarium Inv. 21631. Image after Thomas Fröhlich, *Lararien-und*

Fassadenbilder in den Vesuvstädten (Mainz: Philipp von Zabern, 1991) tab. 16

24. Alexamenos graffiti, Palatine Antiquarium, Rome (litho)/Private Collection. Photo: Alamy
25. Chairemon. A funeral stele from Egypt, 3rd to 4th centuries AD: Brooklyn Museum, Gift of Evangeline Wilbour Blashfield, Theodora Wilbour, and Victor Wilbour honouring the wishes of their mother, Charlotte Beebe Wilbour, as a memorial to their father, Charles Edwin Wilbour, 16.90.
26. Woman praying. Paint on plaster. Found in the arcosolium in the Coemeterium Maius, Rome. Image after Jean Lassus, *The Early Christian and Byzantine World* (London: Paul Hamlyn, 1967) figure 7 p. 20.
27. Funerary stele of Licinia Amias. Marble, early 3rd century CE. From the area of the Vatican necropolis, Rome. Source: WikiCommons.
28. Early Christian gravestone of Datus. From Catacombs, Rome, 3rd century AD, Pio Cristiano. Vatican Museums. Photo: Alamy
29. Emperor Constantine the Great (274–337 AD). Photo: PRISMA ARCHIVO/Alamy.

NOTES

Citations below mainly consist of references to ancient sources: these are discussed more generally in the Sources section (p. 251). A guide to Further Reading (p. 257) introduces modern work on the subject.

Chapter 2: Polytheists, Jews and the Supernatural

p. 12 *'"For my thoughts are not your thoughts ..."'* Isaiah 55:8.

p. 13 *spoke to him from a burning bush.* Exodus 3:1–4.

p. 13 *'Achilles, come now ...'* Homer, *Iliad* 21.211–26.

p. 14 *Jacob made the rock ...* Genesis 28:11–12, 18.

p. 14 *a tall stone found in Bactria ...* Pliny the Elder, *Natural History* 37.160.

p. 15 *Yahweh, who sent down fire ...* 1 Kings 18:36–8.

p. 15 *Apollo's infliction of a plague ...* Homer, *Iliad* 1.33–52.

p. 15 *responded with rain ...* Herodotus, *Histories* 1.87.

p. 15 *She merely channelled ...* Judges 4.

p. 15 *'the gods ... are now manifestly ...'* Xenophon, *Hellenica* 2.4.14.

p. 15 *Athena obliged.* Homer, *Iliad* 5.113–21.

p. 15 *In about 701 BC ...* 2 Kings 19:19.

p. 16 *A fable has Fate ...* Babrius, *Fables* B49.

p. 16 *Ecclesiastes in a polytheist way ...* Ecclesiastes 9:11.

p. 16 *... whether humans can figure it out or not.* 1 Samuel 2:6–8.

p. 16 *The bad things were death* ... *Papyri Graecae Magicae* 121.1–14 in Hans Dieter Betz, *The Greek Magical Papyri in Translation* (Chicago: University of Chicago Press, 1986), p. 316.

p. 20 *Araca Marcella* ... *L'Année épigraphique 2009* no. +00613 (Spain).

p. 20 *Gaius Iulius Frontonianus* ... *Corpus Inscriptionum Latinarum* 3.987 (Dacia).

p. 20 *Esuvius Modestus* ... *Corpus Inscriptionum Latinarum* 9.4752 = *Inscriptiones Latinae Selectae* 3485 (Samnium, Italy).

p. 20 *'There would have been many more ...'* Diogenes Laërtius, *Life of Diogenes* 59.

p. 20 *Deeply grieving parents* ... *Atti della Accademia Nazionale dei Lincei* 1901 [1903], fol. 182, nr. 365, p. 106 (G. F. Gamurrini) (Campania, Italy).

p. 20 *'Each of these [votive] objects ...'* Walter Burkert, *Greek Religion*, trans. John Raffan (Cambridge, MA: Harvard University Press, 1985), p. 13.

p. 20 *'Do the gods' will ...'* Homer, *Iliad* 1.218.

p. 21 *Because Prepousa* ... E. Varinlioglu, 'Eine Gruppe von Sühneinschriften aus dem Museum von Uşak', *Epigraphica Anatolica* 1, 75–86, pp. 42–3, no. 2, quoted by A. Chaniotis, 'Illness and Cures in the Greek Propitiatory Inscriptions and Dedications of Lydia and Phrygia', p. 331 in H. F. J. Hormannshoff, Ph. J. van der Eijk and P. H. Schrijvers, eds, *Ancient Medicine in its Socio-Cultural Context* (Amsterdam: Atlanta, 1995), pp. 323–44.

p. 23 *'You, Judah, have as many gods ...'* Jeremiah 11:13.

p. 23 *And Elijah railed* ... 1 Kings 18:21.

p. 23 *... Bethlehem and her Judaean god.* Ruth 1:16.

Chapter 3: Ordinary Jewish People

p. 27 *Josephus says* ... Josephus, *Life* 235.

p. 29 *These are works* ... Mishnah, *Ketubot* 5.5.

p. 29 *... a woman intervened to save her city.* 2 Samuel 20:14–22.

p. 30 *Then my wife Anna* ... Tobit 2:11–14.

p. 30 *Anna went out by the road* ... Tobit 10:7.

p. 30 *Women appeared* ... Nehemiah 8:2–3.

p. 30 *Paul came across Lydia* ... Acts 16:13–15.

p. 30 *We hear of female followers* ... Josephus, *Jewish War* 4.504–6.

p. 30 *the Hasmonean queen Alexandra* ... Josephus, *Jewish War* 1.110–14; *Jewish Antiquities* 13.405–17.

p. 30 *Justin Martyr noted* ... Justin Martyr, *Dialog with Trypho* 88.

p. 30 *Irenaeus mentioned Marcellina* ... Irenaeus, *Against the Heresies* 1.25.6.

p. 31 *'The very women of these heretics ...'* Tertullian, *Prescription against Heretics* 41.5.

p. 31 *Note that Jesus ...* John 4:4–27.

p. 31 *Sirach has, incidentally, a positive summary ...* Sirach 38:24–39.

p. 32 *Jesus was a tekton ...* Mark 6:2–3.

p. 32 *In Exodus we learn ...* Exodus 13:8–10.

p. 32 *The historian Josephus ...* Josephus, *Life* 8.

p. 32 *The system of tenant farming and day labour ...* Luke 16; Matthew 20:1–16.

p. 33 *Taxes, whether paid to the temple ...* Matthew 17:24.

p. 34 *John the Baptist hinted ...* Luke 3:12–13.

p. 34 *Jesus ... urged people to pay.* Matthew 22:21; Mark 12:17; Luke 20:25.

p. 34 *'... to God what is God's.'* Mark 12:13–17.

p. 34 *Jesus willingly paid the Jewish temple tax.* Matthew 17:24–5.

p. 35 *'always meet together ...'* Philo, *Apology* 7.12–13, from Eusebius, *Preparation for the Gospel* 8.7.

p. 35 *'The wisdom of the scribe ...'* Sirach 38:24–5.

p. 35 *He examines the wisdom ...* Sirach 39:1–11.

p. 36 *'Not without the sincerity ...'* Philo, *On Sacrifices* 11.

p. 37 *There were three main events ...* Deuteronomy 16:16.

p. 37 *For example, popular opposition ...* Josephus, *Jewish War* 2.174.

p. 37 *Cumanus ...* Josephus, *Jewish War* 2.230–31.

p. 37 *A crowd rushing ...* Josephus, *Jewish War* 2.234.

p. 38 *'most Jews saw nothing wrong ...'* Gideon Bohak, *Ancient Jewish Magic: A History* (Cambridge: Cambridge University Press, 2008), p. 136.

p. 38 *'They found sacred charms ...'* 2 Maccabees 12:38–40.

p. 38 *Misogynist rabbinic texts ... Pirkei Avot* 2:7.

Chapter 4: The Justice of Yahweh

p. 41 *You are always righteous ...* Jeremiah 12:1.

p. 42 *The Lord your God will raise up ...* Deuteronomy 18:15–18.

p. 42 *He railed against idolatry ...* Hosea 8:4, 8:13.

p. 42 *'For I desire steadfast love ...'* Hosea 6:6.

p. 42 *He criticised the priests ...* Hosea 5:1–4.

p. 43 *'Return, Israel ...'* Hosea 14:1.

p. 43 *'Woe to you ...'* Amos 6:1–7.

p. 43 *'Woe to those who plan iniquity ...'* Micah 2:1–2.

p. 43 *'Shall I acquit ...'* Micah 6:11.

p. 43 *'skimping on the measure ...'* Amos 8:5–6.

p. 44 *I hate, I despise* ... Amos 5:21–4; cf. Amos 4; Isaiah 1:13; Jeremiah 6:20.

p. 44 *You are always righteous* ... Jeremiah 12:1.

p. 44 *'Yet you say ...'* Ezekiel 18:25–32.

p. 45 *'I the Lord ...'* Jeremiah 17:10.

p. 48 *Hosea called Israel to account* ... Hosea 10:13–15.

p. 48 *'"Because you have not listened ..."'* Jeremiah 25:7–11.

p. 48 *Jesus, son of Ananias, ...* Josephus, *Jewish War* 6.301–14.

p. 49 *As the Babylonians* ... Jeremiah 25, 27, 29.

p. 49 *The God of Israel* ... Jeremiah 32:36–9.

p. 50 *'The days are coming,'* ... Jeremiah 23:5–6.

p. 52 *'Yahweh will conquer ...'* Isaiah 42:13.

p. 55 *'In that Day ...'* Isaiah 24:21.

p. 55 *Multitudes, multitudes* ... Joel 3:14–16, 2:1–32.

p. 55 *'The Day of the Lord ...'* Obadiah 1:15.

p. 55 *'Seek the Lord ...'* Zephaniah 2:3.

p. 56 *With the righteous* ... 1 Enoch 1:9.

p. 56 *'And Jupiter will look ...'* Lactantius, *Divine Institutes* 7.18.2.

p. 56 ... *'those who survive ...'* P. Rainer 19813, 39–43; cf. P. Oxy 2332, 63–71.

p. 56 ... *the dead would be resurrected* ... Ezekiel 37:1–11.

p. 56 *'Multitudes who sleep ...'* Daniel 12:2–3.

p. 56 *I tell you, you sinners* ... 1 Enoch 102:9.

p. 57 *'I know that you can ...'* Job 42:2–3.

Chapter 5: Polytheists in Their World

p. 60 ... *Lucian, who ridiculed* ... Lucian, *Icaromenippus* 25.

p. 60 ... *Marcus Aurelius recalled* ... Marcus Aurelius, *Meditations* 1.6 and 1.3.

p. 60 ... *Seneca and Cicero both insist.* Seneca, *Letters* 117.6; Cicero, *Tusculan Disputations* 1.30.

p. 62 *'Once upon a time ...'* Pliny the Elder, *Natural History* 12.2.3.

p. 63 *A remarkable example* ... Acts 14:8–18.

p. 63 *'The greater part of the people ...'* Seneca at Augustine, *City of God* 6.11.

p. 65 *We possess polytheists' prayers* ... Examples of hymns at Ramsay MacMullen and Eugene N. Lane, *Paganism and Christianity 100–425 CE: A Sourcebook* (Minneapolis: Fortress Press, 1992), pp. 50–63.

p. 65 *Proverbs of Publilius Syrus* ... Publilius Syrus 2, 123, 274.

p. 65 *'when they daily rise ...'* Didascalia Apostolorum 13.

p. 66 *'the sacrifice of victims ...'* Pliny the Elder, *Natural History* 28.3.11.

p. 66 *Eternal Lord* … From MacMullen and Lane, *Paganism and Christianity*, p. 80.

p. 66 *While I am unable* … *Corpus Inscriptionum Latinarum* 13.7661.

p. 66 *'on walls, too …'* Pliny the Elder, *Natural History* 28.4.19–20.

p. 67 *By command of the Lord Asclepius* … From MacMullen and Lane, *Paganism and Christianity*, p. 37.

p. 67 *'you can study the numerous inscriptions …'* Pliny the Younger, *Letters* 8.7.

p. 67 *'from the very god himself'*. *Inscriptiones Latinae Selectae* 3160, cf. 3704.

p. 67 *Gaius Clodius paid a vow* … *Corpus Inscriptionum Latinarum* 6.145 (Rome).

p. 67 *Rogatianus had a vision* … *Lupa* 19210 (Apulum, Dacia).

p. 67 *And in one case* … *Les inscriptions latines de Belgique* 32 (Tavier, Germania Inferior).

p. 67 *'a thing we know …'* Pliny the Elder, *Natural History* 28.21.

p. 67 *The attitude towards God* … Plutarch, *A Pleasant Life Impossible* 1101D–F.

p. 68 *The entire area was sprinkled* … Artemidorus, *Interpretation of Dreams* 2.33.

p. 68 *The cult of Mithras* … Justin Martyr, *1 Apology* 66.

p. 68 *'I must note that …'* Lucian, *The Dance* 15–16.

p. 69 *All the local girls* … Xenophon of Ephesus, *Ephesian Tale* 2.

p. 69 *'But to balance all this …'* Strabo, *Geography* 17.1.17.

p. 69 *'the city look like nothing …'* Tertullian, *Apology* 35.1–2.

p. 69 *The very extensive description* … Apuleius, *Metamorphoses* 11.8–11.

p. 71 *Claudius Silvanus* … *P. Cair.* J. E. [*sic*] 38622, per Christopher A. Faraone and Dirk Obbink, *Magika hiera: Ancient Greek Magic and Religion* (New York: Oxford University Press, 1997).

p. 72 *Cenacus complains* … R. S. O. Tomlin, 'Roman Britain in 1978: Inscriptions', *Britannia* 10 (1979), pp. 340–42 per Faraone and Obbink, *Magika hiera*.

p. 72 *'Once you are dead …'* *Corpus Inscriptionum Latinarum* 4.5279.

p. 72 *'I did not exist …'* *Inscriptiones Latinae Selectae* 8162ff.

p. 72 *He mentioned dream interpretation* … Justin Martyr, *1 Apology* 18.

p. 75 *'I was never anxious …'* Epicurus, fragment 43.

p. 75 *Widespread adherence* … Cicero, *Tusculan Disputations* 4.7.

p. 75 … *'the common people …'* Lucretius, *On the Nature of Things* 945.

p. 76 *Paul spread his message* … Acts 17:17 – Athens.

p. 76 *Paul once rented Tyrannus's lecture room* … Acts 19:9 – Corinth.

p. 76 *Aristotle forthrightly said* … Aristotle, *Nicomachean Ethics* 1142b2–7.

p. 77 *You often see him, Cosmus* … Martial, *Epigrams* 4.53.

p. 78 *posting themselves at street-corners* … Dio Chrysostom, *Discourses* 32.9.

p. 79 *People were more likely to think* … Seneca, *Letters* 5.1–2, 29.1; Martial, *Epigrams* 4.5.3; Petronius, *Satyricon* 14.

p. 80 *For there was a feeling* … Aelius Aristides, *Oration* 48.32 per MacMullen and Lane, *Paganism and Christianity* 7.4, p. 81.

p. 82 *'All are to obey …'* and *'No one is to ask …'* P. London 2710, cited by Hans-Josef Klauck, *The Religious Context of Early Christianity: A Guide to Graeco-Roman Religions* (Minneapolis: Fortress Press, 2003), p. 49.

p. 82 *The problem of sub-groups* … 1 Corinthians 1:10.

p. 83 *'"What form of entertainment …"'* Apuleius, *Florida* 5.

p. 84 *'The gods will be gracious …'* *Sylloge inscriptionum Graecarum³* 985.

p. 84 *The letter of James* … James 4:13–14.

p. 84 *Recognising this, the Christians* … Pliny the Younger, *Letters* 10.96.7.

p. 84 *'Should not this have been classed …'* Tertullian, *Apology* 38.1–2.

p. 85 … *'festivals and sacrifices …'* Plutarch, *Moralia: Obsolescence of Oracles* 417C.

p. 86 … *'have thoroughly persuaded themselves …'* Eusebius, *Preparation for the Gospel* 4.1.

p. 86 *'The chief fruit of piety …'* Porphyry, *To Marcella* 18.

Chapter 6: Paths to Change

p. 89 *'The Levitical priests …'* Ezekiel 44:15.

p. 92 *Phineas, son of Eleazar* … Numbers 25:6–13.

p. 92 *As a result, he is singled out* … Psalm 106:30–31.

p. 93 *'I [Elijah] have been very zealous …'* 1 Kings 19:10.

p. 93 *Various psalms praised* … 25:4, 31:23.

p. 93 *'For the Lord loves the just …'* Psalm 37:28–9.

p. 93 *'Even if all …'*, *'When Mattathias saw …'* and *'Everyone who is zealous …'* 1 Maccabees 2:19–28.

p. 94 *First, in their intense purity* … 1 Maccabees 2:41–2.

p. 94 *Then they believed lies* … 1 Maccabees 7:10–16.

p. 94 *This priest is usually identified* … 1 Maccabees 10:18–20.

p. 96 *'You do not delight in sacrifice …'* Psalm 51:16–17.

p. 97 *Josephus says there were six thousand* … Josephus, *Jewish Antiquities* 17.42.

p. 98 *'for they taught that the soul …'* Josephus, *Jewish Antiquities* 18.13–14.

p. 100 *The widespread popularity* … Josephus, *Jewish War* 2.164–5; Hippolytus of Rome, *Refutation of All Heresies* 9.24.

p. 100 *For example, Simon son of Boethus* … Josephus, *Jewish Antiquities* 17.78.

p. 102 *Listen to me, you descendants of Jacob* … Isaiah 46:3–4.

p. 102 *'This is what the Lord says …'* Isaiah 44:6.

p. 102 *'Let my persecutors ...'* Jeremiah 17:18.

p. 102 *Josephus spoke of a Fourth Philosophy ...* Josephus, *Jewish Antiquities* 18.23–6.

p. 102 *'If you fear the Lord ...'* 1 Samuel 12:14–15.

p. 103 *'Heaven would be their zealous ...'* Josephus, *Jewish Antiquities* 18.5.

p. 103 *'Phineas son of Eleazar ...'* Numbers 25:6–13.

p. 104 *Then, Joab murdered ...* 2 Samuel 20:6–10.

p. 104 *the Sicarii clubbed together ...* Josephus, *Jewish War* 7.254–5.

p. 105 *'I will make you ...'* Genesis12:1–3.

p. 105 *'Stay in this land ...'* Genesis 26:3–4.

p. 106 *'And I, because of what ...'* Isaiah 66:18–21.

p. 106 *'Foreigners who bind themselves ...'* Isaiah 56:6–7.

p. 106 *The story of Naaman the Syrian ...* 2 Kings 5.

p. 106 *As late as the Book of Enoch ...* 1 Enoch 10:22.

p. 106 *The centurion Cornelius ...* Acts 10:1–22.

p. 107 *He noticed many ...* Josephus, *Jewish War* 2.463, 2.559–61, 7.45.

p. 107 *He also attested ...* Josephus, *Jewish War* 6.426.

p. 107 *Philo urged Jews ...* Philo, *Special Laws* 1.52–3, 4.178.

p. 107 *Tacitus, from the polytheist ...* Tacitus, *Histories* 5.1.

p. 107 *Josephus has only one example ...* Josephus, *Jewish Antiquities* 20.34–53.

p. 107 *Following Deuteronomy 10:16 ...* Jeremiah 9:25–6.

p. 108 *Ezekiel also emphasised ...* Ezekiel 44:9.

p. 108 *This man told the king ...* Josephus, *Jewish Antiquities* 20.34–53.

p. 108 *He went on to call ...* Philo, *Questions and Answers on Exodus*, Exodus 2:2.

p. 108 *The survival in rabbinic ...* 'Gore Toshab', Babylonian Talmud, *Yebamoth* 47b.

p. 109 *Among pious Jewish people ...* Acts 10–11.

p. 110 *'All of the Hellenistic philosophical ...'* A. A. Long, *Hellenistic Philosophy: Stoics, Epicureans, Sceptics* (Berkeley: University of California Press, 1986), p. 6.

p. 110 *It is symptomatic ...* Josephus, *Jewish War* 2.119; *Jewish Antiquities* 18.11 cf. *Jewish Antiquities* 13.171, where he calls these groups 'sects'.

p. 111 *Philo described synagogue ...* Philo, *Dreams* 2.127; *Contemplative Life* 26.

p. 111 *When he addressed the Gauls ...* Quoted by Ramsay MacMullen, *Paganism in the Roman Empire* (New Haven: Yale University Press, 1981), pp. 97–8.

Chapter 7: Charismatics and Messiahs

p. 114 *'Deceivers and impostors ...'* Josephus, *Jewish War* 2.258–9.

p. 115 *Josephus had personal experience* ... Josephus, *Life* 8–12.

p. 115 *'The morning bathers ...'* Tosefta, *Yadayim*, 2:20.

p. 116 *John apparently thought of himself* ... Matthew 3:4 and 2 Kings 1:7–8.

p. 116 *Josephus stated that John's* ... Josephus, *Jewish Antiquities* 18.116–19.

p. 116 *Even Pharisees and Sadducees* ... Matthew 3:7.

p. 116 *For him, righteousness encompassed* ... Luke 3:12–13.

p. 116 *'I will send my messenger ...'* Malachi 3:3.

p. 116 *People considered* ... Matthew 14:5.

p. 116 *Andrew, one of the disciples of Jesus* ... John 1:35–40.

p. 116 *Unlike the false prophets* ... Matthew 11:2.

p. 116 *In Ephesus Paul found* ... Acts 18:25.

p. 117 *In 36 a man of Samaria* ... Josephus, *Jewish Antiquities* 18.85–7.

p. 117 *... he persuaded a multitude* ... Josephus, *Jewish Antiquities* 20.97–8.

p. 117 *Acts says 400* ... Acts 5:36.

p. 117 *Clearly, he was claiming* ... 2 Kings 2:7–8, 13–14.

p. 117 *a more reasonable four thousand* ... Josephus, *Jewish Antiquities* 2.261–3; Acts 21:38.

p. 117 *The Lord will go out* ... Zechariah 14:3–5.

p. 118 *Felix, the Roman governor* ... Josephus, *Jewish War* 2.261–3; *Jewish Antiquities* 20.169–70.

p. 118 *Other times, the charismatics* ... Josephus, *Jewish Antiquities* 20.167–9.

p. 118 *Felix was clearly suspicious* ... Josephus, *Jewish War* 2.259–60.

p. 118 *He was eventually killed* ... Josephus, *Jewish War* 6.300–309.

p. 118 *priests, prophets and kings.* Exodus 29:29, 40:15; Ezekiel 28:14; Isaiah 61:1; and 1 Samuel 10:1, 16:123, respectively.

p. 118 *Even a non-Jew* ... Isaiah 45:1–5.

p. 120 *Judas, son of Hezekiah,* Josephus, *Jewish War* 2.56.

p. 120 *Simon of Peraea,* Josephus, *Jewish War* 2.57–9.

p. 120 *... a shepherd named Athronges* ... Josephus, *Jewish Antiquities* 17.278–84; *Jewish War* 2.60–65.

p. 120 *as Elijah did for Elisha.* 1 Kings 19:16.

p. 120 *'The Spirit of the Sovereign Lord ...'* Isaiah 61:1.

p. 121 *A messiah announcing* ... Psalms of Solomon 18.

p. 121 *It was these people* ... Dead Sea Scroll *Damascus Covenant* 14:19.

p. 121 *'He will atone for the children ...'* Dead Sea Scroll 4Q541.

p. 122 *He shall be called the Son of God* ... Dead Sea Scroll 4Q246.

p. 122 *And also his son* ... Dead Sea Scroll 4Q246 1.9–2.10.

p. 122 *[The hea]vens and the earth* ... Dead Sea Scroll 4Q512.

p. 123 *Josephus, writing perhaps* ... Josephus, *Jewish Antiquities* 18.63–4.

p. 125 *'Love the Lord your God ...'* Mark 12:29–31.

p. 126 *But his biographers* ... Mark 8:27–30; Matthew 16:13–16.

p. 126 *'What comes out of a person ...'* Mark 7:20.

p. 128 *Outside the Gospels and Acts* ... Romans 9:5; 1 Peter 1:11; Revelation 11:15 and 12:10.

p. 128 *It is notable that most documentation* ... E.g., Luke 3:15.

Chapter 8: Christianity in the Jewish and Polytheistic World

p. 130 *The Twelve minus the traitor* ... Acts 1:12–14.

p. 130 *The last surviving blood relatives* ... Eusebius, *Ecclesiastical History* 3.20.

p. 130 *Mary and the other women* ... Acts 12:12.

p. 131 *A council of elders is mentioned* ... Acts 15:22.

p. 131 *He was called as a prophet* ... Acts 9:1–17.

p. 131 *He forbade promiscuous mobs* ... Philo, *Flaccus* 4.

p. 132 *There are a vast number* ... Philo, *Flaccus* 136.

p. 132 *'Unlawful assemblies must not ...'* Digest of Roman Law 47.11.2.

p. 132 *'By the Decrees of the Emperors ...'* Digest of Roman Law 47.22.1.

p. 132 *According to Philo* ... Philo, *Embassy to Gaius* 40.311–12.

p. 133 *Josephus reports* ... Josephus, *Jewish Antiquities* 14.214–16.

p. 133 *Advocates of early Christianity* ... Acts 6:9, 9:2, 9:20, 13:5 and many other citations.

p. 133 *Adherents thought of themselves* ... Ephesians 2:19.

p. 133 *A household meal formed* ... Tertullian, *Apology* 39.

p. 133 *For Christians are not distinguished* ... Epistle of Mathetes to Diognetus 5.1–5.10.

p. 134 *Tertullian seconded this* ... Tertullian, *Apology* 42.1.

p. 134 *Although there is evidence* ... Acts 17:16–18, 8:5, 17:13, 24:12.

p. 134 *Jewish non-adherents* ... Acts 24:5, 28:22.

p. 134 *Polytheist opponents called them ... first used in Antioch.* Acts 11:26.

p. 134 *... and the general citizenry hated them* ... Josephus, *Jewish War* 7.45.

p. 135 *Probably local citizens of Antioch* ... Acts 11:28.

p. 135 *'However, if you suffer ...'* 1 Peter 4:16.

p. 136 *'[Jesus] said to them ...'* Luke 24:44.

p. 137 *The first instance* ... Genesis 9:8–17.

p. 137 *Yahweh confirmed the covenant* ... Genesis 15:18 (Abraham), 17:19 (Isaac), Exodus 2:24 (Jacob) 24:8, 31:18 (Moses).

p. 137 *'Then [Moses] took the blood ...'* Exodus 24:8.

p. 137 *At the Last Supper* ... Luke 22:20; Matthew 26:28; Mark 14:24.

p. 137 '"The days are coming ..."' Jeremiah 31:31–3.

p. 137 'For I, the Lord, love justice ...' Isaiah 61:8.

p. 137 Their Teacher of Righteousness ... Dead Sea Scroll Damascus Covenant 6.19b.

p. 138 'This is my covenant with you ...' Genesis 17:10.

p. 138 The act was mentioned only once again ... John 7:22–3.

p. 138 Scripture proclaimed ... Leviticus 26:41; Deuteronomy 10:16, 30:6.

p. 138 'Circumcise yourselves ...' Jeremiah 4:4.

p. 138 And he emphasised ... Jeremiah 9:25.

p. 138 'So then, if those who ...' Romans 26:26; 1 Corinthians 7:19.

p. 138 'For in Christ Jesus ...' Galatians 5:6.

p. 138 The Gospel of Thomas ... Thomas, Sayings 53.

p. 139 Justin Martyr ... Justin Martyr, 1 Apology 1.67.

p. 139 Still, in the beginning some ... Colossians 2:16–23.

p. 139 Many also participated ... Matthew 26:17 and many notices, e.g. Acts 2:1, 20:6, 27:9; 1 Corinthians 5:7–8, 16:8.

p. 139 Finally, it is important ... Luke 24:53; Acts 3:1.

p. 140 'Then David said to Nathan ...' 2 Samuel 12:13; Jeremiah 3:11–13; Job 33:27–8.

p. 140 Many scriptural references ... Job 19:25–7; Hosea 6:1–2.

p. 140 Ezekiel's dry bones ... Ezekiel 37:11–14.

p. 140 At that time Michael ... Daniel 12:1–3; also 2 Maccabees 12:43–5.

p. 140 in the case of Enoch and Elijah. Genesis 5:24; 2 Kings 2:11.

p. 140 People were ready ... Luke 9:7–8; Mark 8:28; Matthew 16:1.

p. 140 The early Christian martyrs ... Acts 7:54–9; Josephus, Jewish Antiquities 20.200.

p. 140 other martyrs of the Jewish people. E.g., 2 Maccabees 6:1–31.

p. 141 Philo in his ... Philo, Apology 7.6.

p. 141 as it was among those ... Dead Sea Scroll 4QPs37, col. II, 9–10.

p. 141 Now listen, you rich people ... James 5:1–6.

p. 141 For example, they subscribed ... Philo, Apology 7.3.

p. 141 Relationships to polytheists ... Acts 13:46, 18:6, 19:8–10, 28:28.

p. 141 Teaching in parables ... E.g., 2 Samuel 12:1–15.

p. 141 The geography of many ... 2 Kings 5:8–10.

p. 142 [Jews] petitioned the king ... 3 Maccabees 7:10–16.

p. 142 'one must instruct every man ...' Abot de-Rabbi Nathan, ed. S. Schechter, A iii, 7b–8a.

p. 144 That is not to say ... Suetonius, Life of Claudius 25; Acts 18:2.

p. 144 The idea that Jesus ... Apuleius, Florida 15.

p. 144 *Some mystery religions* ... Diogenes Laërtius, *Diogenes* 6.39.

Chapter 9: Hostility to Christianity

p. 148 *'All things have been committed ...'* Matthew 11:27.

p. 148 *'You, Lord, are ...'* Isaiah 64:8.

p. 148 *'Come down from ...'* Matthew 27:39–41.

p. 148 *Hellenistic Greeks crucified* ... E.g. Josephus, *Jewish Antiquities* 12.255–6.

p. 149 *Alexander Jannaeus ... Varus ... Quadratus* ... Josephus, *Jewish Antiquities* 13.380, 17.295, 20.129.

p. 149 *Governors of Judaea crucified* ... Philo, *Flaccus* 72.

p. 149 *During the Great Revolt* ... E.g. Josephus, *Jewish War* 3.321, 5.449–51.

p. 149 *'the most pitiable of deaths'.* Josephus, *Jewish War* 7.203.

p. 149 *'a stumbling block to Jews'.* 1 Corinthians 1:23.

p. 149 *'If someone guilty ...'* Deuteronomy 21:22–3.

p. 149 *Paul tried to explain* ... Galatians 3:13.

p. 149 *Indeed, in this view* ... Josephus, *Jewish War* 3.321.

p. 149 *Because of martyrdoms* ... *Assumption of Moses* 8:1.

p. 150 *But he was pierced* ... Isaiah 53:5–12.

p. 150 *'truth, righteousness, justice ...'* Dead Sea Scroll 1QS8.

p. 150 *'God presented Christ ...'* Romans 3:25.

p. 151 *The suffering and death* ... 4 Maccabees 6:26–30, 17:17–22.

p. 151 *The early Christians* ... Romans 3:25, 5:9, 8:3; Hebrews 2:17, 9:14, 9:28, 10:10, 13:12; Revelation 1:5.

p. 151 *Jesus's sacrificial blood* ... 1 Corinthians 5:6–8; Justin Martyr, *Dialog with Trypho* 111.

p. 151 *Then came the Festival* ... John 10:22–33.

p. 152 *'We have heard Stephen ...'* Acts 6:11.

p. 153 *'The Lord your God ...'* Deuteronomy 18:15.

p. 153 *'You are just like ...'* Acts 7:53.

p. 153 *'Anyone who blasphemes ...'* Leviticus 24:16.

p. 153 *As in the Gospel* ... E.g., Matthew 10:17; Luke 4:28, 12:11; John 9:22–3, 12:42, 16:2, 24:12; Acts 14:1, 17:2, 19:7–8 and many other notices.

p. 153 *'If you Jews were making ...'* Acts 18:12–17.

p. 154 *'Therefore, my friends ...'* Acts 13:38–9.

p. 154 *Fellow children of Abraham* ... Acts 13:26–30.

p. 154 *Paul and his companion* ... Acts 13:13–52.

p. 154 *At Iconium* ... Acts 14:1–7.

p. 154 *At Lystra* ... Acts 14:8–20.

p. 154 *In Thessalonica a mob* ... Acts 17:1–9.

p. 155 *'I have worked much harder ...'* 2 Corinthians 11:23–6.

p. 155 *'In all probability ...' 'when [piety, reverence and religion] are gone ...'* Cicero, *De natura deorum* 1.3–4.

p. 156 *'haters of the human race'* Tacitus, *Histories* 5.5.1; cf. Josephus, *Apion* 2.148 and Diodorus Siculus 34.1.2.

p. 156 *Four thousand were expelled* ... Tacitus, *Annals* 2.85.

p. 157 *'Gather together our scattered ...'* 2 Maccabees 1:24–9.

p. 157 *'If they wish to be members ...'* Josephus, *Jewish Antiquities* 12.125–6.

p. 157 *On the first day* ... Lucian, *Alexander the False Prophet* 38.

p. 158 *Some people plotted* ... 3 Maccabees 3:2–7.

p. 158 *[Those accused as Jews]* ... Philo, *Flaccus* 95–6.

p. 159 *There was a very large* ... Josephus, *Jewish War* 7.43.

p. 159 *'When the people heard this ...'* Josephus, *Jewish War* 7.45–51.

p. 160 *People were quite prepared* ... Matthew 17:1–3.

p. 160 *The people of Lystra* ... Acts 14:8–18.

p. 160 *They saw that as* ... 1 Corinthians 1:23.

p. 160 *'You, therefore, have no excuse ...'* Romans 1:1–3.

p. 161 *There are many who* ... Origen, *Against Celsus* 7.9.

p. 163 *'Flee from idolatry ... offered to demons.'* 1 Corinthians 10:14, 19–20.

p. 163 *The poor wretches [Christians]* ... Lucian, *Peregrinus* 13.

p. 163 *As Walter Burkert pointed out* ... Burkert, *Greek Religion*, p. 255.

p. 163 *'Men wisest in all divine ...'* Livy 39.16.8–9.

p. 164 *How often, too* ... Tertullian, *Apology* 36.2, 49.4.

p. 164 *'a people skulking ...'* Minucius Felix, *Octavius* 8.

p. 165 *'There are none more apt ...'* Tertullian, *Apology* 35.8.

p. 165 *[T]he stories told about us* ... Athenagoras, *Apology* 13, 14, 15, 31.

p. 165 *Paul noted miscreants* ... 1 Corinthians 5:1–2, 11, 13.

p. 165 *The second letter* ... 2 Peter 2:19, 2, 13–14.

p. 167 *'We know that in our own regions ...'* Origen, *Commentary on Matthew*, from MacMullen and Lane, *Paganism and Christianity*, p. 222.

p. 168 *Seizing perceived malefactors* ... Josephus, *Jewish War* 7.46–53; Philo, *Flaccus* 41.

p. 168 *Luckily for Paul* ... Acts 19:23–41.

p. 168 *An analogous episode occurred at Thyatira.* Acts 16:16–21.

p. 168 *Pliny, the Roman special governor* ... Pliny the Younger, *Letters* 10.96–7.

p. 169 *Ignatius of Antioch* ... Irenaeus, *Letter to the Romans* 3.3; *Letter to the Magnesians* 10.1–3.

p. 169 *'since the Jews ...'* Suetonius, *Life of Claudius* 25.4.

p. 169 *'After this, Paul left Athens ...'* Acts 18: 1–3.

p. 170 *Tacitus writes an account ...* Tacitus, *Annals* 15.44.

p. 170 *'The Jews regard ...'* Tacitus, *Histories* 5.5.1.

p. 170 *'In [Nero's] reign ...'* Suetonius, *Life of Nero* 16.2.

p. 172–4 *Pliny to Emperor Trajan; Emperor Trajan to Pliny.* Pliny the Younger, *Letters* 10.96–7.

p. 175 *Roman law punished actors ...* Paulus, *Opinions* 5.26.2.

p. 175 *'but if they begged him ...'* Suetonius, *Tiberius* 36.

p. 175 *'But the question ...'* Ulpian, Book 7 *de officio proconsulis* 15.2.1.

p. 175 *Closer to the Christian situation ...* Josephus, *Jewish War* 7.43.

p. 175 *'And this is the sole accusation ...'* Justin Martyr, *1 Apology* 24.

Chapter 10: Christianity's Appeal: Magicians, Miracles and Martyrs

p. 179 *The conversion of Paul ...* Acts 9:1–18.

p. 180 *'We must say that ...'* Origen, *Against Celsus* 1.10.

p. 180 *'My message ...'* Origen, *Against Celsus* 3.10; 1 Corinthians 2:4–7 with *Against Celsus* 3.19.

p. 180 *'For we did not follow ...'* 2 Peter 1:16.

p. 181 *We have seen how ...* 2 Maccabees 6:18–19; 4 Maccabees 17:9–12, 21–2.

p. 181 *The prophet Jeremiah ...* Jeremiah 31:31–4.

p. 182 *Apuleius wrote ...* Apuleius, *Apology* 26.6.

p. 182 *The Roman legal scholar ...* Paulus, *Opinions* 5.23.15–16.

p. 183 *Pliny the Elder understood this: ...* Pliny the Elder, *Natural History* 30.1, 30.2, 28.10, 28.19.

p. 183 *'For...sorcerers advise ...'* Plutarch, *Moralia: Table Talk*, book VII, 5.706D.

p. 183 *In Hebrew history ...* 2 Chronicles 16:11–13.

p. 184 *'I desire to speak to the Almighty ...'* Job 13:3–5.

p. 184 *'Honour physicians ...'* Sirach 38 1 and 15.

p. 184 *After strolling to and fro ...* Petronius, *Satyricon* 131.

p. 185 *Everyone knows about ...* Lucian, *Lover of Lies* 16.

p. 185 *'put to the nose of the possessed man ...'* Josephus, *Jewish Antiquities* 8.46–8.

p. 185 *Called in to cure ...* Acts 19:13–16.

p. 186 *'Long ago was discovered ...'* Pliny the Elder, *Natural History* 25.10.

p. 186 *'To the astonishment of all ...'* Pliny the Elder, *Natural History* 28.30.

p. 186 *Dealing with snakes ...* Luke 10:19; Mark 16:17–18.

p. 186 *'Consult a spirit for me,' ...* 1 Samuel 28:7–15.

p. 187 *There are many who ...* Origen, *Against Celsus* 9.

p. 187 *The wife would ...* Plautus, *Braggart Soldier* 685–701.

p. 188 '[Our minds are] always ...' Pliny the Elder, *Natural History* 28.4.21.

p. 188 'When you enter ...' Deuteronomy 18:9–13.

p. 189 *The priest shall bring* ... Numbers 5:11–31.

p. 190 *He went to the prophet Elisha* ... 2 Kings 5:1–14.

p. 190 *Magical acts were entangled* ... Pliny the Elder, *Natural History* 30.1–2.

p. 191 *Josephus noted King Solomon* ... Josephus, *Jewish Antiquities* 8.45.

p. 191 'There is yet another branch of magic ...' Pliny the Elder, *Natural History* 30.11.

p. 191 *No sooner has [a priest]* ... Juvenal, *Satires* 6.542–7.

p. 191 'Others are mocked ...' Lucian, *Gout* 171–4.

p. 191 *Apuleius called the people* ... Apuleius, *Florida* 6.

p. 191 *If, then, we shall be able* ... Origen, *Against Celsus* 1.24.

p. 192 'God granted him knowledge ...' Josephus, *Jewish Antiquities* 8.45.

p. 193 *He was baptised* ... Acts 8:9–13, 14–24.

p. 193 *He appeared in Christian* ... *Acts of Peter* 3.4.

p. 193 *There was a Samaritan* ... Justin Martyr, *1 Apology* 26.

p. 193 *Alexander seated himself* ... Lucian, *Alexander the False Prophet* 15, 19.

p. 194 *Pliny agreed that* ... Pliny the Elder, *Natural History* 25.10.

p. 195 *I was almost four* ... *Corpus Inscriptionum Latinum* VI 19747 = *Inscriptiones Latinae Selectae* 8522.

p. 195 *Whether we want to cull* ... 1 Kings 18:18–40.

p. 195 *The confrontation of Paul* ... Acts 13:4–12.

p. 195 *... the rival sons of Sceva.* Acts 19:11–20.

p. 195 *In the Acts* ... *Acts of Peter* 31–2.

p. 195 *Dio, writing in the third century* ... Dio 52.36.1–3; cf. Ulpian 15.2.1–3 and Paulus *Opinions* 5.21.1–2.

p. 196 *Embedded in Justinian's code* ... *Justinian Code* 9.18.7 AD 358, 9.18.4 AD 321.

p. 196 *As Tertullian saw* ... Tertullian, *Apology* 21.17.

p. 196 *In accounts of confrontations* ... Justin Martyr, *Dialog with Trypho* 69.7; Origen *Against Celsus* 4.33.

p. 196 *Peter raised the dead* ... Acts 9:36–41.

p. 196 'Then Peter said ...' Acts 3:6.

p. 196 'God did extraordinary miracles ...' Acts 19:11.

p. 196 'She kept this up ...' Acts 16:18.

p. 197 *God struck down Ananias* ... Acts 5:1–10.

p. 197 *Aelius Aristides stated* ... Aelius Aristides, *Heracles* 40.12.

p. 197 *Eunus, the leader* ... Diodorus Siculus, *History* 34/35.11.

p. 198 *At Stymphalus in Arcadia* ... Pausanius, *Description of Greece* 22.8.

p. 198 *The god commanded ... Corpus Inscriptionum Graecarum* 5980 = *Inscriptiones Graecae* 14.966a = *Sylloge Inscriptionum Graecarum* 2 807.

p. 198 *in the fifth century* BC. Pausanius, *Description of Greece* 2.12.2–9.

p. 198 *There was a girl ...* Philostratus, *Life of Apollonius* 4.45.

p. 198 *Apollonius's biography ...* Philostratus, *Life of Apollonius of Tyana* 4.20.2–3 and 4.44.2.

p. 199 *He was said to have ...* Suetonius, *Life of Vespasian* 7.1.

p. 199 *Celsus in his diatribe ...* Origen, *Against Celsus* 1.68.

p. 199 *Miracles also had ...* 1 Kings 17:17–24; 2 Kings 4:8–37, 13:20–21.

p. 199 *A man came from ...* 2 Kings 4:42–4.

p. 199 *He also performs ...* 2 Kings 4:1–7.

p. 200 *Marcus Aurelius wrote ...* Marcus Aurelius, *Meditations* 12.28.

p. 200 *'Many of the Samaritans ...'* John 4:39–40.

p. 200 *The list of miracles ...* E.g. Mark 3:35–41, 10:46–52; Matthew 11:1–15; Luke 13:10–17; John 6:5–14.

p. 201 *For with a word ...* Tertullian, *Apology* 21.17.

p. 201 *He also testified ...* 1 Corinthians 15:6.

p. 201 *'Our Saviour's works, moreover ...'* Eusebius, *Ecclesiastical History* 3.37.3.

p. 202 *'Moreover, by the works ...'* Justin Martyr, *Dialogue with Trypho* 11.

p. 202 *Peter took down a sardine ...* Acts of Peter 13.

p. 202 *Celsus wrote that Jesus ...* Origin, *Against Celsus* 1.38.

p. 202 *And I shall refer ...* Origen, *Against Celsus* 1.46.

p. 203 *'Surrender of one's life ...'* MacMullen, *Paganism in the Roman Empire*, p. 135.

p. 203 *'Yet it was the Lord's will ...'* Isaiah 53:10–12.

p. 203 *A tradition grew up ...* 4 Maccabees 6:27, 17:21–2; 2 Maccabees 6:18–31.

p. 203 *As the psalmist sang ...* Psalm 116:15.

p. 203 *'Do not be afraid ...'* 2 Maccabees 7:29.

p. 204 *'held out under every variety ...'* Josephus, *Jewish War* 3.320–21.

p. 204 *'they cheerfully resigned ...'* Josephus, *Jewish War* 2.152–3.

p. 204 *The cases of the consul ...* Livy 8.9.

p. 204 *even being cited by Augustine ...* Augustine, *City of God* 5.18.

p. 204 *The practice of self-immolation ...* Strabo, *Geography* 15.1.4.

p. 204 *According to Lucian ...* Lucian, *Peregrinus* 23 & 40.

p. 205 *In Spain, the barbarian ...* Strabo, *Geography* 3.18.

p. 205 *Tertullian, seeking polytheist ...* Tertullian, *Apology* 50.

p. 205 *According to Christian tradition ...* John 15:18, 20; Matthew 5:11–12.

p. 205 *The first martyr ...* Acts 7:51–8:1; Leviticus 24:15–16.

p. 206 *'it is plain that ...'* Justin Martyr, *Dialogue with Trypho* 110.

p. 206 *Tertullian famously stated* … Tertullian, *Apology* 50.13.

p. 206 *'That very obstinacy …'* Tertullian, *Apology* 50.14–15.

p. 206 *Some, such as the Acts of Perpetua* … *Acts of Perpetua* 1.1.

Chapter 11: When Prophecy Fails

p. 208 *Followers expected his Second Coming* … Luke 9:27; Matthew 16:28.

p. 209 *He had to make constant assurances* … Romans 13:11–12; 1 Corinthians 7:29; 1 Thessalonians 4:13–18, 5:2.

p. 209 *By the end of the first century* … 2 Peter 3:3–9.

p. 209 *Other writers kept up* … E.g. Hebrews 10:37; James 5:8; 1 Peter 4:7.

p. 209 *'With the Lord …'* 2 Peter 3:8–9.

p. 211 *They treated Christianity* … Tertullian, *Apology* 3.5.

p. 211 *'Aristides, a most eloquent …'* Jerome, *Illustrious Men* 20.

p. 211 *He claimed that* … Tertullian, *Apology* 1.7.

p. 211 *Origen properly noted* … Origen, *Against Celsus* 1.46.

p. 211 *For example, some thought* … 1 Corinthians 8:1–9.

p. 211 *The Gospels themselves embodied differing interpretations* … Matthew 10:5, 15:24; Luke 2:29–32.

p. 211 *'philosophers agree about nothing …'* P. Oxy. 3008.

p. 211 *He got involved* … Artemidorus, *Interpretation of Dreams* 4.33, p. 206.

p. 212 *Hegesippus … stated that* … Hegesippus in Eusebius, *Ecclesiastical History* 3.32.7–8.

p. 212 *We do not need to uplift* … Seneca, *Letters* 41.1–2.

p. 213 *'neither give nor have evil …'* Seneca, *Letters* 95.50.

p. 213 *Be assured that…* Epictetus, *Enchiridion* 31.

p. 214 *It is the goal of wisdom* … Apuleius, *On Plato and His Doctrine* 23.

p. 214 *Celsus pointed out* … Origen, *Against Celsus* 6.71.

p. 214 *we are told that Jesus* … Origen, *Against Celsus* 6.16.

p. 214 *This, supposedly* … Origen, *Against Celsus* 7.58.

p. 214 *There he found what he was looking for* … Tatian, *Address to the Greeks* 29.

p. 215 *Tertullian … writes that* … Tertullian, *On the Soul's Testimony* 1.1–2.

p. 215 *'weave together erroneous opinions …'* Origen, *Against Celsus* 3.16.

p. 215 *'No wise man …'* Origen, *Against Celsus* 6.73.

p. 215 *And I make no new statement* … Origen, *Against Celsus* 4.14.

p. 216 *'One ought first …'* Origen, *Against Celsus* 1.9.

p. 216 *Supposedly this was directed* … Tertullian, *On the Soul's Testimony* 1.6.

p. 216 *'foolish and low individuals …'* Origen, *Against Celsus* 3.49.

p. 217 *'Let no one come to us …'* Origen, *Against Celsus* 2.44.

p. 217 *'Most people are unable …'* From an Arabic translation of Galen, cited and translated in Richard Walzer, *Galen on Jews and Christians* (London: Oxford University Press, 1949), p. 57.

p. 217 *The appeal was to …* Origen, *Against Celsus* 3.44, 3.55.

p. 217 *'For why is it an evil …'* Origen, *Against Celsus* 3.49.

p. 217 *Christians are sorcerers …* Origen, *Against Celsus* 6.14, 3.50.

p. 218 *So Paul at Corinth …* Acts 18; 1 Corinthians 3:18.

p. 219 *At the community meal …* 1 Corinthians 11:20–22.

p. 219 *Those same people tried …* James 2:3.

p. 220 *My brothers and sisters …* James 2:1–4.

p. 220 *'envy and selfish ambition'* James 3:13–16.

p. 220 *'boast about themselves …'* Jude 1:16.

p. 220 *He used the human body …* 1 Corinthians 12:12–27.

p. 220 *He also affirmed …* 1 Corinthians 8.

p. 220–21 *He was, as Eusebius pointed out …* Eusebius, *Ecclesiastical History* 3.24.4.

p. 221 *None of these …* Acts 4:13.

p. 221 *Christ's Apostles were …* Eusebius, *Ecclesiastical History* 3.24.2–3.

p. 221 *Subjected to persecution …* Acts 15:1–35; Galatians 2:11.

p. 222 *For example, the four daughters …* Acts 21:8–9.

p. 222 *Agabus roamed as far as Antioch …* Acts 11:27–8.

p. 222 *Herod also threatened Peter …* Acts 12:3–11.

p. 222 *Christians had fled …* Eusebius, *Ecclesiastical History* 3.5.3.

p. 223 *The group unanimously chose Simeon …* Eusebius, *Ecclesiastical History* 3.11, 4.22.4.

p. 223 *But this 'cousin' …* Matthew 13:55; Mark 6:3.

p. 223 *Eusebius deduced that … early second century.* Eusebius, *Ecclesiastical History* 3.32.4–8.

p. 223 *They somewhat grudgingly … Jews living there.* Acts 11:1–18, 15:1–35, 8:1–25.

p. 223 *… although they did …* Acts 1:19.

p. 223 *Even as late as …* Eusebius, *Ecclesiastical History* 3.35.1.

p. 223 *He was influential …* Eusebius, *Ecclesiastical History* 3.23.6.

p. 223 *These people were …* Quadratus of Athens c.AD 120, preserved in Eusebius, *Ecclesiastical History* 4.3; cf. Jerome, *Illustrious Men* 19.

p. 223 *Ireneaus, for example …* Eusebius, *Ecclesiastical History* 3.36.1.

p. 223 *Acts recognised …* Acts 13:1.

p. 223 *Paul listed in addition …* 1 Corinthians 12:28–9.

p. 224 *The author of the letter …* Ephesians 4:11.

p. 224 *Apostles, prophets* ... 1 Corinthians 12:1–31.

p. 224 *But authority fragmented* ... Eusebius, *Ecclesiastical History* 3.32.8.

p. 224 *And I shall not hesitate* ... Papias of Hierapolis, *The Interpretation of the Oracles of the Lord*, Preface, quoted by Eusebius, *Ecclesiastical History* 3.39.3–4.

p. 225 *These are the things* ... 1 Timothy 6:2–5.

p. 225 *Preach the word;* ... 2 Timothy 4:2–4.

p. 225 *'They are like unreasoning animals ...'* 2 Peter 2:12.

p. 226 *'Let no one do anything ...'* Ignatius, *Letter to Smyrnaeans* 8.

p. 228 *About 5 per cent* ... This and what follows is based upon Ramsay MacMullen, *The Second Church: Popular Christianity, A.D. 200–400* (Atlanta: Society of Biblical Literature, 2009).

p. 231 *Here lies a dear* ... *Corpus Inscriptionum Latinarum* 11.4629 = *Inscriptiones Latinae Christianae Veteres* 3658.

p. 232 *'To the immortal powers ...'* *Corpus Inscriptionum Latinarum* 10.5957 = *Inscriptiones Latinae Christianae Veteres* 3913.

p. 232 *To the Underworld Spirits* ... *Corpus Inscriptionum Latinarum* 10.7914 = *Carmina Latina Epigraphica Sardinia* no. 17 late fourth century AD Tharros (Capo San Marco) Sardinia.

p. 232 *Why do you pay such honour* ... Jerome, *Against Vigilantius* 4.

p. 233 *'I certainly go to idols ...'* Quoted by Augustine, *Exposition on the Psalms* 88 *Patrologia Latina* 37.1140 (14).

p. 234 *To paraphrase Lactantius* ... Lactantius, *Divine Institutes* 4.3.4–6.

p. 234 *'made the least possible tear ...'* Ramsay MacMullen, *Christianizing the Roman Empire, A.D. 100–400* (New Haven: Yale University Press, 1984), p. 21.

p. 234 *The conversions* ... Tertullian, *Apology* 21.31.

p. 234 *Adjusting to the needs of ordinary people* ... Wayne A. Meeks, 'Social and ecclesial life of the earliest Christians', pp. 145–73 in M. M. Mitchell, F. M. Young, eds., *The Cambridge History of Christianity: Origins to Constantine* (Cambridge: Cambridge University Press, 2006), p. 171.

INDEX

Page references for illustrations are given in *italics*

A

Aaron 42, 89, 92, 94, 98, 103
Abraham 105, 137, 138, 238
Achilles 13
Acts of Perpetua 206
Acts of Peter 193, 195, 202
Acts of the Apostles 10, 117, 129, 169,
  253
  Christian name 134
  exorcism 185–6
  god-fearers 106
Adiabene 107, 238
Aelius Aristides 60, 80, 197, 238
Agabus 135, 222
agape meal 68, 84, 219, 226, 227, 229
Age of Sects 92
Albinus 118, 238
Alcimus 94
Alexander (philosopher) 211
Alexander (polytheist charismatic)
  157–8
Alexander (Procurator of Judaea) 238
Alexander of Abonoteichus 24, 25,
  73, 193–4, 238
Alexander the Great 4
Alexander Jannaeus 91, 142, 149
Alexandra 30
Alexandria
  crucifixion 149
  Cynics 78
  Jews 39, 156, 158–9
  martyrs 204
  Therapeutae 97
Amasa 104
Amos 43, 44
amulets 16, 38
Ananias (Christian) 197
Ananias (Jewish merchant) 108
Ananias, Jesus ben 48, 118, 238
Anaximander 74
Anaximenes 74
Andrew 116, 130

Anna (Tobit's wife) 30
anointing 118, 120–1
Antinous 85
Antioch 238
    Christians 134–5
    god-fearers 107
    Jews 156, 159, 168, 175
    women 30
Antiochus 159
Antiochus IV Epiphanes 5, 52, 53, 90,
    93, 109
Antisthenes 79
Aphrodisias 106
apocalypse 140, 239
    Essenes 95, 96–7
    John the Baptist 116
    see also Second Coming
Apocrypha 10, 239
Apollo 15
Apollonius of Tyana 73, 145, 198
Apollos 116, 218
Apuleius 69, 73, 83, 86, 182, 191, 194,
    213–14, 239
Ares 62
Aricia, Italy 229
Aristarchus 167–8
Aristides 197, 211
Aristotle 76, 110
Artemidorus 211, 239
Artemis 68, 167, 198
Asa 184
Asclepius 25, 60, 63, 66, 80, 160, 198
Assyrians 4, 15, 26, 44, Plate 1, Plate
    21
astrology 75, 144, 145, 171, 175, 188
atheism 162–3, 164
Athena 15
Athenagoras 165, 169, 239
Athronges 120

atonement 36, 150–1, 181
    and martyrdom 203–4, 205
Augustine 204, 233
Augustus 132–3

B
Baal 23, 239, Plate 2
    and Yahweh 15, 24–5, 195, 197, 199,
        Plate 3
Baal Peor 92
Babylonians 4, 26, 38, 44, 48
Bannus 115, 239
baptism 115, 116, 226
Bar Kochba revolt 47, 49
Barnabas 63, 153–4
Bartholomew 130
Ben Sirach 31–2, 35, 248
bishops 219, 226–7, 228
Bithynia 168, 172–4, 205–6
blasphemy 151–3
blood sacrifice 150–1
Boethian sect 100
Bohak, Gideon 38
Buddhism 197, 200
burial customs 230–3, 230, 231
Burkert, Walter 20, 163

C
Canaan 2
Canaanites 15, 23, 26, 48, 239
Cantabrians 205
Capernaum 31
Carpocrates 30
Celsus 161, 228, 239
    magic and miracles 191, 199, 202
    and philosophy 214, 215–17
    preaching 161
    prophets 187
    punishment after death 162

cemeteries 230–3
charisma 114, 240
charismatic leaders 114–18, 122, 129,
    145
    see also Jesus of Nazareth;
        messiahs; prophets
chi-rho *231*, 232
Chilon of Sparta 76, *Plate 10*
Chrestus 169
Christ 129
Christianity 6, 8–9, 11, 80, 92, 169,
    237
    agape meal *Plate 19*, *Plate 20*
    burial customs 230–3, *230*, *231*,
        Plate 27
    Constantine 1, 2, 9, 234, 237
    and destruction of temple 208
    early adherents 131, 133–5, 145–6,
        Plate 23
    Eucharist 164, 219, 227–8
    hostility to 147–77
    intellectual approach 210–16
    and Jews 134, 135–43, 145–6, 209,
        223, 235
    leadership and organisation 130–1,
        210, 216–33, 227, 234
    magic and miracles 200–2
    martyrs 205–6, 232–3, *233*
    monotheism 11
    and philosophy 210–16, 217, 234
    and polytheism 81, 83–4, 109, 141,
        143–6, 157–8, 159–68, 209, 228–
        33, 234, 235, 236–7, *Plate 25*
    praying position *Plate 26*
    and Romans 80, 169–76, *Plate 24*
    Second Coming 9, 127, 208–9, 217,
        218, 235
    sources 10, 252–4
    and women 30–1, *Plate 19*

    see also Jesus of Nazareth
Christians 134–5, 147, 169
Chryses 15
churches 228, 229
Cicero 60, 75, 155
circumcision 8, 45, 107–8, 137–9
Clement of Rome 226, 240
Clitumnus 66–7
Clopas 223
Coemeterium Maius, Rome *Plate 26*
communal meal 68, 84, 219, 226, 227,
    229
Constantine 1, 2, 9, 234, 237
Corinth 165, 196, 218
First Corinthians 124
Second Corinthians 124
Cornelius 106, 109
Cosmus the Cynic 77
Croesus, King 15
crucifixion 148–50, 160, 205, *Plate 22*
Cumanus 37, 240
Cybele *Plate 8*
Cynics 72, 75, 77–80, 83, 86, 111, 211,
    240, *Plate 11*
Cyprus 223
Cyrus, King of the Persians 4, 118,
    119, 120

D

daemons 63, 213
dance 68
Daniel 56, 120, 140, 240
David 2, 48, 50, 121, 222, 240
Day of Atonement 139, 151, 240
deacons 139, 219, 226, 227
Dead Sea Scrolls 10, 92, 94–5, 120–3,
    128, 135, *Plate 17*
death 17, 20, 72, 162
    burial customs 230–3, *230*, *231*

necromancy 186–7
Deborah 15, 29, 48
Decius Mus 204
delayed-rule model 54–7
Demetrius 167–8
Democritus 74
Deuteronomy 35, 107–8, 149, 240
Di Manes 231–2, *231*
diaspora 38–9, 104–6
  and Christianity 223–4
  revolt 49
  Therapeutae 97
Didache 141, 219, 225, 241, 254
dietary rules 8, 27, 36, 45, 139
Dio, Cassius 195
Dio Chrysostom 78, 241
Diogenes of Sinope 22, 77–8
Diogenes Laërtius 20, 76
Diognetus 60, 212, 241
Diomedes 15
Dionysus 83, *Plate 5*
divination 62, 187
Dura-Europos 227

E
Ecclesiastes 16
Ecclesiasticus 31–2, 35, 248
Egypt 4
  Egyptian religion 85
  festivals 68–9
  gatherings 131–2
  Jews 23, 38–9, 151
  Therapeutae 30, 97
  Zeus Hypsistos 82
Egyptian, The 117–18, 127, 241
Elagabalus 85
Eleazar (exorcist) 185
Eleazar (Jewish martyr) 149, 151,
  181, 203, 205, 241

Eleazar (Pharisee) 108
Eleazar (Sicarii) 104
Eleazar (son of Aaron) 89
Eleusis 80
Elijah 92–3, 103, 126, 140, 241
  and Elisha 120
  and Jesus of Nazareth 144
  and Jezebel 23
  and John the Baptist 116
  and prophets of Baal 15, 24–5, 195,
    197, 199, *Plate 3*
Elisha 120, 190, 199
Elymas 195
Empedocles 74
End of Days *see* eschatology
Enoch 55–7, 106, 120, 140, 241
enslavement 23, 26
Ephesians (Pauline letter) 224
Ephesus 116–17, *166*, 167–8, 223
Epictetus 213
Epicureans 60, 75, 110, 157–8, 171,
  242
Epicurus 75
eschatology 88, 91, 160, 204, 231, 242
  see also apocalypse; Second
    Coming
Essenes 58, 92, 95–7, 104, 105, 136,
  181, 242
  and Christianity 142
  eradication 208
  martyrdom 204
  women 30
Euagon 186
Eucharist 164, 219, 227–8
Eunus 198
Eusebius 1, 86, 201–2, 221, 223, 224,
  242
Exile 4, 23, 26, 44, 45, 137, 242, *Plate 1*
Exodus 32, 35, 242

exorcism 31, 73, 144, 184–6, 192
Ezekiel 44–5, 56, 89, 108, 140, 242

F
Fadus 117, 242
Fate 16, 59, 61, 72, 73, 96, 100, 144
Feast of Weeks 37, 100, 139, 254
Felix 118, 195, 242
Festival of Tabernacles 37, 45, 100, 249
Festival of Unleavened Bread 32, 37, 38, 45, 100, 139, 151, 246
festivals
    Jews 37–8, 45, 92, 100–1, 139
    polytheism 67–70, *Plate 8*
Festus 242
Flaccus 131–2
Florus 242
Fortune 61, 72

G
Gaius 167–8
Gaius Clodius 67
Galatians 124
Galen 202, 217, 243
Galileans 100
Galilee 26, 27–8, 243
    Jesus of Nazareth 126
    Pharisees 208
    temple tax 34
    see also Judaea
Gallio 153, 243
Gaul 85, 111
Genesis 35
Givat ha-Mivtar *Plate 22*
Glycon 24, 25, 73, 193–4
god-fearers 24, 30, 106–7, 108, 134, 181, 243
Golden Ass (Apuleius) 73, 86

Gospel of Thomas 124, 138, 253, 254
Gospels 10, 123, 124, 145, 210, 211, 253
    messiah 128, 129
    miracles 201
    social justice 141
Great Revolt 28, 29, 47, 48, 49, 91, 94, 97, 99, 103, 208, 243
    crucifixion 149
    martyrs 204
    prophetic men 118
Greek language 39, 51
Greeks 4, 6, 23, 26
    crucifixion 148–9
    see also Hellenism
group identity 17–18, 50, 109–10

H
Hadrian 85, 176, 211
Hasidim 47, 90, 94, 95, 243
    see also Essenes
Hasmoneans 90–1, 108–9, 222, 243
Hathor 23
healing 183–4, 190
Hebrews 243
    see also Israelites; Jews
Hegesippus 100, 212, 243
Hellenism 23
    Galilee 28
    Jerusalem 27
    Judaea 51, 53, 89, 91
    and Maccabees 91
Hemerobaptists 100, 115, 244
henotheism 83
Herculaneum *Plate 14*
Hercules 63, 160
Herod Agrippa 222
Herod Antipas 28, 116, 125, 128, 205, 244

Herod the Great 91, 100, 244
  temple 37, *Plate 4*
Hezekiah, King 15
Hillel 142–3
Hippolytus 30, 95–6, 244
Hosea 42–3, 48
Huldah 29
Hypsistos 24, *81*, 82–3, 144
Hystaspes 56

I

Ianuarius 67
Iconium 154
Idumea 27
Ignatius 169, 226, 244
incubation 66
Iraq 117
Irenaeus 30, 244
Isaac 105, 137, 244
Isaiah 46, 49, 108, 128, 244
  anointing 118, 120
  covenant with Yahweh 52, 54,
    101–2, 105–6, 137
  and crucifixion 150
  Day of the Lord 55
  Dead Sea Scrolls *Plate 17*
  god and humans 12
  and king 50
  martyrs 203
  miracles 199
Isis 80, 85–7, 144, 178, 179, 229, 244,
  Plate 13, *Plate 14*
Israel 2, 4, 105
Israelites 2–6, 8, 148, 244
  Baal worship 23
  Exile 4, 23, 26, 44, 45, 137, 242, *Plate
    1*
  Judaea 26
  Lachish *Plate 21*

Lost Tribes of Israel 4
monolatry 45
monotheism 1
  see also Jews

J

Jabin 15
Jacob (Israel) 13–14, 105, 137, 244
James, brother of Jesus 130, 140, 205,
  218, 220, 221–2
James, brother of John 130, 160, 164,
  222
James, son of Alphaeus 130
James (epistle) 83–4, 141, 219, 220
Jamnia 208
Jehovah *see* Yahweh
Jeremiah 245
  Babylonians 48, 49
  circumcision 108, 138
  covenant with Yahweh 41, 44, 45,
    48, 54, 102, 137, 181
  and king 50
  worship of other gods 23
Jerusalem
  Assyrian attack on 15
  The Egyptian 117–18
  Hellenistic and Roman influence 27
  Romans 6
  see also temple
Jesus ben Sirach 184
Jesus of Nazareth 1, 6, 8, 9, 32, 76–7,
  92, 123–9, 176, 236
  circumcision 138
  crucifixion 127–8, 148, 149–51, 205
  family 221–2, 223
  and Jews 147
  and John the Baptist 116, 125
  and Lazarus 196, *Plate 28*
  magic and miracles 196, 197, 200–2

and polytheists 114
Second Coming 9, 127, 208–9, 217, 218, 235
and snake handling 186
sources 123–5
and taxes 34
and women 30, 31, *Plate 18*
see also Christianity
Jews 7, 8, 88, 236, 245
anointing 118, 120
becoming Christians 8, 9, 11, 112, 134, 135–43, 145–6, 181, 209, 223, 235
charismatic leaders 114–18, 122, 129
converts 107–9
covenant with Yahweh 7, 11–25, 35, 40, 41–58, 88–92, 105
diaspora 38–40, 104–6
Exile 4, 23, 26, 44, 45, 137, 242, *Plate 1*
exorcism 185–6
family 32
festivals 37–8, 45, 92, 100–1
gatherings 34–5, 131–3
and god-fearers 106–7
hostility to Christianity 147–55, 176
and Hypsistos 83
lives 26–40
magic and miracles 188, 189–93, 197, 198, 199
martyrs 203–4, 205
men's work 31–2
messiahs 118, 120–3
monotheism 101–2, 112
persecution of groups 141–2
and philosophy 111–12
and polytheism 106–10, 155–9, 163
prophets 42–4, 47, 79–80, 86, 92–3

and Romans 171
sacrifices 36–7, 150–1
sects 92, 95–100, 101, 102–4
sources 10, 252
Torah 35, 46
women 29–31, 38
see also Great Revolt; Hebrews; Israelites
Jezebel 23
Joab 29–30, 104
Job 57–8, 184, 245
Joel 55
John (disciple) 130, 160, 218, 223
John the Baptist 92, 115–17, 245
execution 28, 116, 125, 128
and Jesus of Nazareth 125, 154
and tax collectors 34
Jonah 106
Jonathan Maccabeus 53, 90–1, 94, 120
Joseph, brother of Jesus 130
Joseph and Asenath 107
Josephus of Jerusalem 10, 245, 252, 253
ancestral customs 8, 39
and Bannus 115
charismatic leaders 48, 114–16, 127, 128, 181–2
converts 108
crucifixion 149
Essenes 95, 96, 110
exorcism 185
and father 32
Fourth Philosophy 102, 110–11
Galilee 27
gatherings 133
god-fearers 106–7
and Jesus of Nazareth 123, 127
and John the Baptist 115–16
Judas the Galilean 102–3

magic and miracles 191, 192, 195, 198
martyrs 204
Pharisees 97, 98, 110
philanthropia 109
Sadducees 99, 110
Zealots and Sicarii 103, 104
Joshua 48, 197, 199
Judaea 4–6, 7, 26, 46, 88
  Age of Sects 92
  banditry 28–9
  Bar Kochba uprising 49
  charismatic leaders 114–18, 122, 129
  crucifixion 149
  Great Revolt 48, 49, 91, 208
  Hellenism 51, 53, 91
  kings 46, 50, 51
  Maccabean revolt 49, 50, 53, 90–1, 93–4
  messiahs 120–3
  political opposition 156
  population 26–7
  priesthood 46–7, 50–1
  taxes 33–4, *33*
Judah 2, 4
Judah Maccabeus 38, 53, 90–1, 94, 120
Judas (disciple) 130
Judas, brother of Jesus 130, 218, 221
Judas, son of Hezekiah 120
Judas the Galilean 102–3, 222
Judas Barsabbas 130–1
Judas Iscariot 130
judges 2, 245
Julius Caesar 67
Julius Eutecnius 111
Jupiter 56, 62
  see also Zeus

Jupiter Dolichenus 80, 87
justice
  Jews 17, 41–58, 96–7, 98, 99–100, 103
  polytheism 70–2
Justin Martyr 111, 210–11, 215, 245
  Christians 169, 175
  martyrs 206
  miracles 202
  polytheists and death 72
  Simon Magus 193
  Sunday meetings 139
  women 30
Justinian 196
Justus 223
Juvenal 191

K
kings 46, 50, 51, 53–4, 222
  anointing 118, 120, 121
Kiryat Sefer, Israel *Plate 15*
Kourion, Cyprus *Plate 16*

L
Lachish *Plate 1*, *Plate 21*
Lactantius 234
laity 219, 226, 228
Laodicea 111
Lar 64, 65, *Plate 6*
Last Judgement *see* eschatology
Lazarus 196, *Plate 28*
Leviticus 17, 35, 36, 245
Lilith 13
Livia *Plate 25*
Long, A. A. 110
Lost Tribes of Israel 4
Lucian 60, 163
  Alexander of Abonoteichus 193–4
  Cynics 77, 78

dancing 68
magic 184–5, 191
Peregrinus 204–5
Lucius 179
Lucretius 75
Luke 123, 124, 130, 253
  see also Acts of the Apostles
Lystra 63, 154, 160

M

Maccabean revolt 5, 49, 50, 52, 53, 90–1, 93–4, 109, 157, 222
3 Maccabees 141–2
Macedonia 4
MacMullen, Ramsay 203, 228, 234
magic 88, 145, 182–3, 197, 200, 236, 237
  astrology 144, 171, 175, 188
  Christianity 196–7, 202
  divination 187
  exorcism 184–6
  famous magicians 192–5
  healing 183–4, 190
  Jews 38, 58, 188, 189–92
  and miracles 197
  necromancy 186–7
  polytheists 15
  prophecy 187
  Romans 171, 195–6
  see also prophets
Malachi 116
Marcellina 30
Marcus Aurelius 60, 194, 200
Mars 62
Martial 77, 79
martyrs
  Christianity 140, 175, 205–6, 232–3, 233
  Jews 149, 151, 203–4

polytheism 204–5, 206
remembrance of 232–3, 233
Mary, mother of Jesus 130, 148, 221
Masada 208
Masbotheans 100
Mattathias 53, 90, 93–4
Matthew 130
Maximus of Tyre 76
medicine 183–4, 190
messiahs 118, 120–3, 129
  see also Jesus of Nazareth
Middle Platonism 60, 111–12, 245
miracles 88, 197–202, 236, 237
  Christianity 126, 140, 200–2, 211
  Jews 24–5, 126, 129, 198–9
  and magic 197
  polytheists 25, 129, 198
Mishnah 10, 29, 246, 249
Mithras 68, 80, 86, 246
Modein 53, 90
monolatry 45
monotheism 11, 45, 101–2, 112
  Christianity 8, 9, 136
  Jews 1, 8
  polytheism 24, 83, 144
  see also Zeus Hypsistos
Morgan, Teresa 60
Morpheus 13
Moses 105, 137
  and blasphemy 153
  burning bush 13
  covenant with Yahweh 35
  magic and miracles 188, 197, 199
  Passover 151
  as prophet 42
  Ten Commandments 1
Mount Gerizim 117, 152, 248
Mount Olympus 13

Mount Sinai 1, 7, 13
mountaintops 13
mystery religions 80, 144, 246

N
Naaman the Syrian 106, 190
Naomi 23
necromancy 186–7
Nero 170
New Testament 3, 10, 136
    god-fearers 106
    proselytes 107
    see also Acts of the Apostles;
        Gospels; Paul
Numbers 35, 189–90, 246

O
Obadiah 55
offerings 19, 20, 71, 72, *166*, 167
Old Testament 10, 249
    see also Prophets; Psalms; Torah
Oracle of Hystaspes 56
Oracle of the Potter 56
oracles 72
Origen 161, 167, 180, 202, 211, 217,
    246

P
Palestine 2–6, 85, 246
    see also Canaan
Pandarus 15
Panormus *81*
Panticapaeum 106
Papias 224
parables 35, 141
Parmenides 74
Passover Feast 32, 37, 38, 45, 100,
    139, 151, 246
patriarchy 7, 29, 32

Paul 10, 75, 134, 135, 211, 253
    circumcision 138
    conversion 179, 180, 201
    at Corinth 75, 82, 165
    crucifixion 149
    and disciples of John the Baptist
        116–17
    and Elymas 195
    at Ephesus 116–17, 167–8, 224
    and false doctrine 225
    and idolatry 163
    and Jesus of Nazareth 124, 127,
        128, 129
    and Jews 153–5
    leadership 131, 218–19, 220–1, 222,
        223–4, 226
    and magic 185–6, 195, 196–7
    mistaken for god 63
    and polytheists 160, 163–4
    and Second Coming 208–9, 210
    social justice 141
    at Thyatira 168
Paulus 182
Pella 222
Pentateuch *see* Torah
Pentecost 37, 100, 139, 254
Peregrinus 204–5
Persians 4, 46, 51
Peter 130, 160, 193, 218, 222
    and Cornelius 106, 109
    death 223
    and magic 196, 197
    see also Acts of Peter
Peter (epistles) 164, 165–6, 180, 209,
    219, 225
Petronius 79, 184, 194, 251
Pharisees 92, 97–8, 99, 102, 104, 142,
    181, 208, 246
    and charismatic leaders 115

and Christianity 142–3
and diaspora 105
and Jesus of Nazareth 152
and John the Baptist 116
Philadelphia 83, 106
Philemon 124
Philip (disciple) 130, 193, 218, 222
Philip II 4
Philippians 124
Philistines 26
Philo of Alexandria 10, 106, 247, 252,
253
atonement 36
circumcision 108
Jewish gatherings 34–5, 132–3
Jewish groups 95, 110, 111
and philosophy 181, 213
and polytheists 39, 109
proselytes 107
social justice 141
Therapeutae 97
philosophy 59, 86
and Christianity 210–16, 217, 234
and Fate 72
and Jewish sects 110–11
and polytheism 60–1, 62, 70, 74–80,
110, 111–12
Phineas 92, 103
Phoenicia 223
piety model 47, 50, 52
Pilate 37, 117, 128, 149
Plato 74, 110, 192, 214
Platonism 23, 60, 75, 213–14, 247
see also Middle Platonism
Plautus 187
Pliny the Elder 60, 95, 247, 251
Essenes 145
magic 183, 186, 188, 191, 194
prayer 65–7

stone pillow 14
trees 62
Pliny the Younger 3, 10, 169, 196,
210, 247, 249
agape meal 84
Clitumnus sanctuary inscriptions
66–7
executing Christians 168, 172–4,
175, 176, 205–6
and Jesus of Nazareth 123
Plutarch 60, 67–8, 76, 85, 247
Poimandres 145
Polycarp 206, 223
polytheists 1, 7–8, 88, 236, 247
becoming Christians 8, 9, 11, 81,
83–4, 109, 134, 141, 143–6, 178–9,
180–1, 228–33, 234, 235, 236–7,
Plate 27
burial customs 230–2, 231,
Plate 27
delayed-rule model 56
Fate and Fortune 72, 73
festivals 67–70, Plate 8
gatherings 131
god-fearers 106–7
holy men 73
hostility to Christianity 147, 157–8,
159–68, 176–7
and Jews 39, 107–10, 155–9
justice 70–2
magic and miracles 129, 191, 192,
193–5, 198
martyrdom 204–5, 206
and monotheism 24, 83
mystery religions 80
ordinary people's lives 59–87
and philosophy 59, 70, 74–80, 110,
111–12, 209, 210–16
praying position Plate 25

and religious change 80–7, 110,
112, 113
religious experience 61–5
sacrifice *Plate 7*, *Plate 9*
and supernatural 11–25
worship 65–70
Pompeii
Cynics *Plate 11*
death graffiti 72
election graffiti 131, *132*
festivals *Plate 8*
Forum 161, *Plate 12*
lararium 64, 65, *Plate 6*
Tavern of the Seven Sages 76, *Plate 10*
Pompey the Great 5, 6
Pontius Pilate 37, 117, 128, 149
Pontus and Bithynia 168, 172–4,
205–6
Porphyry 86, 247
prayer 62, 65–6, *Plate 25*, *Plate 26*
preaching 134, 141, 161
Cynics 77, 79, 83, 111
see also charismatic leaders;
prophets
Prepousa 21
priest-and-king model 46, 47, 48, 50,
53–4
priestly model 47, 48
priests 46–7, 50–1, 52–3, 89, 222
anointing 118, 120
Prometheus 13
prophets 42–4, 47, 86, 129, 147–8, 187
anointing 118, 120
and anti-covenantal tendencies
92–3
and Cynics 79–80
Day of the Lord 55–6
Old Testament 135

see also Jesus of Nazareth
Providence *see* Fate
Psalms 46, 93, 96, 101, 135, 203
Psalms of Solomon 121
Psidian Antioch 153–4
Ptolemies 4
Publilius Syrus 65
purity
charismatic leaders 115
Essenes 96
Jesus of Nazareth 126–7
Jews 27, 36, 47, 51, 57, 88, 95
Pharisees 97–8
polytheism 66
Pythagoras 72, 144, 192, 247

Q
Quadratus (Christian apologist) 201,
223, 247
Quadratus (governor of Syria) 149,
247
Quintilius 247
Qumran 96, 128, 135–6, 137, 150, 208
see also Dead Sea Scrolls

R
rabbinical tradition 9, 10, 98
reason 74
resurrection 56
righteousness
Essenes 95–7, 181
Jesus of Nazareth 125–7
Jews 41, 44–8, 52, 55–8, 88, 92–5,
98, 100
John the Baptist 116
Pharisees 97–8, 181
Therapeutae 97
rivers 13
Rogatianus 67

Romans 5–6
  and associations 84, 131–3
  Christianity 1, 9, 10, 80, 234, 237,
    Plate 24
  crucifixion 148, 149
  destruction of temple 4, 8–9, 208
  Galilee 28
  Great Revolt 48, 208
  hostility to Christianity 169–76, 177
  imperial cult 85, 166–7
  Jerusalem 27
  and Jesus of Nazareth 127–8
  and Jews 156–7
  Judaea 28–9, 37–8, 46, 51, 88
  and magic 188–9, 195–6
  martyrdom 204
  and Sicarii 103–4
  taxes 33, 34
Romans (Pauline letter) 124, 128,
  163–4
Rome
  Christians 205, *Plate 26*, *Plate 28*
  fire 170
  Jews 39, 156, 169
Ruth the Moabite 23

S
Sabbath 8, 32, 92, 101, 139
sacrifices
  Christianity 167, 174, 175
  Jews 36–7
  polytheists 62, 65–6, 69, *Plate 7*,
    Plate 9
Sadducees 89, 92, 99–100, 105, 116,
  208, 248
Samaritan, The 117, 128, 248
Samaritans 4, 100, 142, 152, 200–1,
  223, 248
Samuel 102, 186–7

San Callisto Catacomb, Rome *Plate
  20*
Sapphira 197
Sarapis 68
Sardis 106
Satan 136
Saul 2, 186–7
Scamander 13
Schilles 20
science 74
Scribes 97, 136, 248
Second Coming 9, 127, 208–9, 217,
  218, 235
Second Temple Period 3, 4, 248
Seleucids 4–6, 46, 53, 88
Seneca 60, 63, 76, 79, 205, 212–13,
  248
Sennacherib 15, *Plate 1*
Septuagint 252, 253
  see also Tanakh
Seven Sages 76, *Plate 10*
Shavuot 37, 100, 139, 254
Sheba 29–30
Shema 125
sica 103, *Plate 16*
Sicarii 92, 103–4, 127, 208
Simeon 223
Simon (disciple) 130
Simon ben Giora 30
Simon Maccabeus 53, 90–1
Simon Magus 30, 143, 145, 192–3,
  195, 248
Simon of Peraea 120
Simon, son of Boethus 100
Simonians 193
Sirach 31–2, 35, 248
slaves 23, 26
Smyrna 223
snake handling 186

social justice 235
  Christianity 140–1
  Essenes 96, 181
  Jesus of Nazareth 125, 126, 127
  Jews 44, 48, 51, 54
  John the Baptist 116
  Judas the Galilean 103
Socrates 74, 155, 204, 205, 214
Solomon 2, 191, 192, 248
Stephen 140, 152–3, 205
Stoicism 60, 72, 75, 212–14, 248
Strabo 68–9
Stymphalus 198
Suetonius 10, 123, 169, 170–1, 199,
  210, 249
Sukkot 37, 45, 100, 249
synagogues 90, 226, *Plate 15*
Syria 6, 39, 149, 223
Syrus 249

T
Tabernacles, Feast of 249
Tacitus 10, 123, 127, 196, 249
  Christians 169, 170, 171, 210
  converts 107
  Jews 156
Talmud 10, 92, 100, 249
Tanakh 249
  see also Old Testament; Septuagint
Tatian 169, 214–15
Tavern of the Seven Sages, Pompeii
  76, *Plate 10*
taxes 33–4, *33*, 39
Teacher of Righteousness 94–5, 123,
  135, 137, 141, 249
temple 36, 37, 39, 45, 46, 98–9, *Plate 4*
  Antiochus 53
  and Christianity 139
  destruction by Romans 4, 8–9, 208

  disagreements 91, 92
  Maccabean revolt 53, 91
  taxes 33, *33*, 34
  Zadokites 89
Tertullian 111, 134, 210–11, 216, 249
  Christian gatherings 84, 133
  festivals 69
  Jesus of Nazareth 196, 201
  martyrs 205, 206
  persecution of Christians 164, 165
  polytheist converts 215, 234
  women 30–1
Theagenes of Thasos 198
theodicy 44–5
Therapeutae 30, 97, 104–5, 249
First Thessalonians 124
Thessalonica 154
Theudas 117, 128, 249
Thomas 130
Thrasybulus 15
Thyatira 168
Tiberius 175
Torah 35–7, 39, 46, 50, 65, 90–1, 101,
  107, 109, 111, 135–6, 139, 142–3,
  240, 242, 249
  Antiochus 53, 109
  Essenes 96
  Jesus of Nazareth 125–6
  magic 188
  Pharisees 97–8, 104, 152, 181, 208,
    246
  purity 36
  Therapeutae 97
Trajan 172–4, 176
Tralleis 106

V
Varus 149, 254
Vespasian 185, 199

Vigilantius 232–3
votive offerings 19, 20, 71, 72, *166*, 167
vows 19–21, 62

W
Weeks Feast 37, 100, 139, 254
wells 13
Wisdom of Solomon 254
women
Christianity 30–1, *Plate 19*
Essenes 30, 96
god-fearers 30, 107
and Jesus of Nazareth 30, 31, *Plate 18*
Jews 30, 31, 38
magic 194–5
and philosophers 76
Therapeutae 97

X
Xenocrates 74
Xenophon 73

Y
Yahweh 1, 7, 8, 12, 254
and Baal 15, 24–5, 195, 197, 199, *Plate 3*
covenant with 7, 11–25, 35, 40, 41–58, 88–92, 101–2, 105–6, 137, 181
justice 41–58, 96–7, 98, 99–100, 103
Yavne 208
Yom Kippur 139, 151, 240

Z
Zachlas 73
Zadok 89, 98–9, 250
Zadokites 89, 94
Zealots 92, 103, 127, 208
Zechariah 117
Zeno 75
Zephaniah 55
Zerubbabel 203
Zeus 13, 62
see also Jupiter
Zeus Hypsistos (Zeus Most High) 24, *81*, 82–3, 144